Experiencing Broadband Society

Participation in Broadband Society
Edited by Leopoldina Fortunati / Julian Gebhardt / Jane Vincent

Volume 2

PETER LANG
Frankfurt am Main · Berlin · Bern · Bruxelles · New York · Oxford · Wien

Julian Gebhardt / Hajo Greif / Lilia Raycheva / Claire Lobet-Maris / Amparo Lasen (eds.)

Experiencing Broadband Society

PETER LANG
Internationaler Verlag der Wissenschaften

Bibliographic Information published by the Deutsche Nationalbibliothek
The Deutsche Nationalbibliothek lists this publication in the Deutsche Nationalbibliografie; detailed bibliographic data is available in the internet at http://dnb.d-nb.de.

ISSN 1867-044X
ISBN 978-3-631-58406-4
© Peter Lang GmbH
Internationaler Verlag der Wissenschaften
Frankfurt am Main 2010
All rights reserved.

All parts of this publication are protected by copyright. Any utilisation outside the strict limits of the copyright law, without the permission of the publisher, is forbidden and liable to prosecution. This applies in particular to reproductions, translations, microfilming, and storage and processing in electronic retrieval systems.

www.peterlang.de

Acknowledgements

The editors wish to thank Peter Lang AG, Berlin for their support in establishing a new series on new ICT and society called Participation in Broadband Society.
This publication is supported by COST Office and their staff is acknowledged for their assistance together with the COST Action 298 Chair Bartolomeo Sapio and Vice Chair Tomaz Turk. The members of COST Action 298 Working Group "Humans as e-actors" are thanked for their support during the production of this book. These are: Leopldina Fortunati, Julian Gebhardt, Hajo Greif, Sander Limonard, Claire Lobet-Maris, Andraž Petrovčič, Lilia Raycheva, Panayiota Tsatsou, Olga Vershinskaya and Jane Vincent.

COST – the acronym for European *CO*operation in the field of *S*cientific and *T*echnical Research- is the oldest and widest European intergovernmental network for cooperation in research. Established by the Ministerial Conference In November 1971, COST is presently used by the scientific communities of 35 European countries to cooperate in common research projects supported by national funds. Web: www.cost.esf.org

 ESF provides the COST Office through an EC contract

 COST is supported by the EU RTD Framework programme

 COST 298 – Participation in the Broadband Society

Table of Content: Experiencing Broadband Society (Volume II)

Julian Gebhardt, Hajo Greif, Lilia Raycheva, Claire Lobet-Maris and Amparo Lasen
Introduction: The Broadband Society and its Citizens 9

Theme I: Uses and practices of new media

Tim Van Lier and Jo Pierson
Identification of community practices and co-creation by pre-adolescents: the case of Ketnet Kick 27

Beatriz Galán, Maidana Andrés Legal, D.I. Pedro Senar
Design and communication for local development: technological decisions in collaborative scenarios 49

Theme II: New media and the social differentiation of their use

Marina Borovik and Ludmilla Shemberko
Social Sciences Information User Behaviour and Searching Strategies in Multifarious Environment 69

Sarah Gallez, Anne-Claire Orban, Céline Schöller and Claire Lobet-Maris
Teenagers on the Net: Generational Divide, Autonomy, Liberty and Responsibility 83

Maria Sourbati
Non-Users in the Information Society
Learning from the older generation 107

Theme III: ICT use and sustainable development

Inge Røpke, Kirsten Gram-Hanssen and Jesper Ole Jensen
Households' ICT use in an energy perspective 121

Kerstin Wüstner
Attitudes towards mobile phone communication technology 143

Theme IV: New technologies, new challenges

Sharon Baurley, Erik Geelhoed, Philippa Brock and Andrew Moore
Communication wear: User feedback as part of a co-design process 169

Larissa Hjorth
Beyond the frame: The place of mobile and immobile media 187

Authors 201

Julian Gebhardt, Hajo Greif, Lilia Raycheva, Claire Lobet-Maris and Amparo Lasen

Introduction: The Broadband Society and its Citizens

In the broadband society an increasing, albeit limited, number of people are taking advantage of the new technological possibilities of generating, obtaining and communicating information. Their purpose and hope is to expand and enhance their interpersonal relationships and their agency as social beings in general. In this context, the term "broadband society" is used to characterise a society in which not only information has become the primary economic commodity, which is the key characteristic of the information society or knowledge society, as these terms were defined by Machlup (1962) and Bell (1973), but where people's access to information potentially anytime and everywhere is becoming a common and – to a certain extent, in certain contexts – indispensable feature of their everyday lives (Baron 2008). Although it should be kept in mind that there are many people without access to, or use for, broadband technologies. Nonetheless, new forms of social ties and cooperation have been emerging in recent years, such as online communities (Wellman 1999; Rheingold 2000), social network sites (Boyd & Ellison 2007) and other Web 2.0 applications (O'Reilly 2007), involving many new users who, every day, add new modalities and styles of mediated social relations to their lives. Moreover, new content and forms of narrative have been developed within this framework, creating a large corpus of stories (Lesser et al. 2000). Although these and other related phenomena certainly imply significant changes in social processes in contemporary societies, the aim of this book is not to establish a conclusive and unequivocal definition of what the broadband society really is. Instead, this collection of papers seeks to convey in a manageable form, recent thinking and research on the social and cultural aspects of broadband technologies. The aim of this book and its contributions is to demonstrate, by example, the importance of investigating, collecting, recording and reflecting upon the social experiences and practices of using information and communication technologies (ICT) in the emerging contexts of the broadband society.

Why now a book on the many different ways in which people experience old and new media in the broadband society? There are several reasons, not least because after almost two decades of both thinking about and discussing theories the editors of this volume perceived the need to capture the attitudes and behaviours expressed by everyday users in this new socio-technical landscape that broadband technology is supporting. This includes discourse on conceptual frameworks, social regularities and formal models (e.g. Hackett et al. 2007; Lievrouw & Livingstone 2006), as well as conducting research projects focused on quantitatively and qualitatively assessing the uses of ICTs (Jenkins 2006; Bakardjieva 2005; Silverstone & Hirsch 1992; Glotz et al. 2005; Ito et al. 2006; Katz & Aakhus 2002). As Bourdieu (1977) pointed out, there is no better way to achieve this goal than to reconstruct the practices of use of technologies in order to understand the transformation of their social meaning and functions as well as the transformation that occurs in the everyday lives of individuals. The editors of this collection of scientific papers are part of a European network that was among the first to investigate these practices in the beginning of the 1990s (Haddon 1998).

In particular, inquiries into how people experience ICTs in the broadband society are becoming more urgent. This is important now that these technologies also convey meanings, symbols, values and vivid emotions (Vincent & Fortunati 2009; Lasen 2005) to an unprecedented extent, and in an ever more refined fashion that transcends the scope of formal theories of information, of usage surveys, of domestication and usability studies, or of media case studies and ethnographies. Thus, a more integrated approach appears to be required. In fact, the issue of everyday life experiences of ICTs is attracting increasing attention from the scientific community within and between multiple disciplines (Höflich & Hartmann 2006, Wellman & Haythornthwaite 2002; Gebhardt 2008). The purpose of this book is to identify and address current research questions directed at this issue, examining various multi-disciplinary approaches towards the common goal of understanding the various social practices of ICT use. However, this book does not put its main focus on fashionable topics such as social networks that are now attracting a lot of research and debate but that will sooner or later be on the downside of the hype cycle (Nyiri 2008). Instead, this book addresses and provides evidence of a variety of apparently mundane practices and experiences of ICT use that nonetheless are shaping people's lifeworlds. It does so by bringing together the work of international researchers who gathered in Moscow for the conference "The Good, the Bad, and the Unexpected. The User and the Future of Information and Communication Technologies", organised by the European network COST 298 in May 2007. In this volume, a selection of the outcomes of the discourse among the scholars participating in this event is presented in the form of original material on their respective research topics. This conference was distinctive not only to the extent to which it was an international and interdisciplinary event focusing on ICT use and participation in the broadband society, but also in the ways in which it aimed to produce a true conceptual integration of different approaches and disciplines on this broad, but highly relevant theme.

The ICT world comprises personal and social relationships, devices, signs and communication and information practices and users. These issues were explored by scholars from various disciplines, including social sciences, computer science, engineering, arts and design. The papers that are presented and discussed here cover a variety of topics, including current theoretical frameworks and contemporary research projects concerning the way in which users are affected by, and respond to, the manner in which broadband technology is being employed. This also takes account of issues related to evolving societal forms and environments in the information society, such as on-line communities and ways of analyzing people's emotional experience of ICTs and their social implications. The current aim is to build upon the dialogue and networks that emerged from this conference, crossing and integrating many different scientific and research approaches, as well as conceptual perspectives, with the goal of developing new ontological and epistemological positions on the experiences and practices of ICT use.

Overview of Book

The purpose of this book is to investigate the role of broadband ICTs from an anthropocentric point of view. What social and personal problems in communication have people tried to overcome by using and interacting with broadband technology? What new problems may arise in the course of acting and interacting with ICTs? What are the social structures and processes that are involved in and affected by this use? In this book the authors examine new technologies, albeit in a similar way to that suggested at the beginning of the last century by Sombart (1911)., He discussed how technologies in various societies presented different and peculiar opportunities to 'rationalise' the organisation of daily life, to resolve practical problems, to provide solutions for reducing fatigue, the amount of time spent and the costs that people encounter in their everyday life. Therefore, the chapters in this volume cut across a broad variety of social issues and geographical domains. They highlight the attitudes and actions of both users and non-users, they inquire both into mundane and into innovative uses, and they probe for political and operational consequences. The chapters' foci range from individual to collective issues, and from (post-) industrialised to developing societies. The themes also cut across psychological, sociological, cultural, and environmental levels of analysis. At their heart, though, is the common theme of how broadband ICTs have contributed – in both intrusive and subtle ways – to the reshaping of people's experience of everyday life.

Central Themes

The volume covers four main themes and empirical areas of research. The themes can be named as follows: Firstly uses and practices of new media, with particular focus on underprivileged groups; secondly new media and the social differentiation of their use; thirdly ICT use and sustainable development and fourthly new technologies, new challenges.

The first of these themes introduced in this book debates the possibilities that social software may open for the less powerful or even deprived groups in society, such as children or rural communities in less developed countries respectively, but it also concerns the possible contributions from those social groups to the further development of social software applications.

The second area presented in this book refers to and discusses the situation of e-actors with regards to the specific difficulties of their using the Internet and other ICTs. The term "e-actors" does not only refer to people as users of ICTs, but to the manifold roles and situations that people experiment with in their relationships with these technologies, including the roles of citizen, customer, consumer, co-designer, stakeholder, and others. Unlike in much of current scholarly literature on ICTs and society, here it is not the proactive and innovative user who takes centre stage, but the one who has to cope with a technology that has not been designed with his or her needs in mind. For example, different age cohorts are confronted with different impediments to ICT use. E-actors live in specific relationships to the new media, according to their social alignments (for a more in-depth discussion of the notion of e-actors, see Fortunati et al. 2009, which comprises more contributions from the same conference). It is thus important to identify the issues relevant to different generations of e-actors in order to shed new light on the co-construction of socio-technical systems based on computerisation and on the social and cultural differentiations these systems produce (Scott & Marshall 2005).

The third area concerns the often overlooked relation between ICT use and sustainability issues, that is, possible environmental and health risks, which is mediated by perceptions, attitudes and practices of e-actors. Since ICTs are increasingly subject to the "throw away ethic" and strategies of obsolescence in contemporary consumer societies which are producing large amounts of e-waste (Slade 2006), the reflections on this problem presented in this book can be interpreted as a response to a perceived lack of public concern.

Finally, the fourth area addresses questions of the possible new relationships between users and advanced mobile communication functionalities, such as the features of, and affective responses to, communication-wear, that open up entire new fields of activity and interaction to e-actors. Having identified these four areas, we have arranged the contributions in four sections, a more detailed explication of which follows.

Theme 1: Uses and practices of new media

In this section, authors discuss recent research on online communities, presenting selected case studies from two rather different countries and cultures, namely pre-adolescent youths in Belgium and marginalised urban and rural communities in Argentina. The research projects introduced here offer powerful examples of how the same technologies with which people may arrange their activities and resolve vital problems in their everyday life in different cultural contexts are in reality shaping socio-technical systems with specific meanings and functions. These studies also tackle the issue of methodology for collecting and analyzing the data in such different settings. Although significant developments in the Internet world such as Web 2.0 have emerged in the last few years, they have only recently received attention in terms of sustained investigation by the social sciences. Thus the papers we present in this section give a valuable contribution to a deeper understanding of this growing area. They both deal with the evolution of the Internet culture, as it is being revitalised by the social software phenomenon.

The section is opened by the chapter of *Tim Van Lier and Jo Pierson, Identification of community practices and co-creation by pre-adolescents: the case of Ketnet Kick*. The authors provide a critical and nuanced image of online communities and their potential social implications for youngsters and vice versa, reflecting the specific way in which children become members of online communities, and contributing to the recent focus among many scholars on the practices of children in using and developing new ICTs. To this end, Van Lier and Pierson first investigate what the concept 'community' means to children in an environment which rapidly changes day by day. Second, they take an interdisciplinary perspective to discuss theories on pre-adolescent communities, in order to better understand the socio-psychological dynamics that characterise teenagers' behaviour. Third, they investigate the determinants of (online and offline) communities and try to identify what children may find important in a community. Van Lier and Pierson seek to identify precisely where and how children experience the sense of a mediated community. Are children after all, engaging as e-actors in the community landscape and if so, how are they dealing with these electronic communities? After outlining their theoretical background, these authors present and discuss findings from their own case study 'Ketnet Kick'. 'Ketnet Kick' is a successful collaborative game developed by the Flemish public broadcasting company VRT (Flanders, Belgium) and games developer Larian. In terms of methodology, the instruments applied in this research are numerous. In a first stage, diaries and questionnaires were used to identify the media profiles of children involved in the research. Then, six focus group interviews and ten in-depth dual-interviews were carried out. In total 71 children living in Flanders were studied. Van Lier's and Pierson's research shows how children interpret the notions of online community and Web 2.0. The children's everyday life context is a key factor in determining their media practices and needs. In this context, it appeared that, in applications designed for pre-adolescents – i.e. children between the ages of eight and ten –, a sense of community is enabled through collaboration and co-creation of content. On the other hand, the act of communicating online is not the ultimate goal for these children. Rather, they strive for common experiences and are cooperating for common purposes.

Van Lier's and Pierson's perspective is complemented by a chapter written by *Beatriz Galán, Maidana Andrés Legal, D.I. Pedro Senar, Design and communication for local development: technological decisions in collaborative scenarios*. This chapter is focused on the role of ICTs as tools for spreading innovative social practices promoted by organisations of the civil society, and as media for overcoming territorial isolation, social exclusion and environmental degradation through low scale investment solutions, within a framework of community co-construction. The use of ICTs and particularly of Web 2.0 constitutes an important component of the knowledge transfer to communities that had been developed by the authors' research group at the Universidad de Buenos Aires. Coming from a Technology and Society research background, the authors describe how they developed what they call an "animation device", based on Web 2.0 , in order to connect the needs and resources of a specific local community with other social networks and thus to overcome its isolation. This device is seen as an agent of development, and its designers as social animators. Since applications that combine resources of a self-managed data base with weblog interfaces and processes of technology are rare, this team has innovatively contributed the first step towards the appropriation of ICTs by emerging community organisations, supporting them to the point at which they reach autonomy in content management. The purpose of these authors is to empower the innovating activity of non-governmental organisations on a low scale, utilizing the increasing diffusion of ICTs, and in particular the resources provided by fibre optic lines as the technological infrastructure necessary to autonomously carry out content management. At the end of their chapter, the authors offer some results of their efforts, represented by the institutional strengthening of the community involved in the project through the appropriation of Web 2.0.

Theme 2: New media and the social differentiation of their use

Three different approaches to exploring the relationship between computers/internet and social networking are presented here. They form a kind of mosaic that depicts different facets of users, according to their different social and demographic characteristics. At the same time the chapters below capture specific experiences of being e-actors and using new technologies in different Eastern and Western European countries, namely in Russia, Belgium and UK.

The section starts with the chapter *Social Sciences Information User Behaviour and Searching Strategies in Multifarious Environment* by *Marina Borovik* and *Ludmilla Shemberko*. It is an investigation into users' searching strategies in social science databases in Russia, and into the way in which users change their behaviour to improve their interaction with retrieval systems. The authors present a multidimensional approach to the analysis of information users in the field of social sciences, outlining the situated cultural practices of e-science and of the social construction of knowledge. The authors provide an interesting picture of the involvement of internet users in the creation of the broadband society in Russia, with special attention to their needs and searching behaviours in the electronic repositories of information and knowledge. The results of a survey involving 3,500 e-users are delivered, showing that in the field of social sciences even frequent users are not always able to utilise the potential offered by new information technologies for searching databases and digital repositories. Even here, among experts, the common phenomenon of under-utilisation of available technological resources is observable. In order to differentiate the picture, the search strategies of different categories of users are described and a number of observations of users' searching behaviour on the Web and in various social science databases are offered for discussion.

The second chapter, *Teenagers on the Net: Generational Divide, Autonomy, Liberty and Responsibility*, by *Sarah Gallez, Anne-Claire Orban, Céline Schöller* and *Claire Lobet-Maris* takes us to Belgium and depicts a totally different group of e-actors: teenagers. In this chapter, youngsters' attitudes and practices in the internet sphere are examined, and some common sense assumptions about this so-called "digital generation" are challenged. In fact, according to the authors, youngsters in Belgium do not at all form a single, homogeneous generation, but are characterised by social and cultural diversity both with regard to their internet usage practices and to the social meanings they give to their practices. The authors proceed to demonstrate the highly variant and diverging investments into the Internet, such as into blogs, chats and games, along the lines of gender, age and socio-cultural status. Another commonly held view that is challenged by the authors is the presumed globalisation of the digital generation that instead seems to navigate and interact on a predominantly local scale, where youngsters shape the net as an explorative social dimension between the public and private sphere, set apart from the adult world. The paper is based on a recent qualitative study conducted within the framework of the research project TIRO – Teens and ICT, Risks and Opportunities –, sponsored by the Belgian Science Policy Office (BELSPO). The main topic of this research is the rules and regulations shaped and used by teenagers (12 to 18 years) to guide them in their practices and attitudes in the Internet sphere. In the first part of their chapter, the authors question the generational divide that shapes teenagers' ICT practices and its influence on youth's socialisation and regulation. Based on these sociological and cultural observations, the authors, in the second part of the chapter, analyse the traditional legal framework that is meant to regulate the teenagers' digital sphere, and question its current appropriateness. Again, a problem of under-utilization is detected among the very group that is generally considered to comprise the most advanced e-actors. However, the main profile of the broadband user does not include teenagers, but rather more mature youngsters.

The section is concluded by the chapter *Non-Users in the Information Society. Learning from the older generation*, written by *Maria Sourbati*. Here, the opposite age group is addressed, by investigating into the social construction of the elderly, and by analysing the current rhetoric of the emerging public discourse about them. In the post-modern society, the elderly have become subject to a radical reversal of their social representation and image. Once being considered the repositories of wisdom, their role has become redrawn as that of individuals unable to cope with the changes and the possibilities offered by the new technological artefacts available in their society. Sourbati critically discusses political perspectives on the 'non users' of new information and communication technologies (ICTs), showing a lack of an anthropocentric approach to the relation between new media and the elderly. She examines how older non-users of today's new media are represented in the policy discourses about the Information Society. Elderly people's relationship with new media technologies is commonly framed in terms of age-based understandings, of static and binary notions of media access, and of an individualistic perspective on the non-users (Ling 2008). Older adults are deemed unable to obtain the literacy required to access and use new media technologies and services mainly because of their age, while, at the same time, they are considered as potentially major beneficiaries of access to online services. This kind of prevalent conceptualisations can be seen to define non-users as a homogenous group of isolated individuals, media use as a solitary activity, and the nature and benefits of access as a matter of absolutes. Drawing on broadly interactionist perspectives, this paper suggests that non-users are better understood as interacting individuals who relate to the media in various ways, including forms of engagement with them that are mediated by other people. The paper concludes by considering what bearing these understandings have on policy formation.

Theme 3: ICT use and sustainable development

The third section explores the future agenda of the broadband society and the environmental risks that it is, and will be, confronted with. Even if the oft-repeated diagnosis that labour becomes immaterial and social interactions virtual is true, all that labour and interactions have to rely on is material infrastructures, whose production, presence and maintenance produce more or less directly tangible material effects: energy consumption, waste, and, arguably, also electromagnetic field emissions. Two studies, one from Denmark and one from Germany, are included in this section.

This section is opened by the chapter *Households' ICT use in an energy perspective*, authored by *Inge Røpke, Kirsten Gram-Hanssen* and *Jesper Ole Jensen*, which deals with the issue of sustainability of the broadband society model in terms of the increasing energy consumption concomitant with the growing number of ICT appliances and the intensification of ICT use. The chapter's starting point is the perceived lack of connection between two of the prominent social agendas of our time: the development of the information society and the question of how to prevent human-made climate change. The chapter is intended as a contribution to integrate these two agendas. As this issue has not received much attention in previous research, the paper has more of an explorative character. Firstly, some of the available studies on the relationship between ICT use and energy are reviewed, introducing a consumption perspective. Secondly, the integration of ICTs in everyday practices and the dynamics behind these changes are outlined, adopting a historical perspective. Thirdly, a figure of the relationships between the changes in everyday practices and the related energy impacts is presented, followed by descriptions of direct energy consumption related to household ICTs, of indirect energy consumption outside households, and of derived impacts both within and outside households. The paper concludes with some remarks on political implications and questions for further research.

The second paper, *Attitudes towards mobile phone communication technology*, by *Kerstin Wüstner*, presents an empirical study conducted by the author in Germany that analyses the polarisation that occurs between citizens' attitudes towards potentially harmful effects of mobile phones. The author takes a closer look at the negative side of the perception of mobile phones, that is, at underlying concerns and fears that citizens might have towards this technology. Although the vast majority of people possess and use mobile phones, and although mobile phones are a mostly taken-for-granted part of everyday life, a rising number of people, even among mobile users, shares critical attitudes and expresses fear of possibly harmful effects, mainly produced by mobile antennas and masts. While this group is convinced of negative health effects of the electromagnetic fields (EMFs) emitted by these devices, others appear to be more indifferent, or even are convinced that the limit values that have been set up by the authorities are safe. In the discussion about possible effects, people's attitudes are often in conflict. Precisely what concerns do people express? Are there gender differences between the concerned and the not so concerned groups? Do the attitudes of users and non-users of mobile technologies diverge consistently? These questions are empirically addressed within the theoretical framework of social representations of technology (Fortunati & Contarello, 2005; Contarello et al. 2008).

Theme 4: New technologies, new challenges

The last section addresses contemporary developments in new ICTs, among them the merging of fashion cultures and mobile technologies, shared attitudes on communication wear and the new visual, aural and haptic economies emerging from mobile media convergence. In these contexts, very immediate issues of users' taste, self-image and even sensory perception take centre stage as challenges for design and the provision of new services.

This last section is opened by *Sharon Baurley, Erik Geelhoed, Philippa Brock* and *Andrew Moore*, who present the chapter *Communication wear: User feedback as part of a co-design process*, showing an interesting line of research that proposes the merging of fashion cultures and the mobile technology sphere. In the Communication-Wear project, a clothing concept is developed that augments the mobile phone by enabling expressive messages to be exchanged remotely, by conveying a sense of touch and presence. It proposes to synthesize conventions and cultures of fashion with those of mobile communications, where there are shared attributes in terms of communication and expression. This research project locates young people as the target of the development of fashion/clothing prototypes by engaging them as co-developers and evaluators. Using garment prototypes as research probes as part of an on-going iterative co-design process, the authors endeavoured to mobilise participants' tacit knowledge in order to gauge user perceptions on touch communication in a lab-based trial. The aim of this study is to determine whether established sensory associations people have with the tactile qualities of textiles could be used as signs and metaphors for experiences, moods, social interactions and gestures, related to interpersonal touch. In this way the study presented here provides a new comprehensive way of looking at the multiple and convergent facets of e-actors.

In the last chapter of this book, *Larissa Hjorth*'s *Beyond the frame: The place of mobile and immobile media*, the development of the electronic self and the electronic portrait of what it is to be human is explored, through analysis of the artistic and filmic organisations for which the brevity of digital media formats affords exciting new opportunities. Hjorth's paper explores the social reasons for this tendency towards brevity, arguing that these reasons should be individuated in the multiplicity of the media that people use on a daily basis. Until a few decades ago, people had at their disposal electronic media such as landline telephone, television and radio. With the new digitalisation and mobilisation of broadband technology, the spectrum broadens towards a variety of other modes of electronically mediated communication. This multiplicity of ICT uses, Hjorth argues, fosters a new brevity of the products that the individual media offer, and even new modes of perception. The rise of mobile media afforded everyday users with the ability to document and edit their stories. However, mobile media promise more than that – the portal to new arising forms of distribution such as MySpace, Facebook, Cyworld minihompy, YouTube etc. These new modes of sharing and context give rise to new modes of mobility. However, in the excitement to document Web 2.0 convergence, some dimensions of mobile media – most notably their oscillation between forms of mobility and immobility, delay and immediacy – are being overlooked. According to Hjorth, mobile media challenge the ocular-centricism of 20th century screen cultures in favour of other effectual economies such as the haptic.

Conclusions

The contributions to this volume, while hailing from a broad variety of disciplines, as well as addressing a multitude of topics, all converge towards one focal point: What it is for different people, under different circumstances and modalities of action, to live in a society that has become essentially reliant on the use of ICTs – even if the modes of using them, and even the possibility of accessing them in the first place, are not evenly distributed. It is precisely this broad variety of experiences of living in this society which is addressed in this book. If the notion of the broadband society, as it emerged from the context of the ICT industries and telecommunications providers, is to have any meaning and practical use as a conceptual tool in social science inquiry, and if a certain technology can be truly said to shape a society to an extent that warrants naming it after that technology, then these uses have to be justified by examples. We consider this book an important step into this direction, starting not from a policy or macro-sociological point of view, but from inquiries into people's experience. In essence, the book's central purpose is to look at the everyday uses of broadband ICTs by everyday people, and to figure out whether there are any remarkably consistent changes in personal routines and social organisation as a result of putting broadband technology resources into the hands of people.

What we can conclude from our collection of examples of different individual and collective experiences with and around ICTs is, firstly, that there are many levels of experience, and that there are many varieties and modes of experience on each of those levels: The use of ICTs may enable a marginalised group to achieve and express a sense of community that has not been accessible to them before, and it may do so in different ways for pre-adolescents and for economically deprived communities in a country's geographical periphery. ICTs may also offer new modes of accessing information, but it remains to be seen whether these new modes truly fit users' cognitive patterns. However, the use of ICTs may even reshape users' ways of perceiving their life-world and of expressing and communicating their emotions.

Secondly, some of the chapters in this volume provide evidence that even non-users of ICTs contribute to shaping the socio-technical framework in which ICTs operate, and are used. Whether these people have simply been left out or whether they consciously decided to refuse ICT use is not completely clear. For some it is about fearing negative health effects although these can hardly be proved or disproved given the short history of broadband ICTs. For others it is about perceiving themselves not to be the target group of the ICT industry's sales strategies. Some find themselves overwhelmed by technological developments whose sheer rapidity even seasoned users find hard to keep up with: non-users' actions do matter, at least in a society in which the principles of equity and participation are valued (Oudshoorn & Pinch 2008).

Thirdly, the shape of the environment in which the citizens of a highly technologised society live is significantly influenced by the presence of ICTs and of the ways in which they are used (Yearly 2008). This fact easily escapes many users' and policymakers attention, as ICTs are frequently imagined as essentially clean technologies, for being considered immaterial, or for being designed as smart means of controlling emissions. The concerns arising in some corners of contemporary society in the post-industrial world are documented here, and should be taken as serious contributions to environmental debates, if not as an invitation to people to consume their broadband gadgets more responsibly, as well as a call to regulatory authorities to rethink and revise their environmental policies.

Each of these conclusions may serve to indicate directions for further research, on at least two levels. Moving from the descriptive approach outlined in this volume, one can move towards macro-sociological and policy perspectives and ask, among other questions: How can different actors' perspectives be integrated into current and upcoming policy debates? How can the differential agency of actors – including all sorts of non-users of ICTs – be addressed in terms of equity and participation? But one can also remain on a more descriptive level and seek to add more empirical pieces to the mosaic, rendering the image of the broadband society more complete. A true explanation of social practices and situations can only come from the detailed and accurate description of the complex articulation of the different elements and actors involved. This endeavour could prove rewarding in itself: in a manner not unlike that of the 18th century natural historians, the attempt to collect and file the manifold specimen encountered in the field may serve as the starting point for well-founded systematic theories to ultimately explain the complex order encountered out there in the broadband society.

References

Lesser E.L., Fontaine M.A., Slusher J. eds. Knowledge and Communities Boston: Butterworth-Heinemann (2000)
Bakardjieva M. Internet Society. The Internet in Everyday Life London: Sage (2005)
Baron N. Always On: Language in an Online and Mobile World Oxford: Oxford University Press (2008)
Bell D. The Coming of Post-industrial Society. A Venture of Social Forecasting New York: Basic Books (1973)
Bourdieu P. Outline of a Theory of Practice Cambridge: Cambridge University Press (1977)
Boyd D., Ellison N. 'Social network sites: Definition, history, and scholarship', Journal of Computer-Mediated Communication 13(1), article 11 (2007)
Castells M., Fernandez Ardevol M., Qiu J.L. and Sey A. Mobile Communication and Society: A Global Perspective Cambridge, Mass: MIT Press (2006).
Contarello A., Fortunati L., Gomez Fernandez P., Mante-Meijer E., Versinskaya O. and Volovici D. 'ICTs and the human body: An empirical study in five countries' eds. E. Loos, L. Haddon and E. Mante-Meijer The Social Dynamics of Information and Communication Technology Aldershot, Hants: Ashgate (2008) pp. 25-38
Fortunati L., Contarello 'A. Social Representation of the Mobile: An Italian Study' ed. K. Dong Shing When Mobiles Came: The Cultural and Social Impact of Mobile Communication Seoul: Communication Books (2005) pp. 45-61
Fortunati L., Vincent J., Gebhardt J., Petrovčič A., Vershinskaya O. Interacting with Broadband Society Berlin: Peter Lang (2009)
Gebhardt J. Telekommunikatives Handeln im Alltag. Eine sozialphänomenologische Analyse interpersonaler Medienkommunikation Wiesbaden: VS Verlag (2008)
Glotz P., Bertschi S., Locke C. eds. Thumb Culture. The Meaning of Mobile Phones in Society Bielefeld: Transcript (2005)

Hackett E., Amsterdamska O., Lynch M., Wajcman J. eds. The Handbook of Science and Technology Studies (3rd Edition) Cambridge: MIT Press (2008)
Haddon L. ed. Communications on the Move: The Experience of Mobile Telephony in the 1990s. COST248 Report (1998) URL: http://www.cost269.org/ (click on Final Report COST248) (accessed January 2009)
Höflich J., Hartmann M. eds. Mobile Communication in Everyday Life: An Ethnographic View Berlin: Frank and Timme (2006)
Ito M., Okabe D., Matsuda M. eds. Personal, Portable, Pedestrian. Mobile Phones in Japanese Life Cambridge: MIT Press (2005)
Jenkins H. Fans, Bloggers, and Gamers: Exploring Participatory Culture New York: New York University Press (2006)
Katz J., Aakhus M. eds. Perpetual Contact: Mobile Communication, Private Talk, Public Performance Cambridge: Cambridge University Press (2002)
Lasen A. Understanding Mobile Phone Users and Usage Newbury: Vodafone R&D Group (2005)
Lievrouw L., Livingstone S. Handbook in New Media London: Sage (2006)
Ling R. 'Should We Be Concerned That the Elderly Don't Text?' The Information Society 24(5) (2008) pp. 334-341
Machlup F. The Production and Distribution of Knowledge in the United States Princeton: Princeton University Press (1962)
Nyiri P. ed. Integration and Ubiquity. Towards a Philosophy of Telecommunications Convergence Wien: Passagen Verlag (2008)
O'Reilly T. 'What Is Web 2.0: Design Patterns and Business Models for the Next Generation of Software' International Journal of Digital Economics 65 (2007), pp. 17-37
Oudshoorn N., 'Pinch T. User-Technology Relationships: Some Recent Developments' eds. E.J. Hackett, O. Amsterdamska, M. Linch, J. Wajcman The Handbook of Science and Technology Studies Cambridge, MA: MIT Press (2008) pp. 541-566
Rheingold H. The Virtual Community Cambridge: MIT Press (2000)
Scott J., Marshall G. Dictionary of Sociology Oxford: Oxford University Press (2005)
Silverstone R., Hirsch E. eds. Consuming Technologies: Media and information in domestic spaces London: Routledge (1992)
Slade G. Made to Break: Technology and Obsolescence in America Cambridge, MA: Harvard University Press (2006)
Sombart W. 'Technik und Kultur' Archiv für Sozialwissenschaft und Sozialpolitik 23 (1911). Reprinted in ed. Moldonado T. Tecnica e cultura. Il dibattito tedesco tra Bismark e Weimar Milano: Feltrinelli (1991) pp. 137-170

Vincent J., Fortunati L. eds. Electronic Emotion. The Mediation of Emotion via Information and Communication Technologies Oxford: Peter Lang (2009)
Wellman B. Networks In The Global Village: Life In Contemporary Communities Boulder: Westview Press (1999)
Wellman B., Haythornthwaite C. eds. The Internet in Everyday Life Oxford: Blackwell Publishers (2002)
Yearley S. 'Nature and the Environment in Science and Technologies Studies' eds. E.J. Hackett, O. Amsterdamska, M. Linch, J. Wajcman The Handbook of Science and Technology Studies Cambridge, MA: MIT Press (2008) pp. 921-948

Theme I:
Uses and practices of new media

Tim Van Lier and Jo Pierson

Identification of Community Practices and Co-creation by Pre-adolescents: The Case of Ketnet Kick

Introduction

We are living in a network society (Castells 2004). Scholars like Castells and Wellman, argue that we live in a paradigmatic shift, for example in the way we are connected to each other. It is the shift from living in "little boxes" to living in networked societies (Wellman & Hampton 1999). People are always and everywhere connected in a positive feedback-loop, according to Wellman. 'The personalization, portability, ubiquitous connectivity, and imminent wireless mobility of the Internet all facilitate networked individualism as the basis of community.' (Haythornthwaite & Wellman 2002, 34). Also digitalisation and online networks cause profound changes in mediated communication and media experiences. Internet services that enable community building have become popular, especially among young people: they grow up using and domesticating these new media (Livingstone 2002). We are heading towards an age of digital natives.

Some scholars also argue that currently, children develop into communicators at an increasingly younger age. The changing environment is transforming the child. Many online communities for children have been conceived, based on this notion. Recently we also observe a rise in interactive and community products and services for children: for example Taatu, Club Penguin, Habbo Hotel, Kid City, the upcoming BBC's Adventure Rock, Toyinima and the Belgian/Flemish case of Ketnet Kick.[1] Gaming, pre-adolescents and virtual social worlds are therefore becoming central research issues.

We need to know how pre-adolescents are acting in this networked society with the possibility of online communities, because we need to provide the right tools to them for an optimal experience. Concretely, we have investigated the meaning of these communities in the current society and how children experience them. Are children experiencing these online communities in a different way? We identified essential practices of children in communities and provide a general insight on this topic. These insights are on the one hand based on a literature study. On the other

---

1 See: www.taatu.com, www.habbo.com, www.kidcity.be, www.clubpenguin.com, www.bbc.co.uk/cbbc/ adventurerock, www.toyinima.be, www.ketnetkick.be.

hand we discuss findings from research in the case study 'Ketnet Kick', a successful collaborative game developed by the Flemish public broadcasting company VRT (Flanders – Belgium) and games developer Larian. First, diaries and questionnaires were used to identify the children's user profiles. Next, six focus group interviews and ten in-depth dual-interviews were done, with in total 71 children in Flanders (Belgium).

Theory on children and online communities

We start with an overview of relevant theoretical aspects related to children and communities. First we give a brief introduction of pre-adolescents' everyday life experiences. Next we give an overview of the different dimensions that, in our view, shape a community. These two components help us in analyzing one particular community case for children: Ketnet Kick.

The child as a game player

This paper focuses on communities for children. There are different theories on the role and position of children in the network society. Often, children are reduced to almighty computer hackers or cyberkids, with the computer as a kind of 'child's machine'. According to Katz (1997), children are at the epicentre of the information revolution and the digital world (Selwyn 2003).

For many children in Western world new media, like internet and games, are no longer unusual or even 'new' but are experienced as everyday, natural and thus domesticated objects. According to Haddon (2004, 183) friends are a central factor in the adoption of new media, and in learning the skills to use them. Wartella and Jennings (2000) talk about 'pervasive media': 'The new media are becoming ubiquitous; that is, touching all aspects of children's lives. As digital circuitry becomes smaller, cheaper, and more plentiful, and as computer networks become larger and more pervasive, new-media implementations are likely to show up anywhere, including the nursery and the playground.' They are often the 'early adopters': 'As 'early adopters' of new media, children and youth are, in many ways, the defining users of the digital media' (Hartmann 2003, 104). However children are not experts but mediators of technologies. They don't know everything of these new technologies, but they use and try to figure out how they can use it in their advantage. The combination of the topics of children and new media are nowadays very relevant to research, but first we certainly need to understand pre-adolescents.

Towards an understanding of pre-adolescents

We have studied children in *middle childhood,* also called pre-adolescents (concept often used within the marketing discipline). These are children between 6 and 12 years old, an age group often overlooked in user research (Fine 1987, 289). Our study focuses in particular on the age group between 8 and 10 years old, who are considered as the 'forerunners' of pre-adolescence. It has been stated that these children increasingly behave like adolescents (Lorre 2005).

The age phase of middle childhood is a transitional phase, which makes it a difficult to research subject (Thornburg 2001) since the children are evolving and changing: psychologically, physically as well as socially.

Three general characteristics – intellectual, social and personal – accurately summarize the essence of middle childhood (Hughes 1999, 172). The most important evolution in middle childhood, on the intellectual plan, is that the child's reasoning becomes more ordered, structured and logic. This affects the child's play, which reflects a growing *need for order*. Secondly, schooling increases the child's social involvement with peers. Friends offer support, a role that previously was reserved for the child's family. *Being accepted by their friends* is of increasing importance for pre-adolescents, and is also reflected in play. The social evolutions in pre-adolescence are the most pertinent is also the opinion of Corsaro (1997, 304): 'Children who are seven to ten years of age in these societies spend much of their lives in mixed-age groups caring for and playing with younger siblings and other younger children in their local communities.' They are shifting from the environment of the family to peer groups. Their social environment is enlarged with school, sports- and youth clubs, which they can choose themselves for a large part (Corsaro 1997).

Finally, there is the huge urge towards self-awareness: they feel a need to demonstrate their talents, knowledge and possibilities to others and to themselves. Also in their play, pre-adolescents show a strong *need for 'industry'*: young people love to show their talents to their peers. They show a strong sense for activity. There is also the need for discovery and activity that is facilitated by an adventurous world, wherein games form the centre. Child's play offers an insight in the development of children, as it often reflects the formation of social networks. Pre-adolescents evolve from fantasy role-play to rule-based play, which to a certain extent functions as a model for 'the real world' (Van Nes 2004).

These aspects are also essential to better understand how children experience communities. These characteristics are hereafter discussed in relation to the experience of online communities.

Online communities

To the extent that internet becomes domesticated by people, it is embraced as a communicative platform. It is a place where people interact and develop communities, often referred to as online or virtual communities. In his introduction Rheingold (2000) defined the latter as:

"social aggregations that emerge from the Net when enough people carry on ... public discussions long enough, with sufficient human feeling, to form webs of personal relationships in cyberspace."

This chapter will discuss the idea of online communities viewed as new places for communication. In it we will investigate if and how the meaning of online and offline communities is different for children. Are online communities also domesticated as a new communication platform for the digital natives?

Towards an understanding of 'community'

The notion of 'community' or network sociality is a very charged concept (Rheingold 2000; Wittel 2001; Turkle 1997). Many scholars already have tried to make a definition. In this brief theoretical part we quote the most essential characteristics of communities. This helps to analyse the different kinds of communities and to better understand the nature of the community.

Already in the fifties Tönnies describes community and society as two overlapping social spheres (Fox 2004). He makes a distinction between 'Gemeinschaft' and 'Gesellschaft'. The 'Gemeinschaft' is a tightly knit community of individuals, while the 'Gesellschaft' is a more individualized, dispersed society (Tönnies 1957).

These notions were part of typifying the age of modernization of society, combined with the negative consequence of often-fragmented social contacts. Tönnies regards the decline of the Gemeinschaft – the place of real, organic contact – as a loss for mankind.

We see a community as a group of people that share a 'sense of community' in a communal space, where interactivity can take place.

Different dimensions shaping a community

Place: The concept community is frequently linked with the connotation of a new kind of 'Gemeinschaft', thus a place where people interact intimately witch each other. Tönnies stresses the importance of locality and a place where people can gather. For Tönnies, the ultimate form of a community is the rural village (Tönnies 1957). We see place as a position in space, whereas space means a continuous area. Locality, however, is regarded as a place occupied by certain people or particular activities. It is more in the sense of an area or neighbourhood. Thanks to virtual media, however, it is no longer necessary for members of a community to be in the same locality. Nowadays the digitalisation and new media offer new ways to interact, but this evolution also leads to new patterns of time and space, referring to the notion of 'time space distanciation' (Giddens 1990, 186). The way people meet and interact has thus evolved. The contexts in which the communities originate are changing (supra).

However, the idea that place is no longer relevant for communities needs to be nuanced. The availability of a communal place (a place that can be shared) is still important, yet this place can now also be a virtual one. The place can serve as a recognizable symbol for a community. Fox (2004, 17) is convinced that 'a community is bound by place, which always includes complex societal and environmental necessities'. Our hypothesis is that this is also a very important aspect for online communities for children.

The interpretation of the concept of 'place' in a context of online communities is reflected in the online –offline continuum. The online sphere, which takes place in the virtual, is mediated, whereas the offline sphere, which takes place in the outside world, is physical. Often, a clear distinction is made between the online and the offline, but in reality this is not always the case. Online and offline spheres are most of the time intertwined, in creating one reality and not two different realities for community members (Wittel 2001; Miller & Slater 2000; Wellman & Hampton 1999). Also Ward (1999) sees the online sphere not as an alien world, as something totally different and cut off from the real world. Both life spheres are part of the everyday life experiences of the user. 'The internet has become a part of everyday life, rather than a separate place to be' (Howard et al. 2003). Thus the concept of place can entail a virtual aspect (the online sphere) as well as a physical aspect (the offline sphere), which constantly influence each other (and ultimately) form one 'place' in the experience of the community members. Our hypothesis is that this kind of hybrid sphere is essential for the experiences of communities of children.

Imagined: The community takes form online and offline, but also exists on the level of the mind. Even Tönnies already described such a kind of community – *community of mind* (Li 2004). The latter stresses the importance of a sense of community or the imaginative. The element 'imagination' transcends the physical and virtual place; we move into the individual and collective imagination, as Fox (2004) suggests. A community exits when it has a meaning for people. This is linked to the concept of 'imagined community' by Anderson (1983, 160): 'All communities larger than primordial villages of face-to-face contact (and perhaps even these) are imagined.'

Communion: A community is only a community when the members experience it as something real. There needs to be a 'common feeling' or a 'will-to-community' (Fox 2004). According to Reid (2005, 166): "The illusion of reality lies not in the machinery itself but in the user's willingness to treat the manifestations of his or her imaginings as if they were real."

Members also have to be committed to the community. This commitment, or 'sense of community', is an essential characteristic. McMillan and Chavis characterise this concept as:

"[...] a feeling that members have of belonging, a feeling that members matter to one another and to the group, and a shared faith that members' need will be met through their commitment to be together" (McMillan & Chavis cited in Meng 2005, 139).

This sense of community has a positive influence on the way a community is experienced. In a virtual community, this is even more the case. The members do not always have face-to-face contact. As such, they need to place trust in the community they are belonging to. More accurately, this 'sense of community' can be called the 'spirit of community', or '*communion*':

"[T]he networks of people that constitute the community. This adds new incentive to the debate as it suggests that the spirit of community or communion that is found among networks of people is [...] more important than having a sense of place" (Ward 1999, 95).

The sense of community stresses an important factor in today's experience of communities. It shows that mind and feeling play a central role in communities. This aspect will be central in our analysis of a community for children.

Interactivity: Communities, and especially online communities, are seen as a group of people that interact with each other in a communal place (supra). In the literature on communities, communication is often seen as an essential factor (Wilbur 1997). Also Rheingold speaks in his definition of the importance of discussions between the members of the community (supra).

We suggest that the concept of 'interactivity' is more suitable. In the following part, it is shown that interactivity cannot be reduced to communication. It seems 'interactivity' can play an important role in bringing a community to live. Interactivity can be understood as the degree people have an influence, have choice and are empowered (Manovich 2001, 354). The different forms of interactivity can play a role in the experience of communities. We recognize user-to-user interactivity, user-to-documents interactivity and user-to-system interactivity[2] (McMillan 2002). Interactivity is also a useful concept in comprehending the Web 2.0 story, actions of children and the possibilities for creativity. Our hypothesis is that user-to-user interactivity is not always required in online communities for children. For this we start from the notion of the imagined community.

Merging of online communities and children

The difference between online and offline interaction is an important element in online communities for children. According to Livingstone (2002), children integrate both kinds of communication in order to maintain their social networks. They move freely between both worlds, although most interactions are local (Livingstone 2002). Thus, the internet positively influences children's existing social contacts instead of undermining them.

As such, online interaction is primarily used to forge 'strong ties'[3] (Subrahmanyam et al. 2001). However, the internet also offers opportunities to form 'weak ties'. It is an environment in which one can meet new people, using applications such as MUD's (Multi-User Dungeons), chat rooms, multiplayer games etc. According to Livingstone (2002) as well as to Valentine and Holloway (2002) children are engaged in two-way interaction in 'the real' as in 'the virtual'. The real world and the virtual world are no separate entities. On the one hand the internet can be seen as a tool for developing online friendships. On the other hand others use it as a means to reinforce their existing offline networks or as a welcome addition to their offline hobbies: they like spending time surfing and 'looking in' here and there (Holloway & Valentine 2003, 180).

Games and interpretative communities

Games are an essential aspect of children's lives, real life games as well as digital games (supra). The latter are often regarded as applications that can only be played. However, Fromme (2003) states that games are frequently integrated in the social and cultural activities of the users. For example, children often play with or against each other, and friends often serve as the most important advisors

---

2   user-to-user: to interact with each other or computer-mediated-communication user-to-documents: the way people interact with content and content makers, the way active users interpret and use mediacontent.
    user-to-system: it is the way people interact with the interface. For example: flow = people lose themselves in simulations, like virtual worlds.
3   Related to the concept developed by Granovetter (1973; 1983).

in game-related issues. This contradicts the idea that playing games leads to isolation. They are integrated in the circles of friends and can originate more or deeper social contacts.

"Playing computer games has generally been regarded as an individual, more or less asocial activity, [...] On the contrary there is a wealth of social activity around the games, which are closely integrated in the social relations and cultural networks of the young" (Jessen 1999, 49).

According to Jenkins, games now offer the same satisfaction and fun as before playing outside did: the exploration and knowledge of the environment, activities with a goal and self-control (Buckingham 2002). Jensen (1999) states that children develop a specific culture in which one has to take part, in order to understand it completely. Children, in his opinion, form interpretative communities, for example around games. He uses football as an example to explain the concept of interpretative community:

"[...] cultural phenomena are quite dependent on living cultural, interpretative communities, and even if there are many differences between football and computer games, both are functions of social and cultural communities" (Jessen 1999, 49).

Games could be the way to incorporate online communities in the lives of children and so merging children with online communities.

The case Ketnet Kick

Within this research Ketnet Kick was chosen as a case to examine the community experiences of children of middle childhood. Is Ketnet Kick really a community? How and where is the sense of community experienced?

Ketnet Kick

Ketnet Kick was developed by the Flemish public broadcaster VRT as an online community in the form of a 3D game for children between the age of 6 and 12. The most frequent players are dspecially the children aged between 8 and 10 . Being set up as a user-generated content application for children, it gives them the possibility to play games, but also make drawings, compose music, improve their dancing skills, create content. Ketnet Kick is designed as a feedback loop: children create content that is showed in the game, on the Internet and on TV. Now children can see what the community of Ketnet Kick is creating and can get inspired.

In the case of Ketnet Kick, it is not possible to have user-to-user interactivity, but there is user-to-documents interactivity in the sense of creating content. One can also speak of user-to-system interactivity since the players can lose themselves in a 3D world. They have the illusion of empowerment.

Ketnet Kick is also based on a story. The purpose is to create a lot of content against Kroknet, the adversary of Ketnet. By creating an enemy one creates an opportunity for a sense of community.

The 3D world provides a communal place for a community. The 3D space online provides a place that they can love, feel and experience. It makes it tangible for the children. Ketnet Kick is a community that has more than 100,000 players and therefore consists of a large group of children who are connected online in a virtual world.

Figure 1: Ketnet Kick screenshot

Method

A child-centred focus

This research is situated in 'the new social studies of childhood': research 'with' children instead of research 'about' children. (Greig & Tayler 1999) Children are seen as competent social actors (Holloway & Valentine 2003). Also Piaget cited by Greig and Tayler (1999) presents children as active 'constructors' of their own knowledge. Here we want to explore how children are constructors of their online communities.

In order to get an in-depth insight in the everyday life and online activities of children, we used a set of different qualitative research methods. The aim was to look at the nature of the phenomenon, based on an explorative and inductive approach and thereby discovering the community practices of children. How do children experience communities? What roles fulfil the dimensions: imagination and interactivity in creating and sustaining a sense of community?

These issues were investigated by the exemplary case: Ketnet Kick, developed by the Flemish public broadcasting company VRT.[4] We chose it for a case study because it could provide us more in-depth results. By choosing one case we also tried to capture the context of this one community. We wanted to provide a full coverage of the community experience. The context can help us to understand the practices of the children.

Data collection

The recruitment of the respondents was carried out in schools. In this way our target group was classified by age and was easily accessible as a group. However children are considered as an internally heterogeneous group. To make a distinction, the typology developed by Livingstone and Bovill (1999, 42) was applied, which makes a distinction depending on how children generate their own style of media use:

- *'Screen entertainment fans'*: these children spend a lot more than the average amount of time in front of the TV-screen, watching videos and playing games.
- *'Specialists'*: they spend more than the average amount of time using one specific medium. Three types are identified: the book fans, the PC fans and the music fans. During the research we discerned other types of specialists: the game fan and the MSN-Messenger fan.
- *'Tradionalists'*: They spend a lot of time with the traditional media (television, music, books, etc.) They spend less time using the PC and playing games.
- *'Low media users'*: These children spend less time than the average on all the media.

---

4   See http://www.ketnetkick.be

Firstly structured diaries were distributed in six classes, spread over two schools. The diaries were used to determine the children's profiles and provided after completing an overview of the children's activities. The main advantage of this unobtrusive method is that it encourages the respondents to record, in a very structured manner, the details of their everyday life as a research diary (Toms & Duff 2002; Corti 1993). After all, gaining an insight in the daily user patterns and the associated experiences (annoyances and aspirations) is crucial in the identification of the dimensions of the community experiences. We asked for some socio-demographic information, hobbies, participation in movements or organisations, media access and media use. Next we asked to register their media use for one week. What were they doing, when and with whom? On the basis of the diary we classified the children according to the Livingstone's typology. The data, collected from the diaries, served as an input for six focus groups with in total 50 children. We conducted separate focus groups with traditionalists, screen entertainment fans and specialists. Two complementary focus groups were carried out wherein the respondents were separated by gender: one with just girls and one with boys. The sixth focus group was mixed in gender and profile.[5]

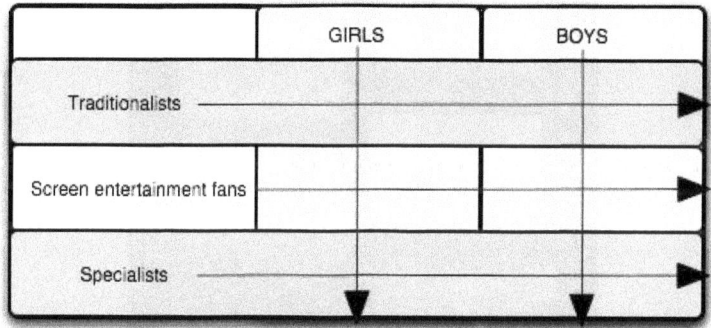

Figure 2: data collection

---

5   The traditionalists contain 8 children of 9 years old, 4 girls and 4 boys. The screen entertainment fans contain 8 children, 4 boys and 4 girls. Two children have the age of eight and 6 the age of nine. The specialists are a group of 9 children with 4 boys and 5 girls, 6 children of nine years old, 2 of eight and 1 of ten. The group is a combination of PC fans, game fans and MSN fans. The group with girls contains 9 children of nine years old. There are 4 traditionalists, 4 screen entertainment fans and 1 PC-fan. The group of boys contain 9 children, 4 children of nine years old, 3 of ten years old and 2 of eight years old. There are 5 screen entertainment fans and 4 game fans. The mixed group contain 7 children, 1 of eight years old and 8 of nine years old. There is 1 traditionalist, 1 game-fan, 2 PC fans and 3 screen entertainment fans.

The focus groups were semi-structured. We used a topic list that consisted of three parts, the world of children, media literacy (especially games and internet) and finally about Ketnet Kick and online communities. Finding the balance between moderating and the free dynamic of the conversation was not always easy to find.he reason for choosing focus groups as a method is related to the fact that group dynamics plays a central role when dealing with communities. *'Groups give children space to raise issues that they want to discuss* (Greig & Tayler 1999, 175). 'However working with children expressed the need for interactive focus groups, since they cannot stay focused for a very long time. Therefore, during the conversations, the children had the opportunity to make drawings of their thoughts and feelings, which were also used as an input for the conversations. We also used incentives to stimulate the thoughts of children. For example we had made a collage of pictures of the main characters of Ketnet Kick to unravel their knowledge and sympathy for the characters.

Figure 3: KNK-collage

We saw how some game-characters were really the start of an animated conversation between the children. This is one of the reasons why we chose a case study closely related to the children, so the conversation could be fun and animated. Conducting research on and especially with children is challenging. During the focus groups, it was sometimes difficult to stimulate the discussion. Listening, however, is very important; it is about them and trying to comprehend them. You need to enter the child's mind. Observation of the children during the conversations was also very fascinating. Often the kids were too enthusiastic, when a relevant topic was discussed. Yet these reactions also told us something on how they experienced the topic. In retrospect however, traditional focus groups do not seem to be the ideal way to conduct qualitative research on children. There is a need for new and interactive research methods (e.g. probing and projective techniques), since it is not so easy to receive information rich judgments from children.

So the focus groups were complemented with 10 in-depth interviews in which two children participated. In these interviews the children were different from the participants in the focus groups. The children in the dual-interviews had some sort of relation with each other (e.g. brother, friend). We chose two people that knew each other to enhance the dynamics of the interview.

All of the data were analyzed by way of the grounded theory approach and the induction method. We wanted to grasp theoretical findings from the empirical data. We transcribed all the conversations in order to code and analyse them. These data, together with extensive desk research, were the basis of this research.

In search of the sense of community in Ketnet Kick

The case of Ketnet Kick (KNK) enabled us to understand how these pre-adolescents make sense of their participation in an online community. KNK is not a community wherein children talk about common topics and interest, due to the lack of user-to-user interactivity within the KNK game. So it is not an ordinary online community like a forum, as it is often stated (supra). The data showed how children experience Ketnet Kick and what they find important.

Identifying the sense of community is looking for activity under the members online and offline. It is also looking for the influence children are feeling. Can this be recognized in KNK?

Specific elements from the game, like the mysterious island[6], and new games are popular topics in offline conversations.

---

6   Mysterious island: a place in KNK where children are unable to go to. Children even created a myth because some children claim that they reached the island and told this to their friends.

> Iris (9 years old, PC-specialist): 'At a certain moment I was standing before a rock far away from me. I heard from a friend of school, that when you jump very far and when you are almost falling, you have to jump again at the right time. Then it is possible to reach the mysterious island, because he has reached it yet many times. He even found a red bottle.
> Int: 'So you think that children already have reached the island?'
> Iris: 'If it is true of course'

It was amazing that some children started a myth around Ketnet Kick and that it lived between the children. The new and the mysterious are important topics of discussion for our respondents, especially among the children who are real fans. This means that Ketnet Kick is in fact part of their everyday conversations at school and at other places where they meet. This implies that KNK has received a place in the lives of people and that this fascination helps to sustain a sense of community.

The interactive feedback loop in KNK[7] also creates a possibility for a feeling of 'togetherness' among the members online, especially in their battle against the evil Kroknet[8]. In this way we can say that all the children playing the game form an imagined community. In order to belong to this imagined and imaginary community, there is no need for direct contact: all gamers battle for their world, the world of KNK. They are fighting for a symbol. Here we see links with the way Anderson (1983) refers to nationalism as the basis for an imagined community: people do not need to know each other in person to love and even fight for the same country. They unite against a common, external enemy. Yet, similar to nationalism, not every member of KNK is equally enthusiastic. Some take the story very seriously, while for others, this is certainly not the main reason to play the game. Other children see past the magic of the game, and experience it as just a game they play for fun. The experience level is therefore not the same for every child.

Another aspect was the importance of the offline sphere wherein children hang out and spend a lot of time together. Children are often very busy and participate in many movements, like youth movements, sport clubs, music schools. So children often participate in many communities, but children will not form large groups. The friendship-groups are often small groups and very local, but essential, because they will share their experiences offline to their best friends. The offline sphere is

---

7 Children can make content in KNK and show it to other children through the game, website and television. The content can be an inspiration or a tool to make content on their own.
8 Kroknet is the adversary of Ketnet (the public tv-station for children). The aim of KNK is to defend the values of Ketnet by creating a lot of content against the wraptors, evil crocodiles, which want to incorporate their tv-station.

a necessary dimension for keeping the community alive and to foster the *sense of community*, especially with pre-adolescents.

There were children who were spontaneously talking about KNK, in order to get help in finishing the game.

> *Irani (9 years old, MSN-specialist): Sometimes, on the playground, he asks me: 'How far did you get? Do you remember how to get passed that level? Do you know what that means?'*

Their conversations are mainly held among friends. In a game, challenge and satisfaction are important. It is essential that children are offered sufficient help, so that they do not give up too soon. It is remarkable that children partly accomplish this need by asking each other for help or by completing a level together. However this cooperation mainly happens offline. This is demonstrated nicely by the following citation:

> *Jonas (9 years old, screen entertainment): 'We always say: 'How far did you get in the cave game?', and the one who got the furthest gets a piece of candy on Monday.'*
> *Int: 'How did you think of that?'*
> *Jonas: 'We use it with games that have levels, like 'flying' or the cave game or the mystery island. Everyone brings three pieces of candy on Monday, and whoever got the furthest in one game, gets one piece of candy from everyone.'*
> *Int: 'And who thought of that?'*
> *Jonas: 'We were talking about the game, and at one point, someone said that we could do that.'*
> *Int: 'That's fun!'*
> *Jeroen (low screen entertainment): 'In fact it is stupid, because you can never prove that you got that far...'*
> *Jonas: 'Yes you can! When you push F7, you can print how far you got in the game!'*

This citation also shows that sometimes children are making their own rules and create their own KNK experience. Children generally try to fulfil this need offline, by asking each other questions. Yet some children also use online channels for this purpose, for example trough MSN-messenger or through a blog.

However, there are also mechanisms offered by Ketnet Kick to help the children, like Star Square or the 'Ket' of the Day[9], are in their own way, also effective. They can be seen as forms of indirect cooperation and are shaped by user-to-documents and user-to-system interactivity that provides alternative ways for helping the members of the community and sustaining the *sense of community*.

---

9 Star square: this is the main location in KNK. In this square creations of players of KNK are showed and available for all the players Ket of the day: Every week a player of KNK is selected and his avatar is showed in the centre of the Star square.

So this community of collaboration is a kind of community that is adequate for pre-adolescents, because during their play they often search for support of their friends. They help and stimulate each other. They give clues; show each other the way. The aspect of support seems important because it was a dimension that occurred several times during the focus groups. The school's playground was an important place where information and support was shared.

However, the community of practice is also available in KNK but in an indirect way. Children are actually alone together in KNK. They experience the world alone but the world is enriched by the creations of the community through Ket of the day and the Star square. These mechanisms are a way to give children recognition and examples, examples of members of the community itself, to build on.

Laurien (9 years, low screen entertainment): " I always look first to Ket of the Day and then I'll try to make something totally different."

In these kinds of interactivity lies the online community practice of the pre-adolescents. Thus, we conclude that Ketnet Kick is an interpretative community (supra), mainly offline but also online, through co-creation, in which the users play and interpret the game together and offline friends are the most important game advisors. Jessen (1999) also stated that these kinds of communities often arise in a game context. This research confirms this and offers support to his concept.

In conclusion children are online engaged in the imagined KNK community. The KNK community is however also sensed offline in small group of friends. Mainly they help each other and form interpretative communities around the game. Ketnet Kick can thus be seen as an imagined multi-platform and hybrid community (online as offline): on internet, television and around friends.

In search of the appealing practices of Ketnet Kick for children

KNK is appealing because it offers a lot of practices relevant to the age group of middle childhood. Since KNK is a game, it greatly appeals to children. As such, it is an appropriate medium to set up a community for the researched age group because it is through play that children create friendships. During play they create their networks and create a 'netplay society', a concept that is more appropriate according us. As stated above, the element of play is thus regarded as more relevant to a community aimed at children than the element of user-to-user interactivity. The theory about children in middle childhood mentions the role of games in children's live (supra). Jessen states this as well:

'The cultures of games playing involves an ongoing construction of an 'interpretive community' and in this respect it may be better suited to the patterns of children's play than older media such as books, which one is alone in consuming' (Jessen 1999, 49).

Our respondents play various electronic games, but also play a lot of games at school and at home. The interviews confirmed the importance of play for social contact between children. Play is central in the everyday life of children. Although pre-adolescents love to communicate, they perceive the play element as more relevant than communication.

Tieboo (8 years old, high screen entertainment): 'You can also chat with your friends because you found a new game...'
Int: 'Which do you like better: playing together or talking to each other?'
Nick (8 years old, PC-specialist): 'I like playing more than talking.
Int: 'And can you tell me why?'
Nick: 'Playing is much more fun than talking, because you can play with your friends and that is more fun. And else, you only talk to one person.'

The interactivity, in the sense of creating, is thus a useful tool to foster the online community for children. This kind of interactivity is more suited for children of middle childhood who like to be active. They are able to enjoy themselves in KNK. Ketnet Kick also provides room for imagination in an adventurous world and that is just what the life of pre-adolescents is all about.

The data have shed a new light on the experience of communities by pre-adolescents and has put the role of user-to-user interactivity into perspective. The emphasis must lie on imagination, creativity and co-creation. The concept imagined community is appropriate here, but maybe this particular online community experience by children could be labelled otherwise: 'imagion', a contraction of imagination and communion. An imagion is a group of children that has a sense of community and has a place as a symbol, but where the experiences of the group lie in user-to-documents and user-to-system interactivity. When we are dealing with pre-adolescents we also speak of a hybrid experience of the imagion. The imagion is living offline.

We have shown our visual interpretation of imagion in Figure 4 to capture the most important dimensions in one view.

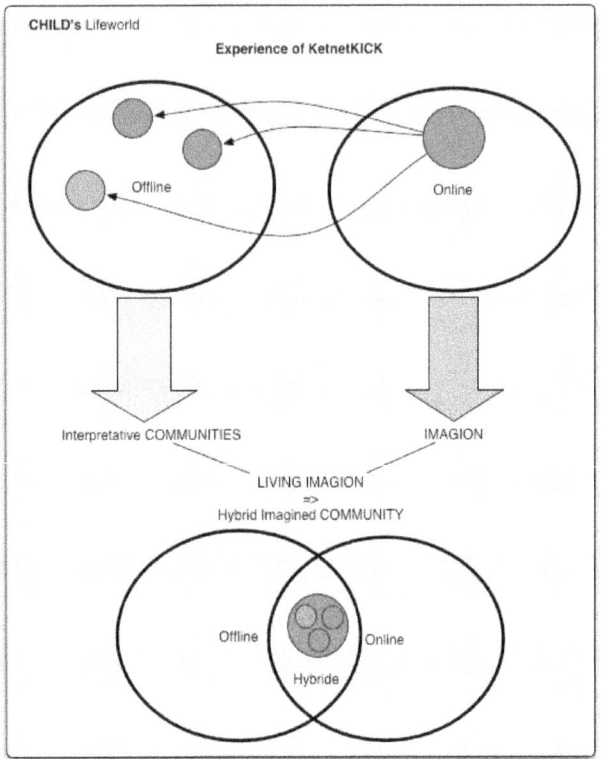

Figure 4: Imagion

Conclusion: communities in the 'netplay' society?

In our analysis we focused on pre-adolescents' relationship to the online communities. We conclude that online communities are to some extent experienced as an important new sphere in the lives of these young people, but we may not underestimate the value of the offline sphere. The online and offline are complementary and both have their specific values. In the case of middle childhood, it is important that we know which sphere provides which values.

Analyzing Ketnet Kick, we can say that children have created a sense of community. They show it with engagement and sometimes some elements in KNK live on their own. One can also notice that children bring the online community more or less 'alive' offline. This indicates the importance of locality and their close friends. If the community wants to be real in the minds of children, it needs to be linked to their own life and experiences; offline interactions can be very helpful. Often, children spontaneously give an offline extension to the online communities. This indicates the commitment to and appeal for the online community. The community lives and goes on in their local community of friends. This indicates another kind of sense of community. The sense of community is very important in the survival of a community. Therefore it is important that the sense of community is stimulated in the appropriate way.

Therefore we suggest that online communities need to be environments, in which children can imagine and play. These are the most striking characteristics for children of middle childhood. The KNK study also demonstrates that online communities can exist without the need for user-to-user interactivity. These findings lead to the idea of an 'imagion', in which the emphasis lies on a sense of belonging and imagination. The online community practices of the children are mainly situated in the creativity. Children also show a tendency to collaborate in this dimension and are active users of user-generated content.

Middle childhood is a transitional phase and also in our research, we found some youngsters who were more active online than others. These are some indications for future research. How do the community experiences evolve in relation to age? Is the online component and need for user-to-user interactivity growing? Still we need to be aware that children remain children and they will always pass through the childhood phase. Children as an audience are not really changed. It is still play (online and offline) that shapes the social network of children and with the incorporation of online community games for children in the social network. In the case of children we could re-interpret the network society as the *netplay society*. Children have new possibilities in the 'netplay society', like interactive communities, that extends their playground, but we may not forget that children remain children. The goal is to incorporate the new possibilities of the internet in the mindset and practices of children. That is why games like Ketnet Kick can form a smooth transition between the 'child's world' and the 'adolescents world'. The concept, 'imagion', can serve as a bridge, to help children, step by step, learning to get involved with the interactive communities.

Central in this research is the combination of two disciplines to generate an interdisciplinary insight: child development on the one hand and the evolution of media and media audiences on the other. The findings acknowledge the current changes regarding child sociology and media use and provide insights on children's digital experiences as a reference for media producers and parents. Moreover, this research stresses the importance of collaboration between researchers and new media designers. It is crucial that notions of online community and Web

2.0 concepts are re-interpreted for and by children. The context of the children's everyday life is a central factor in determining the media practices and needs of children.

Acknowledgements

This article is the result of the Virtual Individual Networks (VIN) project, a joint research project of the Interdisciplinary Institute for Broad Band Technology (IBBT) and several industrial partners. Within this project IBBT-SMIT (Vrije Universiteit Brussel) was responsible for the qualitative user research. I also want to thank my colleagues, Katrien Dreessen and Bram Lievens for their support and ideas.

References

Anderson B. Imagined Communities: Reflections on the Origin and Spread of Nationalism London: Verso (1983)

Buckingham D. 'The Electronic Generation? Children and New Media' ed. Lievrouw L., Livingstone S. The Handbook of New Media London: Sage (2002)

Castells M. The Network Society: A Cross-cultural Perspective Cheltenham: Elgar (2004)

Corsaro W. A. The Sociology of Childhood London: Pine Forge Press (1997)

Corti L. Using Diaries in Social Research Social Research Update Issue 2 Surrey: Department of sociology, University of Surrey (1993)

Fine G. A. With the Boys: Little League Baseball and Preadolescent Culture Chicago: The University of Chicago Press (1987)

Fox S. 'The New Imagined Community: Identifying and Exploring a Bidirectional Continuum Integrating Virtual and Physical Communities through the Community Embodiment Model (CEM)' Journal of Communication Inquiry 28 (2004) pp. 47-62

Fromme J. 'Computer Games as a Part of Children's Culture' Game Studies 3: 1 URL: http://www.gamestudies.org (2003) (accessed January 2009)

Giddens A. The Consequences of Modernity Cambridge: Polity (1990)

Greig A., Tayler J. Doing Resarch with Children London: Sage (1999)

Haddon L. Information and Communication Technologies in Everyday Life Oxford Berg (2004)

Hartmann M. The Web Generation? The (De)Construction of Users, Morals and Consumption Europe: Emtel (2003)

Haythornthwaite C., Wellman B. 'The Internet in Everyday Life: An Introduction' eds. Wellman B., Haythornthwaite C. The Internet in Everyday life Oxford: Blackwell (2002)

Holloway S. L., Valentine G. Cyberkids; Children in the Information Age London: Routledge Falmer (2003)

Howard P. E., Lee R., Steve J. 'Days and Nights on the Internet' eds. Wellman B., Haythornthwaite C. The Internet in Everyday Life Oxford: Blackwell (2003)

Hughes F. P. Children, Play and Development Boston: Allyn and Bacon (1999)

Jessen C. Children's Computer Culture: Three Essays on Children and Computers Odense-Denmark: Odense University (1999)

Katz J. Virtuous Reality: How America Surrendered Discussion of Moral Values to Opportunists, Nitwits, and Blockheads like William Bennett New York: Random House (1997)

Li H. 'Virtual Community Studies: A Literature Review, Synthesis and Research Agenda' Proceedings of the Tenth Americas Conference on Information Systems New York, New York (2004) pp. 2708-2715

Livingstone S. Young People and New Media: Childhood and the Changing Environment London: Sage (2002)

Livingstone S. Bovill M. Young People and New Media: Summary Report of the Research Project: Children, Young People and the Changing Media Environment London: London School of Economics (1999) URL: http://www.psych.lse.ac.uk/young people (accessed January 2009)

Lorre D. Kinderen voor de televisie: Stimulatie presentatie Ketnet brand strategists network September 1st 2005

Manovich L. The Language of New Media Cambridge, MA: The MIT Press (2001)

McMillan S. J. 'Exploring Models of Interactivity from Multiple Research Traditions: Users, Documents, and Systems' eds. Lievrouw L. A., Livingstone S. The Handbook of New Media London: Sage (2002)

Meng M. It Design for Sustaining Virtual Communities: An Identity Based Approach Maryland: University of Maryland (2005)

Miller D., Slater D. The Internet: An Ethnographic Approach Oxford: Berg (2000)

Reid E. 'Virtual Worlds: Culture and Imagination' ed. Jones S. CyberSociety: Computer-Mediated Communication and Community Thousands Oaks, CA: Sage (2005)

Rheingold H. The Virtual Community Cambridge, MA: MIT Press (2000)

Selwyn N. "Doing IT for the Kids': Re-Examining Children, Computers and the 'Information Society" Media, Culture & Society 25 (2003) pp. 351–378

Subrahmanyam K., Kraut R. E., Greenfield P. M., Gross E. F. 'The impact of home computer use on children's activities and development' The Future of Children 10 (2000) pp. 123-144

Thornburg H. D. 'Is Early Adolescence Really a Stage of Development?' Theory into Practice, XXII (2001) pp. 79-84

Toms E. G., Duff W. "I Spent 1 1/2 Hours Sifting through One Large Box...': Diaries as Information Behaviour of the Archives User: Lessons Learned. Journal of the American Society for Information Science and Technology 53 (2002) pp. 1232-1238

Tönnies F. Community and Society New York: Harper and Row (1957, 1887)

Turkle S. Life on the Screen; Identity in the Age of the Internet New York: Touchstone (1997)

Valentine G., Holloway S. L. 'Cyberkids? Exploring Children's Identities and Social Networks in On-line and Off-line Worlds' Annals of the Association of American Geographers 92 (2002) pp. 302–319

Van Nes R. K. Communiceren met jongeren over wetenschap en techniek Amsterdam: Stichting Weten (2004)

Ward K. J. 'Cyber-ethnography and the Emergence of the Virtually New Community' Journal of Information Technology 14 (1999) pp. 95-105

Wartella E. A., Jennings J. 'Children and Computers: New Technology – Old Concerns' The Future of Children: Children and Computer Technology 10 (2000) pp. 31-43

Wellman B., Hampton K. 'Living Networked On and Off Line' Contemporary Sociology 28 (1999) pp. 648-654

Wilbur S. P. 'An Archaeology of Cyberspace: Virtuality, Community, Identity' ed. Porter D. Internet Culture New York: Routledge (1997)

Wittel A. 'Toward a Network Sociality' Theory, Culture & Society 18 (2001) pp. 51-76

Beatriz D.I. Galán, Andrés Arq. Maidana Legal and Senar D. I. Pedro

Design and communication for local development: technological decisions in collaborative scenarios

Introduction

Design for development is an approach that aims to develop a new conceptual matrix in order to actively face the dissociation between technology and society. It is carried out at the CAO Centre (Computer Aided Design Centre) of the University of Buenos Aires and sets in motion the experience of design. It accompanies local communities in the unfolding of strategies of inhabitability linked to the axis of local development: water and sanitation, territorial rooting, creation of satisfactory employment, reconstruction of the productive fabric, food safety, peace, and the accessibility of vulnerable communities to the cultural circuits.

Our project (http://www.investigacionaccion.com.ar) conceives the designer as an agent of technological change who makes it possible to develop a technological-, product- and communication-culture, starting with an animation device based on Web 2.0 which articulates, connects and/or communicates the requirements, needs and/or resources of the territory where it is located with other social networks in other geographies. We present our theoretical and methodological framework. We describe some experiences of technological assistance and hosting from the university to civic initiatives regarding water and sanitation, satisfactory employment, and territorial rooting in isolated areas, geographically or socially speaking, in order to promote the technological and methodological contributions of small-scale solutions.

Presentation of our project: History

Our project RED (Project RED: *Interface between Design and the Community* has worked since 1990 in Computer Aided Creation at the Facultad de Arquitectura, Diseño y Urbanismo UBA. The Formation of a Net-Design Experience as a Device of Animation, Empowerment and Prospective of a System of Innovation. Financed by Secretaría de Ciencia y Técnica de la Universidad de Buenos Aires, the project acknowledges its origin and expansion in the university's process of openness towards the community. It took place parallel to the creation of the *CAO* (Computer Aided Design) Centre.

The hypothesis behind this initiative was that the forming of a critical mass in research in the field of new information and communication technologies, associated with a transfer device, has created a new agenda for research in design. The projects for the transfer of new technologies were like 'windows to everyday life', serving as devices to unveil the behaviours of local communities, obstacles to the appropriation of technologies and the ethics that guided their technological and design practices within the productive system.

Knowledge problems in technological transfers

When accepting the transfer experiences, the use of new technologies did not have to be an objective in itself: we assumed that they, along with design, would be in the horizon of any productive unity or community as a component of their practices. Our task was to find groups, communities and ventures that were working on this process. The notion of 'accompaniment' is considered an essential component of this proposition. We assist in self-management processes which are generators of autonomy that transforms communities into subjects of development. Since concluding the experiences, we have systematised the relationship of design, new technologies and development. These considerations about technology transfer, in local contexts, are based on the accumulated historical experience of technological frustrations due to an assimilation which was incomplete and not well articulated. We suggest that 'appropriation' as the process through which a community develops is a proactive relationship between technology and its own objectives.

We consider that 'strategic innovation' encompasses those acts of technological creativity oriented to the adaptation and adoption of technologies in relation to local community development objectives. It is creativity which is not valued in the field of innovation, but necessary in order to 'metabolise' technologies by means of intelligent learning. Local initiatives, the projects, operate as devices for the restitution of the 'social' character of technology as an adjustment factor between aspirations and resources. Technological animation is the process through which a community is introduced to the use of new technologies according to the development priorities. The theoretical premises were: *technological change as a scenario, participative research action and communitarian construction as methodologies, endogenous development as an objective and the designer as a facilitator of cultural practices.* The design prepares the issue to impose a new dynamic: that of new technologies. Design carries the germ of ICTs and their social and productive dynamics into the core of communities and their productive units. In our proposition, the experience of the socialisation of knowledge is a research topic which repositions and redefines technique within the context of sustainable local development (Galán et al. 2006, 62-66). Authors like Antonio Vázquez Barquero (Vázquez & Madoery 2001, 109) have pointed out that technological progress presents an endogenous behaviour motivated by the effects that it generates on it, the generation of a better understanding of facts and learning.

Role of the local context

During the 1970s, Argentina witnessed the collapse of the import substitution models that had enlivened the development of its national industry; like other countries in Latin America, it did not possess a project of productive development with an endogenous character. Later, the productive system endured the consequences of the neo-liberal policies of the 1990s, which dismantled it almost completely. In 2001, after almost 20 years of stagnation of the productive system, a large percentage of the population was left out of the job market, unable to understand the new productive dynamics, and living under the shelter of state subsidies. The most significant aim of our project was therefore to rebuild the damaged social network, detecting and helping the appearance of new family and community productive strategies by means of technological evolution and focusing on the construction of a science of Design (Piscitelli 2002, 24).

In this direction, we identified different factors, institutions or productive initiatives which are linked to social groups: survival initiatives, related to a family group or a group of families interacting with each other.

- The initiatives of community action strategies by means of associativism in the area of the social economy, based on territory on a 'neighbourhood' scale.
- Initiatives of NGOs that work in the local area and are unaware of each other's knowledge of actions, frequently resulting in overlapping activity.

Relationship between the productive unit and territory: the innovation system

Endogenous growth takes its impulse in a scenario where the knowledge accumulation variable is the determining factor of progress. The local development of a community takes place in a setting where the factors of the accumulation and development of knowledge are present as part of the first step. This determines the progress linking design to knowledge. The basic characteristic of this contribution is to consider technical progress as a factor determined in an endogenous way (Vázquez & Madoery 2001, 90). That is why the deeper is the accumulated and socialised human knowledge, the faster the development of the community. Thus, the productive growth will always tend to be faster, with a positive impact on the local social structure: to have a large proportion of the population educated and sensitised in technological issues, and an economic-productive environment that is favourable to the generation of human knowledge.

The movement has two directions: one, which transmits knowledge from the productive unit to the territory (bottom-up), generating a productive atmosphere (Boscherini & Poma 2000, 24), and another one that tends to transmit the dynamics of the territorial institutional system to the productive units (top-down) (Boscherini & Poma 2000, 24). It is during the development and maturing of the productive units that isolation is broken. The representation of the territory is expanded, since the resources-inputs-opportunities-threats networks are on diverse scales. It is at this crossroads between the local and the contextual in which globalisation is consummated. Then, new alternatives can be imagined, trajectories can be outlined, and strategies can be defined.

The strategic management of design for local development remains defined as a project-based practice whose aim is to achieve structural joining between an external context, articulated in the logic of globalisation, and an internal one whose logic comes from the resources and local answers. This articulation is built through actions of ordering the local resources and the enrichment of externalities generating global visibility for the actors and factors of the district.

The approach to communitarian construction

The approach to communitarian construction is based on the concept of social capital. Pierre Bourdieu distinguishes three forms of capital: economic capital, cultural capital and social capital. He defines social capital as 'the aggregate of the actual or potential resources which are linked to possession of a durable network of more or less institutionalised relationships of mutual acquaintance and recognition'. His treatment of the concept is instrumental, focusing on the advantages of the possessors of social capital and the *deliberate construction of sociability for the purpose of creating this resource*. Bourdieu (1986, 241-258), but it imposes a participative construction on the community's side which implies the task of overcoming the dependence on subsidies: self-esteem, generation of feelings of community, and becoming aware of the individual and collective assets of the neighbourhood.

There are various methodologies under certain common patterns: it is an oriented approach, the assets (not the shortcomings) support the reconstruction of social relations and structures, weakened by decades of migrations, uprooting, disinvestment and isolation (Jorge et al. 2003). It considers poverty as a complex weave of factors, a net of intertwined problems, pertaining to health, the environment, employment and it is necessary to untie the knot of the problem. Part of this problem is ignorance regarding the productive dynamics and the restrictions of the narrow boundaries of the locality.

The approach of 'communitarian construction' (Jorge et al. 2003) is based on the following principles: to be focused on specific initiatives, working on activities according to priorities needs; to be conducted by the community with a broad participation criterion, the community must be owner of the project and the results; to have an entrepreneur-communitarian approach, avoiding the processes of diagnosis without losing a global vision of the problems; to rest on the assets of the community, emphasising the resources and not the deficiencies; to set out from the local scale, towards society, neutralising the isolation and searching for resources out of the local scale; to attack with a strategic vision the barriers that create exclusion (Jorge et al. 2003). The fulfilling of this principle takes time for a discussion for public policies have fragmentary visions of problems that generate exclusion.

The role of design

The valorisation and organisation of the resources, competencies and beliefs of each community lead to a project/programme that implies the unfolding of activities. These involve means which are defined within the framework of communication and product policies. Seen in this perspective, products or interfaces must comply with patterns of cognitive and symbolical as well as technical and economic (Galán et al. 2005, 555-556) performance. This process suggests a re-reading of the contribution of design, bringing in specific resources: by productive mappings and social cartography, contributing to the visibility of territory networks; by elements of communication and visual systems expressing local identities; by local products articulating with the dynamics of demand and by interactive websites transforming local communities in subjects of the information society (Galán 2007, 33).

An important line of our methodology is to value the symbolic capital of communities: 'The symbolic capital is that denied capital, recognized as a legitimate one, i.e., unknown as capital, (…), that constitutes, together with the religious capital, the only possible way of accumulation when the economical capital is not recognized' (Bourdieu 2007, 187-188). Local communities are expanding in their geographical horizons. They must incorporate a more complex vision of the territory as resources and commercial opportunities come from a different scale to the neighbourhood and local ones. Urban markets postulate new patterns to consider in the strategies of communication and construction of identities. Communities find themselves elaborating their identities beyond their own territories, negotiating and struggling in the global space for their threatened existences. This idea was initially raised by Nestor García Canclini, as quoted by Ortiz (1996, 91). This deepening of modernisation, this scenario generated by new technologies, creates a space favouring small communities that were unable to construct their contents in their own national spaces. For example, little districts are valued in the tourism market as an alternative to traditional cities; workcraft production that are not valued by industrial production have a greater presence in the urban market; ethnic communities, in the past discriminated and excluded from economic activity, vindicate production in the market of cultural industries. They do so by communicating values and advantages in a consumption ambiance that values diversity. With the weakening of national borders it is becoming possible to visualise the emerging communities. Latin America is a space featuring the immense diversity of ethnic groups and political expression as a result of which attempts are emerging everywhere to generate a social, sustainable economy as an effort to reproduce life and defend the threatened environment. In these attempts, the embryo of a different ethics of local development could reside and hence the crucial importance of defining new ways in which society, technology and nature can co-exist.

Design has the role of technically supporting communities and animating the possibilities that arise from the new dynamics. Work is unfolding on three fronts: stimulating dynamics and possibilities that emerge because of new technologies: networking; the construction of social and symbolic capital, generating interfaces or applications suited to users who make ICT resources available to communities, undertaking a critical reflection about the impact of these applications on the objectives of development as understood from the point of view of local interests.

Technology is but one aspect of this process. The strategic utilisation of the possibilities enabled by ICTs depends on learning the network dynamics, on negotiation in complex institutional spaces. Reaching out from the public and state university we have got in touch with the most vulnerable sector of civil society. There is a sector that has already successfully appropriated the possibilities offered by Web 2.0. It feeds on knowledge available in the professional market, it has highly professionalized leaders, it manages resources on an international and a national level and, for this same reason, it does not bring forward obstacles in the use of ICTs. The segment we support is much more spontaneous, less professionalized, more genuine in the sense of a vital proximity to the problems they face, and much more vulnerable in terms of financial resources, with no access to the professional market specialised in terms of the service economy.

For the productive units of the social economy, transcending the limitations of the local scale is a key factor in order to gain access to markets and place their products or services in national and international spaces. But this not only depends on their capacity to communicate, but also on the capacity to manage, to develop a logic of distribution, to understand the dynamics of economic sectors and branches, to develop sustainable legal structures, and to take productive responsibilities. Above all, the capacity to become intelligent organisations capable of processing information about consumption scenarios, and translating them into products or services, making them available as regards adequate opportunities and economic circuits in due time and a proper form. In short, incorporating research as a permanent activity. This is only possible by means of a strategic alliance with the public university which plays its role as an agent of development and a technological referent.

Next we offer a brief overview of accessibility to ICTs in Argentina We also present cases taken from the social economy or from civil society that belong to this vulnerable segment and which are undergoing this transformation process in which the Web is playing a key role – whether as a horizon for the project, as a project under way, or already in evolution towards Web 2.0. These initiatives are, in turn, the carriers of certain significant values in terms of what is happening in this vast and vital third sector of Argentinean society.

New technologies in Argentina: some indicators

According to the annual Networked Readiness Index (NRI 2007) prepared by the World Economic Forum, the nation went from 71st place to 63rd place, in the 2006/07 period most countries in Latin America showed an improvement in their use of information technologies in the last year. This study was developed by the Forum in collaboration with the International Business School INSEAD and bases its conclusions on the application and use of information technologies as one of the factors taken into consideration in order to determine a country's competitiveness. Among other factors, we find regulatory frameworks; infrastructures; the preparation of citizens, governments and firms to take advantage of the resources and their real use of cutting-edge technology.

Another factor is the level of access to the Internet, especially broadband. Around 1,583,713 connections to the Internet through broadband were registered in Argentina by the end of 2006, showing annual growth of 66.2% in high-speed connections, according to the third edition of the Cisco Broadband Barometer.

Based on an analysis performed by the Cisco Broadband Barometer, the main results are:

- In the second semester of 2006, the Home segment experienced a 31% rise and the Business segment an increase of 17.7%. According to data from the INDEC for 2005, in Argentina there are 10.07 million homes. If we considered the current amount of broadband technology connections in the Home segment, namely 1.58 million, we may conclude that only about 15.7% of these homes have an Internet connection with broadband technology.
- A fact to take into consideration is the growth in broadband connections in the Education segment, which reached almost 29%. During the June/December semester, total penetration in the Education area was 14.7%. In this period, an increase occurred mainly according to individual initiatives of educational units in the country.
- ADSL access technology grew by 76% during the last year, which makes it the type of connection enjoying the biggest increase, followed by Cable Modem connections with a 49% increase.
- Dedicated Lines rose 24.4% during the last semester, mainly in the segment of small- and medium-sized businesses. As far as satellite technology is concerned, it grew by 12.7% during that same period mainly in the Government and Education segments.
- In the Metropolitan Area of Buenos Aires, connections expanded 23.4% between June and December 2006. Outside this area, connections increased 57.4% during the same period.
- Although the Optical Fibre Corridor formed by the City of Buenos Aires, the provinces of Buenos Aires, Córdoba, Santa Fé and Mendoza keeps concentrating 90% of connections, a higher increase is beginning to be noticed in the tourism and productive areas of the country outside the Metropolitan area.

ICTs and social inclusion

An urban strategy for technological inclusion must turn to the 'bottom-up' model. Castells (1996, 48-49) points out that 'Disconnected areas are discontinuous culturally and spatially' and they must have a combination of political strategies and social software in relation to which we should mention the following:

- Promote Web 2.0 in which citizens and politicians take part.
- Open access to the Internet: generalised and inexpensive telecommunications networks.
- A broad and diverse basis of knowledge.
- The use of open and flexible licenses for knowledge and 'cultural products' (ranging from Copyleft to Creative Commons), which favour the reuse and recombining of software.

Challenges for the Internet on a territorial scale are the hyper-local networks where the power of digital networks and physical networks come together, incorporating what is local and what is global. We believe that the Internet and ICTs are an innovative means that relate to local development and animate the system of social, productive, institutional, economic and territorial structures, creating the conditions for the generation of synergies, and these move the production processes that originate in these synergic capabilities for both the production units that are part of these innovative means and for the community as a whole. We no longer think in economic equations, nor do we reinvent concepts about development; instead, we must tend to achieve a balance between sustainable social growth and the development of human capital.

Although many citizens do not have access to a computer, Argentina features a network of small stores which offer Internet access, even in the humblest neighbourhoods; a population that is literate and interested in new technologies. This conforms a scenario in which an individual owning a Pendrive and an application such as the one we propose has the possibility to edit his or her own site according to his or her own individual or community interests. Another possibility is to enlist NGOs as agents of dynamisation in order to create an environment for the appropriation of ICTs. We therefore stimulate the use of social software. The chosen technology has Open Source features and we support the collaborative paradigm of open access to knowledge.

Something is open when it can be – and has high probabilities of being – discovered, rediscovered, analysed, used and modified by another user. That is a 'language', and as such it makes us understood (uses standards) and does so in a very simple way.

No less important and an 'Achilles' heel' is the graphic interface for which one has to have a clear notion of the cultural characteristics of the local inhabitants, their idiosyncrasies, whether they tending more towards multimedia, image, icons, sounds, or videos. These are the tips that were taken into account when designing the system interface. The contents must be elaborate with the objective of achieving synergy in the identity and the message that is to be transmitted, hence the use of narrations from the locals themselves, videos, maps, networks etc.

When a network works, it connects the agents of change or replicating agents of this initiative. Here it is important to consolidate what we call the *focus of development of open-source technology*. This must be anchored locally; it must share a material space and must be well-defined. This physical space will be one in which to replicate, assist and train in the use of Web 2.0 technology.

Construction of the cases

Experience 1. ICTs in the Delta of the Paraná

Delta of the Paraná is the name given to the final part of the Paraná River system, with an overall surface area of 17,500 km². It is the second in importance in South America, after the *Amazonas* one (Bonetto 1986, 574). It spans from the city of *Diamante* (the province of Entre Ríos) to the mouth of the *Paraná* and *Uruguay* rivers in the *Río de la Plata* estuary. In 2000 it was declared a World Biosphere Reserve, promoted by Argentina at the UNESCO, with the aim of protecting the natural riches of the area, and of stimulating economic activities with a sustainable ecological profile. The first section of the islands – an area strongly dominated by agricultural activities in older times – is these days an area in which tourism and sports activities are concentrated. The 2nd, 3rd and 4th sections are still areas predominantly featuring primary productive activity, where the forestation of salicaceae for paper so far constitutes an almost mono-production, although there are also producers with wicker plantations for handcrafted products, and growing cattle farming activity involving large producers.

The change in activity meant that many who had been small fruit producers had to abandon the Delta or start working as employees since forestation began to demand substantially larger economic units. Those without access to new land lost their quality of independent producers and had to migrate to the city, thereby becoming part of the labour circuit linked to recreational activities or of unemployed sectors.

Hands of the Delta is an artisans' co-operative that congregates 21 family micro-businesses in the area of the Tigre district that work in the production and commercialisation of objects manufactured in rush, wicker and willow. All of its members were born on the islands located between the second and third sections of the Delta of the Paraná.

Each family of artisans manufactures original products based on raw materials that they grow in their homes and fields, and which are transformed in their workshops, using their own production techniques. They know technologies and possess basic tools for this transformation. In order to commercialise these products, this organisation has a location at the *Puerto de Frutos del Tigre* – a commercial space of great diffusion in the area of the Autonomous City of Buenos Aires and the Province of Buenos Aires – which was assigned by the local city council in 1996.

The active policies for the reconversion of areas of the population of the Delta from the production of fruit and vegetables to the production and transformation of wicker and its by-products into products have remarkably broadened the sustainable capacity of the families and small and micro productive projects with behaviour that is respectful of the region's natural and social resources. *Manos del Delta* was established as a co-operative in 1996. As an intermediate organisation it has since covered the role of a link between the delta population and the markets, contributing to the sustainability of each productive enclave.

Actions undertaken

In 2004 an agreement was made between the Co-operative and our project. During the first phase, the brand Manos del Delta was redesigned and a website was designed containing a product catalogue. Through the online catalogue the Co-operative reached out to the national market. Here it is necessary to point out that the sales point is only open three days a week. The artisans remain on the islands for the rest of the week, staying involved in the production they will put up for sale on the weekend. This commercialisation system by means of a web catalogue reinforces their remaining in the territory. The site is static and conventional but someone has been trained to update the catalogue by means of some graphic resources and by editing the contents – which was previously done by means of FTP access – in order to update product prices and images. There is no broadband available in the area but it is currently being installed as a result of steps taken by a local NGO, the Civil Association 'Arroyo Felicaria'.

Today such actions developed together with this institution have improved the local and global visibility, contributing to the construction of networks of institutional relationships. As examples we can mention five international and two national publications which speak about this institution and where members have obtained several types of institutional support: the Premio Jauretche, a benefit for the development of productive projects given by the Ministerio de Desarrollo Social de la Nación in Argentina. At the same time, the A*gentina Solidaria* project financed by the BID Banco Interamericano and developed through the Facultad de Ciencias Económicas of the Universidad de Buenos Aires meets the Cooperativa Manos del Delta through the academia network built by the interaction with our work team and with the project are built a series of innovations in organisation and management which provide a new institutional dynamism that derives from the change in directive commission. Beyond these examples, the accompanying managements developed by our team generated, among other lines of products, the obtaining of means of production, technological complements, productive reorganisation, the incorporation of new ways of making sales, the widening of production standards in terms of the work environment and improving the situation in respect of healthy and safe work.

Asociación Civil Arroyo Felicarias (Civil Association 'Arroyo Felicarias')[1]

The demand itself for local development projects leads from micro-projects to a scale perspective through a network of organisations that articulate themselves by means of technology.

This is the case of the Civil Association and Popular Library 'Arroyo Felicarias' (Located in the north of the province of Buenos Aires. Coordinates Latitude: 34°14'22.58'S Longitude: 58°32'5.41'W). A link with the experience involving Manos del Delta arose because one of its members was a member of the Board of Directors of the Felicarias Association. Understanding the achievements obtained by the Manos del Delta co-operative, they suggested we work on the development of Web 2.0 applications for the purpose of communicating its actions and generating awareness and actions with other entities with similar concerns.

The objectives were:

- To constitute a Pole of Open Source Development that would supply the Delta schools located more than 15 km from the mainland.
- To dynamise the educational, communicative and production activities, proposing a Web 2.0 system as a social tool among young people, teachers and representatives of other NGOs.
- To dynamise by means of Web 2.0 the association's internal and external communication.
- To introduce contents into the wireless connection programme that is being carried out.

We knew from previous experiences that the qualification of human resources and appropriation of the technological tool would constitute a problem. We therefore introduced a training course in Web 2.0 technologies which was attended by people whose task was to design the site, plus one person from the Association. This joint training of designers and members of the Co-operative allowed for integration right from the stage of design, favouring appropriation of the platform. At the same time, Web 2.0 replicators were formed that in this case would be strategic for the Poles of Open Source development.

At the time this text was written, the experience was being carried out in its tuning-up stage. We anticipate that the expectation created by this experience and the Web 2.0 tools have emerged as a result of the positive synergy among other social actors from the Delta. Such is the case of three schools of upper secondary education and one of technical education. The sense of this experience was

---

1 More information here: www.investigacionaccion.com.ar/felicarias

to collaborate with a local organisation of civil society, considering the need to implement the wide fibertel in the Delta. This is necessary for the development of Manos del Delta and other productive units which had to develop most of their websites with a small degree of interactivity. The strategic association between the NGO and the university allows these initial limitations to be overcome.

Design and Technology for the Creation of Environmental Citizenship

Experience 2: The 'El Riachuelo' Foundation.

This experience was carried out for the Project 'WATER + SANITATION', Barrio Villa Jardín. District of Lanús. Buenos Aires. Argentina
The objectives were:

- To develop a digital repository of citizens' initiatives containing successful strategies in the area of water + local sanitation and which may be of public access through the Internet.
- To develop a system based on Web 2.0 that may be maintained and updated by local residents.
- To encourage the use of Web 2.0 tools for the communication of activities and local identity.
- To create a centre for the development of open-source technologies that may collaborate and/or potentiate activities carried out in the area.

Identified problems

In the area of *Villa Jardín* the rate of informatisation is very low, although this stands in contrast with their will to communicate their experience in the field of environmental sanitation, and the social cohesion that has been brought about by this activity. The original population still lives there; it is already the third generation living in this neighbourhood. Not only is it remaining on the same plots of land but also, when the time comes to move, the residents choose to stay in the same neighbourhood.

This peculiar feature of the location has enabled the elders to tell to the younger ones what the neighbourhood was like before the arrival of potable water. It is such a successful and innovative methodology that the news has gone beyond the neighbourhood's boundaries. As a result, other neighbourhood organisations have asked for help in order to start travelling along this same road: to obtain a healthier environment.

On the other hand, it is also a fact that in other locations in Argentina there are NGOs that are beginning to take this same road and that have to go through the same difficulties. They would be the target of this Website 2.0. In this way, thanks to the experience of others they can foresee the difficulties and may successfully avoid them, while managing to bring safe drinking water to their communities.

Actions undertaken

The following points were taken into account when designing the information system for the Foundation:

- Ease of site maintenance and updating.
- The possibility to generate a virtual meeting point for relationships by means of online discussions.
- The site would be a tool for the presentation and communication of the Foundation on the Internet.
- The feature of incorporating young people or people familiarised with informatics as those who directly work with the site, while older adults would be those generating the contents. For example, narratives, photographs, stories, anecdotes.

We worked with the webpage concept, considering its graphical interface and the array of more common elements such as sidebars, navigability, graphic elements.

Special attention was paid to the visibility and usability of the graphic elements, putting more emphasis on their presentation and design. It is important that it may be visualised and understood at a glance. Texts were reduced to a minimum, and sound was incorporated as a communication element. Sound was presented by means of narrations of experiences, using the voices of those who had taken part in them, thus allowing the site to be appropriated as an element in which each one would portray the effects of residents introducing potable water into their homes. We picked resources from social cartography in order to identify zone-milestones within the territory, and these were presented in the form of a map to residents of the area. This was not only done in a graphical format but also on the Web in order to allow them to gradually add their own milestones to it.

The maintenance and updating issue was resolved by means of the graphical interface of a blog. A database of the blog type, programmed in php, was given a graphical interface. Thus, advantage was taken of the system's ease of maintenance, avoiding the use of specific website design and maintenance programmes and forcing a broader qualification of human resources.

The icons in this command console were adapted to the needs of those who would use it. In this way the size and graphics of the access icons to every feature in the blog were defined.

Every step described is performed with free software of the open-source type, as is the site as a whole. The system can be delivered to those who require it, always on the condition that it will remain under the license of open-source software. This is an important issue for one internal guideline for the research group was that this system could be spread to other NGOs that might require it.

For the purpose of establishing relationships with other NGOs, the Foundation was offered a graphical piece, as a quality seal, with which other entities would be called in to discuss, agree and compose the norms that would govern the publication of experiences or projects in the Internet repository.

Work was also carried out on a brand for the neighbourhood in which the experience was developed. In this way, its inhabitants would have an image of their neighbourhood that would nurture a sense of belonging to both the neighbourhood and to the rest of the city.

In a space in which reality is, in great measure, a social construction, moulded by many hands, the designer/animator has the role of an agent of change and for ensuring cohesion of a group, making the behaviour of the neighbours valuable. This case dismantles the generalised beliefs regarding most solutions whereby citizens' participation is limited to denouncing expected state policies. The sense of the project consisted of giving the local group a series of tools and necessary means to make it valuable first, and to afterwards export the implemented methodology in the territory, giving locals a stronger self-esteem and positioning them in another way to be interlocutors of the state in environmental proposals. This information is reflected by the same neighbours who have Web 2.0 technologies becoming generators of information, thereby breaking the static paradigm of bits consumption.

Final comments and prospects

Access to Web 2.0 enables productive initiatives in isolated areas, with different types of exclusion and isolation, to reach distant markets and win resources that are available on the web. In both cases, Riachuelo and Felicarias, we observe that civil society through organisations in our space has the need for and offers the population with different problems of isolation and exclusion a better position, while taking advantage of their accumulated capital in the contexts of reference, in markets or political contexts bringing benefits and fortifying institutions. In one case, Manos del Delta, and Asociación Arroyo Felicarias , the existence of a leader group, respecting consensuses, and accompanied by the public university led to the accomplishment of the proposed objectives: the appropriation of ICTs in their local development objectives. In the case of Riachuelo, there is a greater difficulty of implementing the participation of the neighbourhood. This confirms our hypothesis that the ICTs generate development when there is an effective process of appropriation stimulated by civil society, and leaders with concrete local initiatives, and in conditions of ongoing participation: the local communities are the ones which establish goals and build development horizons.

It is possible to scale a management model which would combine an incubator with accessibility to Web 2.0, based on intermediate entities that act as incubators of local initiatives. This led us to establish a systematic procedure consisting of a hosting service and technical assistance for communitarian initiatives which is administered by means of local associations, complementing the projects and actions of animation of the communitarian action strategies. The proposal values and strengthens intermediate entities as devices for the incubation/maturing of communitarian undertakings. The idea of the incubator implies that the technical assistance should tend to be limited in time, that the initiatives take off and become autonomous, generate their own hard and soft resources. This has encouraged us to additionally define a policy for the domain that ensures ethical-environmental guidelines for the University of Buenos Aires.

This will allow us to scale the experience through a network of design laboratories and ICTs in Latin American universities (Red ITACA 2007) as a component of the management of design transference to emerging communities. If, as we believe, technology has opened up a possibility to recreate the values of modernity as a civilising project, within the Latin American context this process again views design as a privileged agent of change, with maturity in the comprehension of technology, its cultural character and its significance for local development.

References:

Bonetto, A. A. Fish of the Paraná System: The ecology of River System Davies, B. R. y K. F. Walker eds. Dordrecht: The Netherlands (1986)

Bourdieu, P. El sentido práctico (Original title: Le sens pratique, 1980, Les Éditions de Minuit) Siglo XXI Editores: Buenos Aires (2007)

Bourdieu, P., The forms of capital, In Handbook of Theory and Research for the Sociology of Education ed. J.G. Richardson, New Cork: Greenwood Press (1986)
Boscherin, F. and Poma, L., eds. Territorio, conocimiento y competitividad de las empresas, El rol de las instituciones en el espacio global, Miño y Dávila: Buenos Aires (2000)
Castells, M. La Era de la Información Volume I Alianza: Madrid (1996)
Galán, B., Villasante, T.R., Martin Juez, F., Novik, L., Blanch, A., Rossi, A., Naranjo, E. and Toquica Clavijo, M. Diseño & territorio ed. F. Diaz Granados Fac. de Artes: Universidad Nacional de Colombia: Bogotá (2007)
Galán, B., 'Presentación de las Jornadas de Diseño para el Desarrollo Local', non published work, read at the Jornadas de Diseño para el Desarrollo Local SI-FADU-UBA, Buenos Aires, August, (2006)
Galán, B., Maidana Legal, A., Senar, P. and Neuman, M. Diseño para el desarrollo: un enfoque en expansión. X Congreso Iberoamericano de gráfica Digital – SIGRADI. Santiago de Chile, (2006)
Galán, B., Orsil, L. and Neuman, M. 'Diseño para la inclusión: modelo para la toma de decisiones' ENIAD 2002, vol. 1. La Plata-Buenos Aires (2002)
Jorge, E. E., Censi, F. and Bertuchi, J., Capital Social y pobreza: casos y métodos en la 'Construcción comunitaria' (Social Capital and Poverty: cases and methods in 'Communitarian Construction') URL: www.edicionessimbioticas.info/spip.php? article281 2003 (accessed January 2009)
Negroponte, N., Ser Digital. Editorial Atlántida , Buenos Aires (1996)
NRI (2007) URL: http://www.insead.edu/v1/gitr/wef/main/home.cfm (accessed January 2009)
Orsi, L. and Galán, B. Diseño para el medio ambiente: decisiones tecnológicas en escenarios participativos, SIGRADI: Lima (2005)
Orsi, L., Neuman, M., Ruffino, J. P., and Pasin, M. 'La cartografía social como interfase de mediación para el desarrollo en el territorio, l Jornadas de Diseño para el Desarrollo Local SI-FADU-UBA (2006)
Ortiz, R. Otro Territorio, Ensayos Sobre el Mundo Contemporáneo. Universidad Nacional de Quilmes: Buenos Aires (1996)
Piscitelli, A., Ciberculturas 2.0, en la era de las maquinas Inteligentes. Paidós: Buenos Aires (2002)
Vázquez Barquero, A. and Madoery, O. eds. Transformaciones globales, instituciones y políticas de desarrollo local. Buenos Aires: Homo Sapiens (2001)
Red ITACA (2007), Red Iberoamericana de Transferencia de Conocimiento en Competitividad y Autogestión a Comunidades Productivas Emergentes URL: http://www.investigacionaccion.com.ar/site/experiencia.php?linea=00000018 &experiencia=00000073 (accessed January 2009)

Theme II:
New media and the social differentiation of their use

Marina Borovik and Luidmila Shemberko

Social Sciences Information User Behaviour and Searching Strategies in Multifarious Environment

Broadband services in Russia

The introduction of broadband services is expected to usher in a true era of digital convergence when e-users really become the centre of this process and introduce a degree of seamlessness between the work and home environment that has never been possible before. The traditional separation of academic, leisure and work time is fusing into a seamless world. Broadband access is becoming a prerequisite for everything from economic growth to social welfare. Furthermore, it presupposes the capacity to rapidly transmit large quantities of information including data, text and video on the basis of new technologies to provide broadband services. These include services such as interactive e-learning, cooperative composition, electronic publishing, computer conferencing and on-line information searching. The use of broadband technology is becoming an essential part in the process of making telecommunications more "user-friendly".

According to experts estimates in the period up to 2010 all Russian citizens are to be provided with basic telecommunication services across the country while the number of users switched on to the broadband Internet is expected to multiply three-fold (http://www. silicontaiga.org). By 2015 it is planned that Russia will enter the top 10 leaders in the information and telecommunication structure availability. To reach these goals some urgent actions are needed at national and regional level to make the digital divide less sensitive and ensure that everyone not only have broadband access to Internet regardless of where they are but can also use it effectively and efficiently.

Over the last decade the interaction between society and information communications technology (ICT), has become an active area of social science inquiry in Russia. The wide implementation of new information technologies has resulted in a growing number of users as well as in the changes of their information needs and behaviour. There are many factors affecting the efficient use of ICT connected with the changes in the social science approach, including technology, economics, psychology, and linguistics. Modern society has faced many complex problems caused by the rapid rate of technological progress. These problems concern the wider implementation of information technologies regarding the gathering, extraction and analysis of information from the Internet and other sources as well as

69

the improvement of quality of information supply (Choo et al. 1999; Cockburn & Jones 1996; Gordon & Pathak 1999; Hoelscher 1998). In Russia digital resources have grown at a remarkable rate during the last decade, but social science information users do not yet have the technology to make the fullest use of these resources because generally these resources are not connected to each other and users do not make use of effective search strategies.

Another factor concerns the pertinent analysis of the decision-making process in different spheres. In terms of social science decision-making ICT has a non-negligible impact on changing the society in terms of behavioural and mental patterns. Consequently, new information technologies also enhance the adjustment of individuals' adaptability to a higher dynamics of changes in the society. When the information load is increasing at a great speed one can more acutely feel the limitation of such a valuable resource as time. However there is still a desire to find the most relevant resources and to choose an optimal variant for each user. It also means that it is necessary to construct the optimal model of information behaviour and the most effective search strategy for each situation providing an optimal utilization of the information technologies capable to help end-users to solve conceptual and practical problems (Siegfried et al. 1993).

The research study

A sharp growth of new ICT opportunities gives rise to a user's sensation of chaos, stress or at least confusion when faced with the ready accessibility of a huge variety of information resources. To draw an electronic portrait of social science information users it is important to define what type of electronic information they deal with and how they collect, store, use and disseminate information as well as generate new knowledge. In this chapter we report on a study concerned with understanding of user's adaptation to new information searching environments formed by modern technology in general and on user behaviour and search strategies in particular. The goals of this research are firstly to advance the importance of retrieval and wider use of social science information for research, decision-making and teaching. Secondly carry out a case study focusing on search strategies relevant for different user groups. Thirdly to support the further development of the social science information system by improving the user interface design (both in Russian and English) and by developing multi-language linguistic tools that make social science information more accessible, and fourthly to evaluate the ICT impact on user behaviour and search modes in the multifarious environment of social science databases, to explore the strength and weakness of modern technologies as well as to look at the full range of tools employed by information professionals and customers. Our aim is to show that the architecture of social science information systems should be more user-centred, interactive and adaptive.

In the course of the study we conducted numerous extensive interviews with science information users on their information needs, search goals and strategies as well as on their satisfaction with retrieval results. We have used a variety of methods including user queries analysis, search protocols evaluation, user feedback and user testing of different search modes and linguistic tools. This paper is based on the initial findings of the empirical study that examined the user behaviour and search strategies in various social science databases. It is a part of a long-term research project that the Institute of Scientific Information for Social Sciences (INION) has been conducting for the last three years. Data gathered via the questionnaires were analyzed using Statistical Package for the Social Sciences (SPSS) and WinIRBIS Software.

The respondents we have studied were users with various degrees of familiarity with different databases and models of the retrieval behaviours in the multifarious environment of the largest information system in Russia (www.inion.ru). The system's multifarious environment can be described as follows: each database is oriented to its own set of potential users or customers and information on specific topics or multidimensional information on global problems can be available from a single database or several databases. There is also another approach and this is to download information from different sources using search engines and to create a problem-oriented database (Shemberko et al. 1994). The choice of approach depends on the users' searching experience, their activity goals and query complexity.

Results of research

The main purpose of the social sciences information system was the effective use of information resources on national and global problems such as terrorism, energy supply, international migration, drug and slave trades which cannot be solved immediately. These problems were complex, intractable and interrelated, often poorly described and sometimes recognized only after a long period of time or when crucial changes occur. At the same time they put stress on the decision-making processes and institutional capacities. The decision-makers, as a rule, relied on experts and information professionals as well as on researchers, analysts, strategists in order to create a consensus on how best to respond to these problems. Thus, although anyone can be a user of social sciences information there are first priority groups (or categories) such as:

- social science researchers and scientists (28%);
- high school teachers, lecturers and professors (15%);
- postgraduates and young specialists, essentially novices with lack of subject-matter expertise (30%);
- professional persons with considerable subject matter knowledge, skilled in interpreting the information in their fields of interests such as lawyers, bankers, accountants, businessmen, market consultants (9%);
- senior managers, decision makers, leaders (5%);
- journalists, news makers, reporters (3%);
- information specialists as well as information brokers providing information services and assisting others in searching for data and information; they do not create information, but find it and deliver it to other customers (10%).

Findings from the case study on social sciences information users covering the period 2004 – 2006 have identified some characteristics that are of some interest: firstly, the educational level – 12 % had a Bachelor's degree, 35 % had a Master's degree, 47 % had or expected to receive a Ph.D., and 6 % – academics; secondly the age distribution – 26 % were between 19 and 23 years old, while 52 % between 24 and 33, only 8 % between 34 and 50, 12 % between 51 and 60, and 2 % were over 60 years old, and finally gender distribution – 63 % female, 37 % male.

Next, according to the branches of activity the social science information users can be categorised as following: political sciences, state and law – 29,1%, economics and demography – 24,6%, philosophy and sociology – 17,5 %, history, ethnology, anthropology – 5,6%, linguistics – 5,3%, literary criticism – 4,8%, science of sciences – 3,2% and others, including multi-thematic queries – up to 10%.

The experienced searchers or information intermediaries had for years skilfully processed queries regarding large amount of social science information for customers such as academics, top managers and politicians, retrieving information both manual and on-line. The advantages of information retrieval in the social sciences databases seem quite obvious to the majority of scholars: namely access to retrospective information has become faster, more flexible and comprehensive. It is necessary to note that social sciences researchers have traditionally searched for the information themselves: the information retrieval is the major component of their scientific activity. The new information technologies have substantially changed their information behaviour and requirements. Due to the Internet the information retrieval has become less time-consuming, iterative and multifarious.

There is a considerable body of research on user behaviour and searching strategies regarding information retrieval from the Web but far less on searching in social science databases (Lawrence & Giles 1998; Marchionini et al. 1993; Navarro-Prieto et al. 1999; Ross & Wolfram 2000).

Our research was focused on such subjects as the user's work task, information needs and requirements, searching goals, tactics and strategies which could be named and discussed in such categories as query formulation, database definition, keywords and 'catch' terms selection.

We know discouragingly little about the type of searching skills that are needed and how they could be transformed in new technological environment, and it is difficult to define exactly what an experienced searcher should know about information searching that a beginner does not. The analysis of information users has revealed several groups with different level of searching skills – novice, advanced, experienced, experts – that include awareness of the resources available. Other skills were knowledge of databases content and their structure as well as how to critically evaluate the information received and to choose the efficient search strategy.

Searching strategies on information retrieval

The search strategy is one of the most important elements in information retrieval. To satisfy information needs of social scientists and to meet objectives of on-line retrieval, heuristic in nature, it is necessary to choose from the existing alternatives.

Social sciences information users have several sources of ideas and data to draw on. These information sources include graduate studies, journal reading and note-taking, discussions with colleagues, listening to presentations at conferences, relevant databases (national and international) and their current research interests. These sources, however, disparate in time and space, need to be consolidated into a single list of possible topics for exploration. After the information search has been completed the resulting list can be reviewed and up-dated with certain ideas being deleted and others being added or developed. This list can help to keep the user aware of potentially fruitful areas of query construction and of topics on which future researches may be based as well as containing the names of the most productive authors.

At every stage of interaction with the information system the user is in various states of uncertainty that can only be resolved by decision-making which implies a choice from a variety of options and depends greatly on the potential search strategies. Three main patterns of information retrieval behaviour have been revealed each demanding different search strategies: firstly, on-line searching by end-users themselves; secondly, retrieval by an information specialist in the absence of the requester, and thirdly, search by the remote users in cooperation with an information specialist (so called "virtual team"). In our opinion the last one could become the most effective with regard to the results, timesaving, costs and benefits. The information specialist's knowledge of search possibilities guarantees high recall, and by the user's verifying results, the search strategy can be immediately corrected. The major focus should be made on the precision and flexibility of human thinking in the formulation of queries, and on the relationship between the information technology and the languages that are being used to support it.

Social sciences information retrieval quite often demands alternative decisions to expand or narrow search limits, to transfer the query to another database depending on the results received. A lot of search tactics might be employed to build a bridge between the user's query and the information system. At present there are no fully reliable criteria for choosing the best strategy and tactics for each retrieval situation. However our experience of searching social sciences databases shows that the process of information retrieval is full of typical situations. It might be useful, as a starting point, to see if searching one plans to do has already been undertaken by someone else.

In order to elucidate the role of the strategy in information searching it is necessary to define main types of retrieval models that could be used for the scientific purposes of describing, predicting and explaining the user behaviour. Queries which have the same formulation or appear to be the same on the surface are often performed differently in terms of actual retrieval with the help of various information resources and search engines. To some extent the diversity of information included into this or that database allows users to reveal new areas of investigation and unfamiliar approaches. To other users the greater efficiency of information selection and full literature review allows one to save time for research itself; this is very attractive to users. Social sciences users undertaking a search in relevant information systems believe that they can interact with the information resources thus permitting on the spot decisions regarding the choice of adequate terminology and play around tentative ideas while also searching for a resolution to a problem.

The content analysis of 4,052 queries from more than 3,500 users processed during the last three years of the investigation of query processing and retrieval have led to our defining the routine searching strategies employed by social sciences users as follows:

1. Information requirements definition (problem content, subject coverage, geographic and language coverage);
2. Information navigation, search engines and databases selection (database content analysis, retrospective coverage, document types and formats, cost issues, forms of delivery);
3. Query construction strategies (identifying search terms, keywords, synonyms, authors' names and region names, specifying phrases);

4. Interaction strategies (browsing controlled dictionary, subject heading lists and thesauri, scrolling relevant documents, magnitude feedback adjustment);
5. Advanced search strategies (from narrow to broad, Boolean operators, from broad to narrow or specific term search, language and year restrictions, iterative or interactive searching).

Furthermore, the study revealed three models of logical searching based on formal criteria of optimality. These social science logical searching models include: firstly the menu-oriented strategy designed for novice users which is based on query formation by example; secondly the logical construction of retrieval scheme for trained searchers using direct input of 'catch' words (descriptors and keywords) and search field names; and thirdly the so called step-by-step query creation mode that provides the most flexible information strategies for advanced users. The heuristic searching mode could also be the perfect tool for users who fail to find sufficient relevant information.

In order to design the correct searching route through the information resources to reach the desired information a user can break complex search queries down into sub-problems and work on one problem at a time. This is a well-established and productive technique in general problem solving which enables grid information flows. As each sub-problem is solved the separate parts of them can then be knitted into solving the larger problem. As rule such binary searching is a more efficient approach than serial or random searching and helps to spot 'hot topics' before they become mainstream. Yet a rigid adherence to this principle would probably be wasteful, since human beings have additional contextual knowledge about different information resources. That is why the facilitating models that help users to search for information more efficiently or effectively as well as various teaching tools that make it easy for users to learn to search should be incorporated into search procedure[1].

The Importance of Search Terms

Term specificity in social sciences is one of the crucial problems that needs to be solved to achieve optimal information retrieval. A user can try to choose search terms that are on several levels of specificity relative to the topic of interest and then alter a search formulation by using different strategies and moving upwards or downwards through the hierarchy or to move sideways hierarchically to co-ordinate terms. The searcher can perform these strategies by looking through a

---

1 Some models can be found at http://www.library.kent.edu/edu/page/108680

thesaurus or other linguistic tools (such as glossaries, controlled vocabularies, authorized list of terms, subject heading lists and navigation schemes) and promote knowledge discovery by exposing potential linkage between seemingly unrelated subjects.

Every searcher is familiar with the case where a widely used term mysteriously produces no records, or only a very small number – far less than could be expected for that term. In order to search effectively it is important to be aware of the difference between a term and a concept since the two are treated differently in search formulations. A concept, especially in social sciences, can be expressed by several synonymous or related terms and may contain several words that should be combined. Combining search terms with Boolean logic is at the heart of on-line searching. Searches which require exact matches, like Boolean searches, may not retrieve any records. In this case the system should inform and help the user. Several search strategies can be used to manipulate the search formulation until it produces the needed information. It is possible to expand the search formulation or include most (or all) of the concept of a search topic in the initial search formulation, or to add one or more of the query concepts to an already used search formulation, to block or to reject items indexed by certain terms. It is possible to make the search formulation more precise by reducing the number of parallel terms. The fewer variant terms one lists for each concept, the fewer documents are likely to be found that match the request.

One of the main tasks of on-line search is to identify 'good' terms to search with. We have managed to develop a number of social science thesauri that can be viewed as matching or translating tools[2]. These are used on–line or built in the search engines. Vocabulary problems are central to the economics of digital resources processing because an unfamiliar vocabulary reduces search effectiveness. A little bit of effort spent reviewing possible search terms in the linguistic reference databases can eliminate search time. These databases can be used for word by word searching of descriptors, keywords and subject category codes.

Several approaches can be used to generate additional terms in order to enrich search formulation, for example, by looking at neighbouring terms in alphabetically arranged lists of different terms. It is important to remember that a given topic may firstly be discussed in documents wholly devoted to that topic; or secondly they may appear as a subtopic in a document devoted to a broader topic; or thirdly they may have just a part of its content dealing with a document on a narrow topic. Documents of these three types may be of interest to the requester, but documents of only the first type will be retrieved if the only search terms used are those which are exactly descriptive of the topic, not broader or narrower. It is

---

2 See at www.inion.ru

possible to reduce the number of concepts of a search topic in the initial search formulation, or to subtract one or more of the query concepts from an already used search formulation. Besides, any given conceptual element can be broadened by entering additional variant terms or through the use of truncation that is like a wildcard added to the part of a keyword admitting any variant spelling or word endings. It is important to stress that the social science databases are continually being expanded with user participation through the addition of more specific terms that are aspects of those already included into the search formulation.

Our observations on the Web searchers in our study show that ineffective use of information resources is often caused by the lack of understanding of how a search engine interprets a query. The majority of searchers do not use advanced search features, or enter complex queries, or interact with the information system. As a consequence, search engine developers are now trying to automate query formulation, shifting the burden of formulating precise or extensive terminology from the user to the system and to create the multicultural complex of linguistic tools.

Behavioural Searching Patterns

Comparison of the typical retrieval strategies shows a strong similarity in routine user behaviour. However, the ways in which they are used, for example, relevance feedback and other system features vary. These different patterns of information behaviour suggest that it may be hard to predict based upon descriptions of routine strategies alone how users will behave in multifarious environment.

We have tried to specify characteristics of social science information users in order to adapt them to the new information technology. Further we have tried to define some searching strategies which could be helpful for understanding user behaviour and databases design improvement as well as linguistic tool development.

During experimental research various levels of user self-realisation of information search have been found out. The first level is routine in which search problem solving is carried out by analogy to earlier mastered algorithms of activity. Users constantly address to the information intermediary for a detailed explanation of requirements of a research task, algorithm of search, aspire to receive fast results with the least intellectual expenses. They do not want to master various strategies of search. The second level is adaptable in which users fulfil searches on the basis of one of the available logical models known to them. This level assumes the absence of steady user aspiration to self-determination and self-realisation during searching. The third level is reflective in which users try to define the essence of a research problem and aspire to simulate various situations to find more meaningful ways to solve them. They critically analyse search results and are trying to determine the barriers interfering the search of the necessary information. And the last level is creative which allows the searcher not only to use various strategies of information search, but also to generate the new knowledge and new approaches to problem decision.

Challenges in Searching Approaches

In this chapter we have discussed the study we conducted in which social sciences information users responded to an interactive survey in which they were asked about their search topics (or research problems), intended query terms (as a rule very specific), and the search frequency in various databases. The results showed that search topics were spread across 10 –12 subject categories in each social science database. Most of respondents searched on a single topic as determined by their query terms. The mean number of terms in a query was rather high – at 8.5.

The social science databases were intended to be used by scholars themselves. But, as a rule, they can not specify their information requirements in a way appropriate for search formulation. Often they are not aware of the existing thesauri, access methods, structure of databases and search aids that are well-known to information specialists. Furthermore, they often have difficulty grasping Boolean logic, revising ineffective searches and interpreting computer responses. Social science users usually search infrequently and hence forget how and where to enter query formulation. The majority of our respondents reported searching the Internet once or twice a week using no logical operators, and the remainder (11%) reported daily use. Most of them are searching only for themselves and 21% for themselves and others (for patrons, professors, top managers). Not more than 15% employ the Internet in their everyday searching environments. In most cases end-user searches are 50% longer than those of trained intermediaries. Experienced on-line searchers avoid all these problems through training and frequent practice. But still the cost of the services is what users are most concerned about – not the recall or precision of their search.

Concluding Observations

Multilingual search engines are the primary tools to find the Web sites with relevant information and to do the effective searches. Different groups of users submit their queries to various search engines such as Google, Clusty, Lumrix, Multibear, Lycos, AltaVista. Many users prefer to search the Qwika engine where the original content is combined with machine translated content from/ to English; as a rule they do not use more then two search engines and retrieve information in not more than three databases.

The most frequently searched Web sites that provide data and information of interest to the social science users include the INION databases, the EBSCO databases with thousands of e-journals containing millions of articles, the Social Sciences Virtual Library, Social Sciences Full Text (the most important English-language journals published in the U.S. and elsewhere with full text and page images), the EINIRAS Database Network (a virtual Pan-European system of databases for international relations and area studies), the DARE database at UNESCO Social and Human Sciences Documentation Center, the SOLIS database with information on approximately 370 social science periodicals and a lot of others. It is worthy of note that the Social Science Information Gateway (UK Institute: Social Sciences) combining the resources of two services – Altis and SOSIG – offers an easy and powerful tool for discovering the best Internet resources in wide range of subjects, including social sciences, arts and humanities. It provides free Internet tutorials to help users learn how to get the best from the Web.

We conclude this chapter with a number of observations from our experience of user searching on the Web and various social science databases: Firstly social sciences information users search the Web using 2 to 3 searching engines and as a rule not more then two databases; Secondly they spend not more than half an hour searching for the information in Russian language and less than one hour searching information in foreign languages (first of all in English, German, French and Spanish); Thirdly, the searching skills vary and users often consider themselves to be more skilled than they actually are; most participants considered their levels of satisfaction with the search results to be 'good', having no clear idea of how search engines use the queries to search for information.

One of the fundamental issues in search strategy is when to stop. How does one judge when enough information has been gathered? How does one decide to give up an unsuccessful search? When is the optimal time to stop searching in one source and move to the next one? As a rule the lack of time or finance shortage are the main factors stopping the user searching.

In summary, the focus of our research was to look at the impact of ICT in social sciences on two main areas: first the information users and their searching skills and second the information user behaviour and searching strategies. In this chapter we have taken only the first step towards comprehensive study of the consequences of ICT use in social sciences information environment in order:

1. to deepen the knowledge and the capacity of different user groups in information retrieval issues;
2. to reveal science information users needs and their search behaviour for incorporation in ICT policy;
3. to enable development of search patterns for various social sciences information user groups;
4. to stimulate further investigation of most important attributes of social sciences searchers such as work task knowledge and its complexity, abilities to reveal information requirements using natural and retrieval languages, knowledge of the available Internet resources, the level of education and motivation and uncertainty of query formulation;
5. to facilitate exchange of experience on implementation of various search strategies among the information services – national and international – and share their experience in this field;
6. to create closer links between research and practice and to combine more fundamental, small scale research or research focused on specific ICT tools with research that is much more linked to practice.

Finally it is important to note that modern information systems are rapidly being replaced by radically different types of systems that encourage the use of unstructured natural language queries and facilities for automatically (or semi-automatically) reformulating queries through relevant feedback with users.

There is still much to be done before we reach our long-term goals in implementing modern ICT in the field of information retrieval and formation of so-called E-social science. First of all, we need an intelligent multi-language information interface and flexible linguistic tools. In order to design such a system, it is necessary to understand what happens in the human-to-human information interaction, and why it happens, and to define the functions that are required for effective information searching. Unfortunately it would appear that social sciences information users are pleased with the results of their searches – no matter what they retrieved. However, it is quite possible that the spread of information and communications technologies would improve end-user searching and would stimulate the growing demand for teaching and facilitating tools as well as for experienced intermediaries capable to help users online.

References

Choo C. W., Detlor B., Turnbull D. 'Information Seeking on the Web – An integrated model of browsing and searching' Proceedings of the Annual Meeting of the

American Society for Information Science (ASIS) (1999) URL: http://choo.fis. utoronto.ca/FIS/respub/asis99/ default.html (accessed December 2008)

Cockburn A., Jones S. 'Which way now? Analysing and easing inadequacies in WWW navigation' International Journal of Human-Computer Studies 45 (1996) pp. 105-129

Gordon M., Pathak P. 'Finding information on the World Wide Web: the retrieval effectiveness of search engines' Information Processing and Management 35 (1999) pp. 141-180

Hoelscher C. 'How Internet experts search for information on the Web' eds. Maurer, H. & Olson, R.G. Proceedings of WebNet98 – World Conference of the WWW, Internet & Intranet. Charlottesville, VA: AACE (1998)

Lawrence S., Giles C. 'Searching the World Wide Web' Science 5360 (1998) pp. 98-100

Marchionini G., Dwiggins S., Katz A., Lin X. 'Information Seeking in Full-Text End-User-Oriented Search Systems: The Roles of Domain and Search Expertise' LISR 15 (1993) pp. 35-69

Navarro-Prieto R., Scaife M., Rogers Y. 'Cognitive Strategies in Web Searching' Proceedings of the 5th Conference on Human Factors & the Web (1999) URL: http://zing.ncsl.nist.gov/hfweb/proceedings/navarro-prieto/index.html (accessed December 2008)

Ross N., Wolfram D. 'End User Searching on the Internet: An Analysis of Term Pair Topics Submitted to the Excite Search Engine' Journal of the American Society for Information Science 51 (2000) pp. 949-958

The Institute of Scientific Information for Social Sciences of the Russian Academy of Science (ISISS RAS) URL: http://www.inion.ru (accessed January 2009)

Shemberko L., Gromova L., Khisamoutdiniv W. 'Creation of problem-oriented databases by downloading informaton' The Electronic Library 12 (1994) pp. 149-153

Siegfried S., Bates M., Wilde, D. 'A profile of end-user searching behaviour by humanities scholars: The Getty online searching project report no. 2' Journal of the American Society for Information Science 44 (1993) pp. 273-291

Sarah Gallez, Anne-Claire Orban, Céline Schöller and Claire Lobet-Maris

Teenagers on the Net: Generational Divide, Autonomy, Liberty, and Responsibility

Introduction

This chapter is based on recent observations made within the framework of the research project TIRO – Teens and ICT, Risks and Opportunities[1] – financed through the Belgian Science Policy Office (BELSPO). Observations, made over two years of virtual communicative practices with young people on the Internet, particularly the activity of blogging[2], are also taken into account.

TIRO research began more than a year ago. This project is focused on ICT uses (Internet, video games and mobiles) by the 12-18 old teenagers. The central objective of this project is to understand the social praxis around ICT use shaped by young people, to question them concerning the risks and opportunities for their socialization. One of the political issues of TIRO is the implementation of regulatory tools concerning risky activities well re-presentatives of their reality and to elaborate these tools via detailed observations of young people's common practices. TIRO research has a multi-disciplinary approach: sociologists, researchers from the communication sciences and legal experts work together to better understand the practices of teenagers in order to elaborate appropriate regulation. The methodology is mixed with a quantitative survey[3] and several qualitative approaches[4] which complement each other: the quantitative survey is large scale but is based on declarative data[5] decontextualised, without subjective meaning. On the other hand, interviews, focus groups and blog tracking are contextualised and give detailed and comprehensive description of these practices. The particularity of this research is that it is not only research on young people but also with young

---

1 Cfr the website http://www.ua.ac.be/tiro.
2 In the context of a particular study (cfr *Je blogue, tu blogues, nous bloguons*, Clémi, France, http://www.clemi.org/medias_scolaires/blogs/article_blog_ACO.pdf) and certain projects in education concerning the media (BlogoMag, the magazine of blogging edited by *and* for young people, ACMJ).
3 Survey made by Professor M. Walrave and Sunna Lenaerts, University of Antwerp, partner of the project. This survey is based sample of 1300 teenagers.
4 The qualitative phase includes 8 focus groups of boys and girls classified by age, gender and teaching background and a diary research made on a panel of 20 teenagers.
5 Young people have great difficulties to write their practices or to describe gestures that seem spontaneous to them. They have a "procedural memory" (De Smedt et al. 2002).

people that requires a high degree of participation and cooperation from the young people themselves.

From this fairly large research framework, we have decided to narrow the focus in this chapter to the generational divide observed in our preliminary observations. The generational divide is not new but seems to widen and harden with ICT use by young people. The adolescents of the 21st century occupy the space offered by these new media. They express themselves, they chat, consume, play, surf, read, listen... This new social scene seems to be entirely shaped by teenagers outside the world of the adults. Rare are the parents who manage to enter these "new spaces" developed by their children. First, we will study the generational divide as it has been observed in our empirical work. Then, we will contextualise this generational divide with some sociological elements. We will take up the example of weblogs or "blogs" which illustrates on the one hand, the individualization of web practices of youths and their autonomy and on the other hand, the frantic search for peer approval. Finally we will examine the impact on the socialisation of young people of this increased autonomy or of this generational divide.

After these initial observations, we turn to the law in order to ask questions regarding the legal situation of ICT teenagers' practices. The increasing autonomy of young people has provoked breaches in their legal incapacity – breaches that are founded on their supposed capacity discernment. Thanks to new technologies, young people have access to the sphere of public expression and find themselves practically on the same footing as the press. Are young people, within the framework of this enormous power, well served by self-regulation pure and simple? Is their freedom of expression as wide in this regard as the one of journalists? After having examined these questions we will consider the limits of freedom of expression, based on the principle of respect for the rights of others. Two limits appear to us to illustrate questions in the context of a confrontation between adolescents and the new trends in freedom of expression, concerning cyberteasing and copyright. Here freedom shows its hidden face: liability. Adolescents are by definition in a legal state of incapacity. Does this also mean they do not bear any liability? The underlying goal of the civil liability system is one of compensation of the damage suffered by the victim. What is the status of this liability as regards minors, their parents, and teachers, and does the current system of liability measure up to the underlying goal? Would civil liability be clarified and made more workable if it were detached from the notion of guilt, which in any event does not benefit the cause of the victim? With regard to each of these themes, we will discuss pathways for reflection concerning regulations and we will underline the fact that when someone's rights are violated over the Internet, a right of reply offers perhaps an avenue of redress more adequate than litigious procedures.

The tone of this chapter is still quite exploratory, a sign of a research project that is still in progress and which has taken up a fairly radical position to work with young people towards understanding and regulating their practices.

The Internet, a catalyser of the generational divide

The generational divide shaped by ICT use has until now received little interest in the sociological literature, even in the sociology of family[6]. Nevertheless, ICT use by teenagers reveals a deep logic that is demonstrative of the family structure. The French studies which have analysed youth ICT practices, put little accent on the generational divide, but rather they explore two principal topics: identity and sociability constructed through these practises. This focus on this twofold theme can be explained by the fact that adolescence has for a long time been defined by psychologists by its identity characteristics (an age of mutations, construction of self) and its intense and particular sociability (peer pressure, conformism). The sociology of youth has more recently appeared and thus adolescence[7] begins to be considered like a social category in relation to others (Delforge & Vienne 2006).

It is striking to see that Internet use by youths clearly fits into a perspective of the *among-ourselves* (in French: entre-soi), tribal and without adults (Tredan 2005; Metton 2004; Martin 2000; 2004; Médiappro 2006). Studies agree on this point but few worry about it. Concretely, we observe that the adult or the parental figure is absent in youth Internet use. The Internet is learned alone, it is experienced among peers, without recourse to adult. Teenagers, especially the boys, have confidence in their learning capacities, Livingstone (2002) speaks about a *confident generation*. They consider themselves as experts much more than their parents, even if this expertise seems to be more on the order of talk than that of a real Internet literacy. A teenager builds his digital world alone, in an autonomous and individualised way. He personalises his "my computer" (backdrop, welcome message, contact classifications, emoticon...) like personal territory, a sort of prolongation of his personality. He revindicates the right to be the only one to use the computer, to manage its navigation, to develop his relational networks, his leisure and tastes with the Internet independently of family norms and parental control. Like 12 year old Janis who surfs with her neighbour, *"but next year when I start the lycée, I think I'll want to go on the Internet alone and have it at home"*. Discus-

---

6   In Anglo-Saxon literature, some authors in tradition of cultural studies analyse this youth culture via case studies of computer practices, for example, the research of Diane Pacom and Sonia Livingstone.
7   Cfr Fize (1993).

sions between adults and youths about the Internet are very rare, "*actually, no discussion at all!*" add Mathieu, Lionel and Gregory, 16-17, during a focus group.

This adult absence in youths' ICT use can be related to the wider context of a generational divide. Pasquier talks of *generational discontinuity* as a major social factor in juvenile socialisation today. The first factor in this divide is the transformation of the family cell and parent/child relationships. For De Singly, the contemporary family has evolved towards two major transformations, the atomisation of the family regarding the kinship and the autonomisation of the individual regarding the family. The contemporary family lacks *intergenerational horizons* (De Singly 2003; 2004); generations are autonomous from one another, not without ties but on free relationships, respectful, independent and based on logics of individual choices. The second factor is the prolongation of adolescence and its generalisation to all social groups thanks to a longer time spent as a scholar and to the growing youth unemployment (Galland 2002). As a third factor, we note the rupture in cultural transmission between parents and adolescents, reinforced by a double process of individualisation and privatisation on the level of leisure activities, which has been going on since the 80's. Activities which formerly were exercised in the public sphere have shifted over to the domestic sphere and have been individualised. The two adult and youth spheres each henceforth have their practices and territories[8] without really ever having a time or a space in common. The corollary to this process of individualisation that we observe in the contemporary family and leisure activities is that autonomy is becoming a "form of self-discipline" (De Singly 2006) with in counterbalance, a devalorisation of authority, also observed in the Internet use by youths. We have noticed indeed few activities or moments shared by youths and their parents, which are often limited to the evening meal. Two youths on the panel have chosen "the fridge" as the object symbolising their family! Livingstone (2002) has analysed this dual process – individualisation and privatisation – in the Anglo-Saxon context as a parental reaction: by favouring leisure at home and by providing youths with a whole digital and cultural environment, the parents intent to protect their children from the dangers and the insecurity of the street, even if those dangers are more imagined than real. Our observations confirm this « bedroom culture » phenomenon, which seems more prevalent among young girls[9]. Two remarks must be made on those observations: the first is that this norm of autonomy in ICT use does not mean that

---

8   This phenomenon of individualization affects social milieu differently. One example on the level of possession of electronic equipment, 14% of adolescents from privileged milieu have a television in their room against 52% of under-privileged children (Pasquier 2005).
9   This may have maybe to do with the Belgian collective unconscious marked by numerous moral affairs which jolted the entire country.

young's want to take power thanks to ICT or to be independent, an image prevalent at first glance. Rather, they want to build themselves their individualised digital world. Secondly, this divide does not mean that youths and adults are in conflict. It's rather a matter of "indifferent and peaceful cohabitation" (Pasquier 2005, a remoteness including from parents. These two spheres seem "to drive along different highway lanes at different speeds" but are not running into one another[10].

The Internet, a learning stage

Fundamentally, the pattern of youth socialisation is changing. It is no longer founded on the transmission and identification, whereby young people walk in their parent's footsteps (Hersent 2003, 23) but on *experimentation* (Galland 2002). This experimentation is also a central characteristic of adolescence, a period of expectation authorising experiences (Delforge & Vienne 2006). Young people's Internet use seems to be indeed an experimental field and, in that sense, the Internet is not a place where youths "flee" reality but a first stage for learning the life, for better adaptation to their daily existence. This learning stage appears as a middle-land between the public sphere and the private sphere, sometimes "for lack of something better": for lack of public space for youth, they express themselves on the blogs, for lack of seeing each other they "*hang out*" (Boyd 2006) together on instant messenger services, for lack of going out to discover the world, like 17 year old Melissa who is kept home by her mother after two years of silliness in her village, they chat with unknowns. The 14-16 year boys, Bruno, Gary and Aloïs explain that they 'meet' girls on the instantaneous messenger services for not knowing how to proceed in the "real life". They have no desire to stop there but say they learn their tastes and reactions. Or like 12-13 year old Charline, Emmanuelle and Janis who regularly assume the identity of older young women in chatting with others. Metton (2004) illustrated this phenomenon well, for in chatting one can infiltrate other worlds, experiment with the opposite sex for instance and understand scenes from the adult world.

More simply, the offerings on the Internet are massive and diversified and often render adults powerless facing the demands, activities and desires of youths. Parents know less about the web than their children, especially in lower classes (Livingstone 2002) and it is hard to control contents without being seated next to the adolescent.

---

10 For Michel Fize, adolescent culture is not a sub-culture or a counter-culture but another culture; which has never so escaped out of the control of adults and been so organized by the commercial universe (Pasquier 2005).

The weblog, an autonomous and reflexive experience

An obvious example of the increasing autonomy of the young and this generational gap is the weblog. Above all, it represents for youth a space belonging to them. Based on the website's technological offer[11], the young blogger creates his online world, where the tribe finds or assumes its place. This tribe moreover participates in the construction of that personal space and, hence, in the online personality of its author. That personality is incarnated in the pseudonym, the most symbolic mark of identity on the Internet but it is also expressed via the graphic appearance of their blog: the colours, the choice of photos, the arrangement of the notes. Relations, contents and aesthetics thus work in the construction of the blogger's virtual identity, in reflecting sometimes deforming, his personality. Hence it is not uncommon for the young blogger to change the design of his blog or even create a new space from one day to another in order to modify how he presents himself or the self-image he wants to put forward. For example, the weblog "le-jardin-du-bruit-envolé", in a note entitled « *I'm off to a new start* », informs his readers that *"here, this is no longer me... I don't identify with this anymore. [...] I'm beginning a new me"* elsewhere, at another address[12]. In existing as a personal space, the blog rapidly becomes a *territory* with its marks, its codes and rules, that any dissidents are invited to leave. Among the latter figure the parents, doubly strangers in the adolescents' weblogs: strangers to their contents on the one hand and strangers from online practice on the other. This position of allochtoon is also maintained by the parents themselves, little inclined to explore the practice of their adolescents. That disinterest or non-interference of adults into the adolescents' blogs makes the youths' blogosphere a Terra Incognita.

This practice of personal and individualised blogging, with the aim to be connected with his peers, is not lived by the young as a "subjection" or a conformist practice. The youths' reflections about their own blogs testify to this. This reflexivity takes place on three levels. The first is based on the contents of their digital world. This putting his life online, in the form of narrations or images, leads the young blogger to reflect upon himself. Like a world in always under construction, the blog is transformed through the events of the adolescent's life, and the young blogger testifies to this quite explicitly: his blog can be renovated, interrupted, done away with, moved, and pursued elsewhere, depending on the hazards of the adolescent's life. Monsieur-b for example, announces in the month of September a change in his blog: *"new ideas for a new blog and a new year. New things to*

---

11 A website often chosen by relational affinity rather than by technical opportunities and which plays on that community sociability to increase its list of members. Example: the French website Skyrock Blog (http://www.skyrock.com/blog/).
12 A note of 24 September 2006, http://le-jardin-du-bruit-envole.cowblog.fr

discover, to read, to see, to share. A bit of everything, nothing, the strange, the logical, the interesting, nice, special, sad, about me, about you, about us, about the world around us and again many other things for this new blog placed under the sign of change, of novelty,... "[13]. These triggers of reflexivity about contents are often external to the practice of blogging but take place in the face-to-face with oneself that the blog supposes and the confrontation with a third party it imposes.

The second target of the young blogger's self-awareness is precisely, this third party. In putting a blog space online, the youth exposes himself to the view and comments of other blog members. Often sought out and encouraged, the presence of the other manifests itself by means of comments. Greeted in the territory, the visitor (often a peer encountered in the youth's real life) is thus entrusted with the mission of making remarks that reinforce the host, flattering him and describing their friendship. The important thing is maintaining contact not cutting communication. Tripping up in this mission (insults, tag-comments[14]) thus becomes the occasion for brushing up on the territory's implicit rules. Aside from this going beyond the limits, the youth's reflexivity about the public visibility of his personal space can also be triggered by the presence of an "intruder", an unexpected visitor or, again, a "persona non grata" on the blog. In this situation, frequently, the admitted, unmasked or visit of parents on the blogs of their adolescents triggers an awareness of the public nature of the blog. These unwanted presences astonish them (*"how did my parents know my blog address?"*) but above all, make the author feel uneasy. This is the case with Mima, a 15 year old blogger who testifies in her blog that *"what I was doing there, I really have no idea. In fact...I began to fear that too many people come happen upon my blog,...it's so simple to type on Google such and such a high school, such and such a town...dumb things. And in fact, people have already happened upon my blog a few times, by chance. And that really scares me....I want to preserve my anonymity...And then when I saw the commentary by Clic, maybe that pleased me but at night, I got to thinking... Imagine that this Blogomag got to be a little popular. And I lay out my life without a thought, without seriously thinking an instant that someone might it. In reality, I'm saying that I really don't want someone to meet me in the street and recognise me as the writer of such things but it's especially the looks from the people in my entourage that scare me..."*[15].

The third level of reflexivity of young bloggers is situated in the blogging activity itself. These moments of reflexivity are far from being systematic; they

---

13 A note of 27 September 2006, http://monsieur-b.skyblog.com
14 By tag-comments, we mean « publicity » commentaries (Come see my blog, come and leave your com's on my blog), impersonal and left everywhere in the commentaries of adolescent blogs.
15 A note of 12 December 2005, http://c0xynell.canalblog.com

are even rather rare among daily Web-users. On the contrary, as the other two levels of reflexivity, there are trigger situations which set this self-awareness process into motion. "Blogging anniversaries", notes commemorating the first, second and third... year of the blog are opportunities to raise critical question on one's activities, and on the tool itself, its potentialities, inconveniences and limits. The composition of the first note of a blog, or the closing one, also reveals the relationship that the young blogger seems to maintain vis-à-vis his blog. Finally, a last online upset incites the young person to re-position himself in his Internet activity: the virtual notoriety. This notoriety can progress gradually by "word of mouth "on the web, or in a more brutal way by making the youth a Blog Star on the website homepage[16]. In the latter case, the youth's sudden notoriety provokes a more or less critical self-awareness. These three levels of reflexivity with their trigger situations could illustrate well the self regulation process and tools shaped by the youth in their practises.

Generational divide and youth socialisation

Few parents really worry about this generation gap, seeing it as something that has always existed. Some adults speak about this gap positively as the mother of 15 years old Aloïs saying: *"let them to make their lives, they have the right to be autonomous"*. On the contrary, the older youths deplore this parental indifference. They would have wanted more shared moments, discussion and regret the lack of interest on the part of adults. For all interviewed youths, family value is important and they say that they get along well with their parents. But, in practice, they only talk with them, on average, a quarter of an hour a day. And this remoteness, separation seems to grow even wider for the *adonaissant*[17] generations: the lack of understanding that the older adolescents have lived through between themselves and their parents appears to them less worrying than what they perceive between their parents and their younger brothers or sisters 12 or 13 years old. *"My little sister is on another planet of clothes and girlfriends and she hardly sees my mother and father. They never talk to one another and I try talking to her but she doesn't care"* says Matthew, 18 years old. They say that they have had another education, have been more watched over than their younger brothers or sisters, who are on their own and their parents do nothing

---

16 On this subject, the SkyblogStar phenomenon of the French website Skyblog Rock is notorious in French-speaking Europe.
17 Title of the last book of François De Singly, see References.

about it[18]. As 18 year old Isabelle says, *"the difference between me and my little brother is that my parents prefer to leave him alone with his play station games or in front of the computer rather than educating him, for me, my mother always was always behind me"*. They say that they feel themselves to be very different from those teenagers, whereas only 5 or 6 years separate them. Those older youths testify a growing generational divide between parents and the generation of youths now reaching adolescence, the generation born in the MMB (Mobile, MSN, Blog) era. According to those older youths, this a worrying question raised for the future.

This generational gap is questioning, regarding the role the adults traditionally play in the youth socialisation. In the majority of traditional societies the passage from childhood to adulthood is characterised by an initiation rite. This ritual is composed of tests and oral teachings intended to bring about a radical modification in the religious and social status of the initiate. The child learns behaviours, techniques and institutions of adults and discovers his or her role in society. Nowadays, initiation rites are more and more disappearing but the search for meaning remains.

More pragmatically, from a sociological point of view, this generational divide observed in Internet use seems to have three major impacts on the youth's socialisation. The first is the growing influence of what the literature qualifies as the "tyrannical" regulation made by peers but also by the commercial sphere on the social practices of the youth's. The second is a trend of "withdrawal on the self" including on one's own gender. The third is a weak connection with the past, which raises question particularly regarding the scholar culture.

Pasquiers underlines the influence of the commercial sphere and peer pressure on juvenile socialisation. If the family no longer dictates codes and conduct, if the mechanisms of cultural transmission by parents and schools are blocked, then the entourage (the peers) and the commercial sphere take up the slack. The codes of juvenile sociability are particularly, Paquiers even speaks of a *tyranny of the majority*. For this author, finally, what the youth has gained in autonomy regarding his parents, he has lost it with his peers. This peer pressure in Internet use of youths must be studied more. But in pushing this reasoning to the extreme, a youth today does not exist without permanent group approbation, without this horizontal sociability ceaselessly in activity even into their bedrooms. This questions Olivier Tredan who shows that *the permanent gaze of others has a structuring power for these online identities* (Tredan 2005). Where the final freedom for a youth is to

---

18 The older brothers take up the torch, especially for the little sisters, sometimes via close space surveillance calls by short messages during parties.

disconnect himself...[19] From a regulatory point of view, it means a self regulation quite binary, radical and without deliberation. This pressure seems to be a conformism pressure. *"We can with difficulty imagine that there are no relations between the fact that parents transmit less of life instructions and the development of a generational culture which manifests a strong intolerance to individual differences"* (Pasquier 2005, 165).

A second impact related to this generational divide regards a phenomenon of fragmentation and of withdrawal on itself, underlined for example, by the Mediappro research: *"expression, communication and games between peers will maintain relatively isolated networks for a long time, forming a mosaic of small, similar tribes that turn in on themselves"* (Mediappro 2006, 58). We have seen for weblogs, the visitor flatters the blogger for fear of confronting difference. 16 year old Gary on Myspace, only looks for profiles that fit his own profile. A Belgian forum, <barakie.be>, functions on contempt of "the other different of me" and the exclusion. In this vein we have observed, even if we have to remain prudent and nuanced, that girls and boys have theirs favourite practices, among themselves, acting on traditional masculine or feminine elements (typically, strategic, ludic, violent practices like networks games, jokes or gores websites for male /sentimental and emotional practices like chat, instant messenger services for female[20]). During an interview, the girls lend to theirs activities subjective significance, the boys talk about technology, free programmes and consider technology for its own sake. Could we do a hypothesis of a re-emergence of the traditional gender divide, intensified with the technology? In any case, girls seem to be more "secret" in their practices (webactivities from the domestic sphere, based on restrained relational networks, duos or trios) than boys (webactivities based on extended relational networks). We see clearly that *if the parents have lost a great part of their power of regulation, individualities cannot for all that express themselves freely. The search for authenticity unceasingly runs up against adolescent culture codes as well as an – often masculine – definition of situations* (Pasquier 2005)

Finally, how can a generation which is constructing itself in the present, by itself, project itself in the future? Because this separation between youths and adults means also an absence of inscription in the past that gives reflexivity, detachment from self and others. This absence of a clear relationship to the past is very tangi-

---

19 Even if, paradoxically, Internet and chatting specifically allows one to escape this tyranny of the majority. Internet use by youths shows many paradox which are, in many cases, just two faces of a same reality.
20 More generally, the cultural female universe remains little studied. One could point out the Diane Pacom research about young Canadian girls. In this research she observes that young girls, like every social group, create their own universe of significations, values and symbolic representations, different from young boys and women.

ble in the world of school. The literature approaches this problem by pointing out the difficult coexistence between youth culture and school culture. The youth are the world of another culture *not defined by a generational belonging, the culture of work* (De Singly 2006, 28) and the culture "legitimate" and humanist. That means for youth, *a certain form of anti-intellectualism (...) and a valorisation of eclecticism"* (Hersent 2003, 12). Youth's use of the Internet seems indeed to shape a culture of immediacy and the shared emotion with social valorisation of the speed. Furthermore the "feeling" and with it the values as to the authenticity, the self-expression and the "always on" communication of the Internet. This webculture clashes with the traditional humanist culture of the school, which is linked to a past and founded on bodies of knowledge. Professors have to teach cultural objects like history or literary currents which no longer make any sense in the youths' cultural universe. More fundamentally, the "time" of school, a "metronimic society", founded on the historical time, biographical and linear, *"invaded by disciplinary like subjection to schedules, delays, buzzers, duration and order of courses, class days and vacations'* (Lasen 2001, 99) is no longer the time of youth, who lack temporal self-discipline and emprise of historical time in their social life.. These young people who *'do not feel themselves to be "artisans of their destiny" (...) experiment with zigzaging trajectories (...) and imagine a range of virtual choices and not a single linear route"* (Lasen 2001, 285).

The adolescent facing the law: between incapacity and autonomy

From a juridical point of view, the minor is in principle considered to be in a state of general incapacity, which means that he can not validly pass juridical acts alone[21]. In Belgium majority, which ipso facto involves full capacity, is attained at 18 years of age. But is the under 18 year old minor really incapable? The rules on the incapacity of minors date from 1804, the year the French civil code was edited. It tends to protect minors and their potential patrimony against unwarranted acts. There are some exceptions to this rule. Notably, it is accepted that the minor only accomplishes the acts considered to be those of daily life. For that, the minor must possess the capacity of discernment. Capacity of discernment is a factual element which is concretely evaluated by the judge in terms of particular circumstances. In general, courts and tribunals estimate that adolescents do possess capacity of discernment. Since 1804, the autonomy of youths has never stopped increasing. Likewise, the domain of acts considered

---

21 For a detailed analysis of the question of the capacity of minors related to electronic commerce, see Demoulin (2007).

as forming part of daily life and able to be accomplished by the minor alone has considerably widened, so that it would seem wiser to speak of restrained capacity[22] than of incapacity.

Changes brought about by ICT in adolescent autonomy and freedom

Messages circulated by means of traditional medias, for the most part, emanate from professional journalists, bound to respect the deontological rules of the profession. On the other hand, the new media allow any adolescent who wishes to become a broadcaster of content that is potentially accessible to all internet users, in much the same way as to any journalist. Thanks to ICT, the adolescent has attained a public space and a power of expression heretofore unknown. For the adolescent who is a broadcaster, a question arises as to the awareness and knowledge which would allow him to exercise this power in a free, enlightened and responsible way. In a State of law, all freedom ends where that of others begins. It is hence inextricable from liability. How are we to think through the liability of adolescents in knowing that it is the other side of the coin of freedom, all the while taking into account the goals of protecting minors, translated by their juridical incapacity? We shall return to this point. Where the adolescent has attained a potentially large audience, the need for a transmission of knowledge and values on the part of parents and teachers makes itself that much more urgently felt.

If he has become a broadcaster, a fully-fledged actor on the net, the adolescent is also a spectator, a potential reader of everything found on it. The great advantage is that now, no matter what his centres of interest are, the adolescent can satisfy his curiosity rapidly and easily, and without spatial or temporal limits. The problem is that if he has access to the best, he also has access to the worst (racist propaganda disguised in various real events, games inciting hatred, violence, pedopornography…) in passing through the mediocre and everything that can distract him from his initial research. Search engines deliver it all helter skelter, without sorting or preliminary description of the goals of the material's authors. This early confrontation with illicit, dangerous or simply harmful contents makes the necessity of having adequate parameters for verifying the origin and veracity of documents, for sorting and choosing those which nourish research and for avoiding what he is not ready to confront, that much more keenly felt.

---

22 De Page Traité élémentaire de droit civil belge 4th edition ed. Masson Bruxelles: Bruylant (1990) p.1125.

Youth autonomy and self-regulation

From the outset, European and international authorities have favoured self-regulation where new technologies are concerned. This is the case both for texts issued by the European Union[23] and by Council of Europe[24].
While it presents certain advantages, such as being more flexible, more adapted to the context of the new media than State regulation, self-regulation nonetheless runs the risk of accentuating the divide between parents and children. Adolescents surf far from parents who, hypothetically, are reassured in knowing that all sorts of self-regulatory organisations are on guard and that network actors impose their own rules on themselves. Yet in a breach between parents and children which keeps on widening, commercial sector actors are rushing in, seeing youths as potential consumers, infiltrating by *educating them* and *initiating* them into becoming 'good consumers'. In this regard, the Mediasmart site[25] is an edifying example. It defines itself as 'an educational site on medias for children from 6 to 11 years old, created by announcers in collaboration with teachers' associations. It notably includes a set of exercises, brought to the teachers' attention, permitting 'the formation of a critical spirit in students'. The exercises stimulate creativity and are all developed around commercial choices, ways of being convinced about these choices, budget management and so on, stressing uniquely the consumer dimension of children beginning at the age of 6! All the other dimensions of being, which are essential and structuring and which should be transmitted well before 'the capacity to be a wise consumer' are consigned to oblivion. It is significant that precisely this site is pointed to by authorities of the European Union as being an excellent example of education aimed at medias. Youths thus see themselves reduced to their commercial dimension with the benediction of all. They themselves often measure their freedom and their autonomy in gauging their capacity to purchase online.

---

23 Let us point out, for instance, the various texts concerning the 'Safer Internet' program: Decision n° 276/1999/EC of the European Parliament and the Council not in the reference list of 25 January 1999 «instituting a multi-year community program aimed at promoting the safer utilization of the internet and new online technologies in the fight against messages with illicit and harmful content, principally in the domain of the protection of children and minors », OJ n° L33 of 6/2/1999 ; Decision n° 854/2005/CE instituting a multi-year community program aimed at promoting the safer utilization of the internet and new online technologies, OJ n° L 149.
24 We notably point out Recommendation n° R (2001) 8 of the Committee of ministers to the member States on the self-regulation of cyber-contents (the self-regulation and protection of users against illicit and harmful content distributed on the new communication and information services).
25 http://www.mediasmart.org.uk

From a juridical point of view self-regulation, and particularly educational initiatives, should be assessed in terms of legitimacy: has the norm been elaborated by those who represent minors' interests? Should not minors or at least adolescents themselves participate in one way or another in the elaboration of self-regulatory norms?

Autonomy, freedom of expression, press and democracy

In Belgium, freedom of expression is a right guaranteed by the Constitution. For that matter, this right has been explicitly recognised for children by the International Convention of children's rights (article 13). Yet this right is still wider for the press who, given its mission, is granted specific guarantees. This involves the explicit interdiction of censorship, the interdiction of bail, the exclusive competence of Assize Court for press violations (except for press violations inspired by racism or xenophobia) and serial responsibility. Since the Goodwin case[26], we know with certainty that journalists also enjoy rights to secrecy of sources. The press's mission is to inform the population on questions of public interest and so exercise a function of control on public authority (its mission of being the "watchdog" of democracy).

The question that arises is about knowing whether one can transpose the notion of 'press' and, consequently, the specific guarantees of freedom of the press to Internet applications and, notably, to adolescent blogs.

If the Belgian Supreme Court's ('Cour de Cassation') interpretation of the notion of press, which restrains the application to media to the written press via the printing process, appears to go against the will of the Constituent, we do not think that an interpretation as wide as the French interpretation[27] is desirable. In Belgian law, the press should be defined in relation to its mission, to those who exercise it – meaning journalists – and to conditions which are linked to the exercise of journalism (concerted editorial activity, deontological rules, and organised distribution). The constitutional guarantees of interdiction of censorship and bail, of serial liability and of the competence of the Assize Court for press violations thus apply uniquely to those who exercise the mission of informing citizens on all ques-

---

26 Eur Court. H.R., Goodwin v. United Kingdom, 27 March 1994, A&M, 1996, p. 351 and ff., obs. Voorhoof (2003a; 2003b).
27 France has opted for an evolutive interpretation of the notion of the press. Thus, the recent French law « *for confidence in the digital economy* » of 21 June 2004 (abbreviated LCEN) extends the notion of press to every expression of thought whatever the media chosen. The sole exceptions to what is described as press are messages intended for a « a closed group of users ».

tions of general interest, whatever the mode of communication or distribution by means of which they exercise that mission. Consequently, the specific guarantees of the press do not apply to adolescent's blogs.

That said all other expressions by means of the Internet or convergent technologies enjoy the guarantees of article 10 of the European Convention on human rights. The Internet and convergent technologies offer possibilities of expression, of exchanges of ideas, of public debate on a planetary scale undreamed of in the time of traditional medias. The debate is substantially widened: it is no longer reserved just for writers, politicians and journalists and each individual can bring his stone to the edifice. Thus adolescents have attained the possibility of making their voices heard in an immediate way. This widening of the debate is of capital importance for a democratic and, consequently, pluralistic society. In the manner of the European Court of human rights, the national judge should modify[28] his evaluation of the liability of he who expresses himself according to the measure of the importance of that expression in the democratic society, being the ultimate reference of the European Convention on human rights. To do this, he should take a series of parameters into account. He should thus take into consideration the author of the litigious expression, his potential public, and the credibility that the public is liable to accord him. Thus, the liability of a youth who, on his blog, accuses a person of fantasist and slanderous things is not the same as that of a politician who might express himself thusly on *his* blog. The judge should also take into account the person or the organisation targeted by the litigious expression. If it is, for example, a question of the government or one of its members, the judge should permit more severe or even more provocative critiques than if a teacher is in question. Generally speaking, if the person or organisation targeted wields power – and we are not just talking about political power – the critical remarks may be more virulent than for a person or organisation who does not wield power. Finally, judges should take the goal of such communication into consideration. Thus, a message of a commercial character benefits from less protection than a message criticising governmental politics.

Thanks to the direct effect of article 10 of the European Convention on human rights and of the strict conditions that have to be fulfilled by exceptions to the freedom of expression in the Belgian juridical order, one need not associate all non-private expressions with the press in order to guarantee a freedom of expression worthy of the name in a democratic society.

---

28 Most of them do it in a more or less implicit way.

Adolescents facing certain limits to their freedom of expression: cyber-teasing

The personality and identity of adolescents are in development. Their place in the group and group recognition are points of crucial importance for them and is part of their identity construction. One can certainly anticipate reduced powers of resistance in facing attitudes of harassment from a group 'leader'. This would be to maintain their place in the group, to appear 'plugged in'. Further the adolescent's tendency to go along with the teaser, to join together against the chosen victim, the 'scapegoat' of the band, or even to go further in an attempt to be 'cool' also prevail.

Yet this behaviour can have a much more deep impact, in that the victim, with his identity in construction, is more fragile. Exclusion or rejection phenomena, be it only temporary and apparently harmless, can leave indelible traces on the victim without the authors being aware of the scope (or sometimes even of the existence) of the disaster they have caused.

Whenever the teasing is committed by means of ICT, it is not face to face. This absence of direct confrontation removes inhibitions. Hidden, one is more daring; one goes further in aggression, in rejection, in exploitation of the victim's weak points. The fact of not being confronted with the distress he causes allows the blogger to hide his face, to be unaware of what he is doing and, a fortiori, of the consequences that may ensue. ICT also allows a very wide distribution and an almost universal accessibility to what, in former times, would remain in closed committee or, at worst, be known to a few witnesses.

How to react to teasing situations among adolescents? Of course, the (penal and or civil) liability of one or more teasers/harassers can be tested before the courts. But judicial procedures present a certain number of inconveniences, such as slowness and an awkwardness which are in flagrant opposition to the ICT world. Moreover, if sufficient proof of harassment is not brought, the victim may see himself as once again thwarted in his suffering and may live it as an aggravation consequent upon the harassment phenomenon.[29]

It seems to us that an interesting response may be found in mediation. Beyond the fact that such a solution is faster and less burdensome, it reintroduces a face to face situation, facilitating the author's becoming aware of what the victim has endured (the consequences of his acts) and teaches respect for contradictory debate. Mediation initiatives for solving problems between youths by youths, like

---

29 This is called secondary victimization.

'SJAPO'[30], which is present in many schools in Flanders, should be encouraged, favoured and developed. In fact, some youths in schools take a rather long training course to become mediators and form a mediation committee within the school. This training involves education in the principles of respecting others, of openness of spirit, of contradictory debate, of respect of rights of defence, of human dignity ... These principles, which found democratic societies, also inspire most legislation in the area of content regulation. Beyond the fact that the 'mediators' benefit from a rich formation which is a great help to them in learning about life in society in general and about ICT in particular, the whole school, where this system is applied, is made aware of these essential values of democratic societies. We add that this response to conflicts stimulates creativity and reflection as to the types of reparation most appropriate for making amends in these problem cases, solutions which will be different from the payment of damages and interests (inappropriate for minors) or judicial penalties.

Adolescents facing certain limits to freedom of expression: copyright

Unlike the case of Anglo-Saxon law, in Belgian law (as in most continental juridical systems) the very act of creation gives rise to copyright, with no particular formality having to be enacted. This means that a design, a logo, a photo, a poem or a song, accessible online, is not always free of rights, even if no particular system of protection prevents their reproduction. How often have we heard: '*I found this on the Internet. Why can't I just recopy it onto my blog?*'.[31] It seems that, generally speaking, these rights are rather unknown to adults and even more unknown to adolescents. Respect of these rights requires educating teenagers, but first of all adults. Beyond information and education regarding the law itself, we need to inform and educate as to the goals justifying it. The initial goal is to offer recognition, on the one hand, and remuneration for the creation, on the other. This also supposes, on the part of courts, an interpretation in conformity with the goal, so as not to denature the right. For if it is interpreted too broadly it will lose its meaning and tend not to be respected. In general, youths are responsive when they themselves are victims of a violation of author's rights, when one of their poems is recopied on another blog without mentioning the author's name, for example. This sensibility can be the point of departure for education in reciprocity.

---

30 Acronym of 'Samen Jong Anders Problemen Oplossen', could be translated as: Solving problems together, young and differently.
31 It seems that a certain consciousness exists for the musical sector, but that it is largely insufficient in the other sectors.

Adolescents, liability and guilt

Searching for the liable person can be envisaged from the viewpoint of the youth who is the victim of an illicit act or from the viewpoint of a youth who commits an illicit act by means of ICT.

Whenever a youth is a victim of an illicit act committed by means of information and communication technologies, the question is one of knowing who is liable, given the number of actors using the net. This question refers notably to the liability of network intermediaries[32]. We shall not develop this aspect in the present report. We shall simply point out article 299 of the Belgian Penal Code, which requires the mention of a liable editor for all 'written matter'. Unlike what is the case in France, this measure has no equivalent in the new media, so that it is sometimes quite hard to identify who is liable. Extension of this obligation to the new media seems desirable both from the viewpoint of the identification of liability and from the viewpoint of the exercise of the right of reply.

Whenever a young person commits an illicit act, the question can be examined from the angle of both penal liability and civil liability. In this report, we share a few thoughts concerning civil liability.

Civil liability regulation, dating from 1804, has the principal goal of ensuring compensation to the victim for damages he has suffered. A minor can be held liable for his own acts from the moment he has attained the age of discernment. In the view of juridical security, certain authors favour the legal determination of the age from which the minor is presumed conscious of his acts, whatever the particular circumstances. By means of ICT, adolescents can cause particularly weighty damage in that they may potentially reach a large audience, without always being conscious of the public character of their expression.

The notion of wrong which involves liability requires the capacity of discernment on the part of the author. But the complexity of the matter, the multiplication of actors and the generational divide accentuate a general unconsciousness. While nobody should ignore the law, we should envisage, beyond education in juridical rules, education in the values underlying them. Education of youths necessitates the education of teachers and the raising awareness of parents. Only if this education is set up systematically in educational institutions before a certain age (13 years of age for example) can one suppose that such a discernment will be attained from that age onwards.

---

32 This matter is dealt with on European level in the Directive 2000/31/EC of the European Parliament and of the Council of 8 June 2000 on certain legal aspects of information society services, in particular electronic commerce in the Internal Market, O.J.E.C., 17/7/2000, n° L178/1.

If the minor's liability be justified by the autonomy he benefits from and if the liability is proportional to the freedom, the problem of his relative inadequacy for meeting the goal of guaranteeing compensation to victims remains, given the insolvency of most minors.

To make up for this lack of adequacy in compensation to victims suffering damages, the minor's parents' liability may be invoked. Whenever the minor causes damages to a third party, the parents are presumed to have acted wrongfully in the education or surveillance of their child. This presumption of wrong is justified by parental authority and is based on the rather unrealistic idea that if the minor had had a good education and had been watched over correctly, he would not have committed an offence (or an objectively illicit act). Unrealistic from the outset, this idea is getting more absurd all the time and even more pointedly in ICT use, not only given the evolution of principles of education but also the empowerment of youth and the generational divide. Moreover, this system links liability to guilt. The extent of the guilt born by the parents is further accentuated by this present-day tendency, transforming victims into heroes[33]. Yet given the goal of compensation, the system is inefficient insofar as the presumption can be reversed: if the parents can offer proof of good education and diligent surveillance, they will not be held liable and so the victim is not compensated, whatever the extent of damage he suffered.

The teacher's liability[34] can also be invoked in case the student acts wrongfully during the period when he is under the teacher's surveillance. This is founded on the authority the teacher exercises over the student. The teacher is thus presumed to have acted wrongfully in the student's surveillance. The pertinence of the teacher's liability and authority over an adolescent student can be seriously called into doubt in an era where the latter may be on the Internet or using his mobile phone at school. Even if the teacher is protected by immunities (his responsibility is guaranteed by the educational institution or by the State in terms of the type of institution he exercises his functions in), the same critique can be voiced here as it was in case parental liability. Since the presumption may be reversed, in case of reversal, the goal of victim compensation is not attained. If educational institutions are not considered teachers, their liability can nonetheless be invoked in case of teacher's wrong. Thus, in the 'free education system', the educational institution (committing the infraction) is presumed to have acted wrongfully in case of a wrong of one of its teachers. This presumption is undeniable and is hence more capable of responding to the goal of victim compensation.

---

33 See in this connection, the excellent study by Eliacheff et al. (2007)
34 A teacher is conceived as any person charged with a mission of instruction, a mission which has been interpreted very broadly by the 'Cour de cassation' (Cass., 3 Dec. 1986, Pas., 1986, p. 410).

In the 'official education system', the teacher is wrong, he being an extension of the State, ipso facto involves the latter's liability. Of course the own liability of institutions (educational or for the protection of youth) can also be invoked. Thus the burden of proof rests on the victim: it is up to him to show the institution's wrong and the chain of causation between the wrong and the damage. So a bad organisation of the surveillance to be exercised regarding the minor or a bad execution of that surveillance may constitute such wrongs. In the ICT domain, institutions which place computer material in the hands of students or adolescents they are in charge of have every interest in being able to show that they make them aware of the risks that the use of this materiel may involve, for example in making students sign a code of conduct regarding use of ICT in school, in putting in place precise rules for use, in using filters to avoid access to violent, pornographic or other harmful contents.

As we see, in regard to the goal of victim compensation, the formulations involving parental and teacher liability are poorly thought out in that the presumption can be reversed. Moreover, they are inextricably linked to the notion of guilt of those 'presumed liable', which is no more realistic (and never was) and puts a heavier burden on their shoulders. Rather than connecting civil liability to the notion of wrong (and thus of guilt), we should foster an evolution towards a system of objective liability of parents or educational institutions founded on the notion of risk. This would discharge those liable, as well as the minor himself, from the burden of guilt while in any case ensuring reparation for victims. This objective liability might then be linked to obligatory insurance. For educational institutions or youth aid organisations, this insurance might be paid by the subsidies they benefit from, thus distributing the 'risk' to the community.

Contradictory debate and the right of reply

If freedom of the press is an essential component of a democratic society and allows an exercise of control on the powers in place, it is only right that it should be in turn controlled by the citizen to avoid having to cope with an all-powerful press.

The right of reply has its place here and offers a very interesting reaction to any person designated by a media in that it guarantees the contradictory character of debate enhances respect for others and does so without entering into court procedures or posing the delicate question of liability. Existing legislation in the area of the written press and in the audiovisual area also applies to the new media, but the need for regulation adapted to the latter is making itself felt for, in practice, the periodicity condition of written media notably risking posing problems. The adoption of legal measures for introducing the right of reply into online media is recommended by both institutions of the European Union and the Council of Europe and is seen by the latter as a measure ensuring better protection of minors and human dignity in all online services.

In a context where support very often includes spaces for response, reaction and commentaries, one might wonder whether the right of reply still has a 'raison d'être'. We hazard a guess that it is less useful than in the traditional medias, insofar as numerous spaces for response and reaction already exist due to the very nature of public spaces on the net. We are doubtlessly witness to a greater number of spontaneous rectifications or reactions in the spaces set aside for that than ever. Yet, the freedom of spontaneous response is not total: there are always closed sites or closed parts of sites, or moderated sites, etcetera.

But in order that this right might allow us to ensure a better protection of minors and human dignity in all online services[35], there should be awareness of values like respect for others among youths, freedom of expression and the contradictory character of debate, as well as consciousness of the existence of a right of reply as a guarantee of these values. How should this right of reply be exercised by the adolescent minor? Could he act alone or should he have recourse to services and/or consent of an informed adult? To the extent that he expresses himself without parental consent for the content he puts on the web, it seems to us that an adolescent having gained capacity of discernment can also respond alone to critics or inexact allegations without having parental consent. On the other hand, he should have the possibility of talking with an informed parent, teacher, educator or family member, to consider together the best way to answer and learn about the legal conditions of the exercise of that right. Hence the need for information, education and awareness raising of parents, teachers, educators and youth aid organisations concerning the rights and obligations of adolescents using these new medias and, notably, concerning the right of reply.

Conclusions

Such is the paradox of the Net; it is supposed to build bridges between individuals and communities but at the same time, exacerbates tensions between gender, increases individualisation within families and acts as a catalyst for division within tribes based on the self. Adolescents and adults appear to evolve in parallel

---

35 Recommendation of the European Parliament and the Council of 20 December 2006 (2006/952/CE) on the protection of minors and of human dignity and on the right of reply in connection with the competitiveness of the European industry of audiovisual services and online information, J.O.U.E. 27/12/2006, n° L378, p. 72-77.

worlds, each following its course with little regard for the other. Older adolescents themselves invite us to build bridges between these worlds and to re-establish a dialogue so that transmission from one generation to another might carry on: transmission of knowledge, transmission of the way to be and the way to act in society; transmission that is not unilateral (from adults to adolescents) but reciprocal (including what adolescents have to teach adults); transmission allowing opposition and construction of identities.

We have chosen the example of cyberteasing, a common phenomenon among young people that illustrates well the impact of the generational divide. Cyberteasing expresses well the power of peers, the tyranny of the pressure to conform, and the recrudescence of anonymised aggression (anonymous in the sense that there is no physical confrontation) that is part of this phenomenon. Mediation offers an especially interesting response to cyberteasing. In mediation, young people are trained by adults to become mediators by training them in democratic values (respect for others, initiation to contradictory debate, open-mindedness, and respect for the rights of the defence). By this means young people are taught to remember the principles that underlie legislation that applies to content regulation. Such training of young people by adults constitutes a bridge between the two worlds by re-establishing the existence of mutual transmission. Transmission creates confidence and autonomy, since young people who are mediators fulfil the role of conciliators within society (represented by the school). Transmission can stimulate the natural creativity of young people who, after having heard both parties to a conflict, look for solutions that can satisfy the interests of the offending party and the victim. Decisions made by mediators are supervised by adults: a new bridge is created because adults can learn from the restorative creativity about how to solve their own conflicts, and can pick up ideas on how to understand young people. By raising the question of copyright, we invite parents to get involved in the blogosphere of adolescents, and to take an interest in their many creations on the Net. By exploring these, adults create a bridge that is one of respect for the creativity of the generation of teenagers. This bridge built out of listening and respect can be the source of the beginning of education in reciprocity, as it well known that respect creates respect. The question of civil liability for the acts of adolescents also creates links between adolescents and their parents in terms of failure in education and in surveillance. These guilty links, which do not benefit the victim, are not of a constructive nature. Could we not imagine liability as an invitation to shared creativity: if a teenager is at fault (or negligent), this involved youth should have to go with his or her parents in search of a remedy in terms of the victim. In that case, one positive bridge could be constructed between the youth, his parents and even the victim (in the re–establishment of face to face contact). The possibility of the right of reply is something along the same lines, a creative solution that does not involve finding guilt. This possibility does require education about respecting others, about freedom of expression, and about the contradictory nature of debates in democracy, including a guaranteed right of reply as one of the basic values to be upheld. This educational initiative would build yet another bridge which could be crossed in both directions. Mediation and right of reply constitute creative answers to infringements of the rights of persons that demonstrate everyone's creativity. These responses creating confidence and autonomy allow a positive and solid construction of identity. The same cannot be said of the system of civil liability based on the culpability that causes rejection and ill will, attributes that have never been part of bridge-building.

This research creates interesting interactions between sociology, law and communication science showing the force of this cooperation in the elaboration of regulatory tools that are well adapted and able to be appropriated by young people. It gives an empirical evidence of the necessity of anchoring legal reflection in detailed and comprehensive sociological and cultural observation of teenagers' practices.

References

Boyd D. m. 'Identity Production in a Networked Culture: Why Youth Heart MySpace' American Association for the Advancement of Science, St. Louis, MO. February 19, 2006 (2006)
De Smedt T., Klein A., Romain L. Internet et les jeunes Bruxelles· Apprendre les médias (2002)
Delforge H., Vienne P. 'Les horizons culturels de l'adolescence dans le contexte scolaire en Communauté française à Bruxelles' Recherche en Education 113/04, rapport intermédiaire, Bruxelles: ULB (2006)
Demoulin M. 'Les mineurs et le commerce électronique: besoin de protection ou d'autonomie?' Journal des tribunaux 6255 (2007) pp. 105-116.
De Singly F. Les Adonaissants Paris: Armand Colin (2006)
De Singly F. Libres Ensembles Paris: Pocket (2003)
De Singly F. Sociologie de la famille contemporaine Paris: Armand Colin (2004)
Eliacheff C., Soulez Larivière D. Le temps des victimes Albin: Michel (2007)
Eliade M. Initiation, mythes et société secrètes, Naissances mystiques, essai sur quelques types d'initiation Paris: Gallimard (1959)
Fize M. 'Contribution à une sociologie de l'adolescence' Revue de l'Institut de Sociologie 1-4 (1993) pp. 253-268
Galland O. Les jeunes Paris : La Découverte (2002)

Hersent J-F. 'Les pratiques culturelles adolescentes: France, début du troisième millénaire', BBF 3 (2003) pp. 12-21

Jung C. G. L'homme à la découverte de son âme Paris: Albin Michel (1987)

Lasen A. Le temps des jeunes, Rythmes, Durée et Virtualités Paris: L'Harmattan (2001)

Livingstone S. Young People and New Media London: Sage (2002)

Martin O., De Singly F. 'L'évasion amicale. L'usage du téléphone familiale par les adolescents' Réseaux 103 (2000) pp. 45-78

Martin O. 'L'Internet des 10- 20 ans, une ressource pour une communication autonome', Réseaux 123 (2004) pp. 25-58

Mediappro, The appropriation of new Media by Youth, European Research Project URL: http://www.mediappro.org/ (2006) (accessed January 2009)

Metton C. 'Les usages de l'Internet par les collégiens. Explorer les mondes sociaux depuis le domicile' Réseaux 123 (2004) pp. 59-84

Pasquier D. Cultures lycéennes, la tyrannie de la majorité Paris: Ed. Autrement (2005)

Tredan O. 'Les weblogs dans la Cité: entre quête de l'entre-soi et affirmation identitaire', Cahier de recherches de Marsouin 6 URL: http://www.expert.infini.fr/IMG/pdf/Rapport_ Blog_EXPERT-CRAPE-Marsouin.pdf (2005) (accessed January 2009)

Voorhoof D. 'De journalistieke vrijheid en de tussenkomst van de rechter: censuur of noodzaak in een democratische samenleving?' Censures, Actes du colloque du 16 mai 2003 A&M n° spécial Bruxelles: De Boeck & Larcier (2003a) pp. 71-96

Voorhoof D. 'Nieuwe regels betreffende recht van antwoord in Vlaams omroepdecreet' A&M (2003b) p. 407

Maria Sourbati

Non-Users in the Information Society: Learning from the older generation

Introduction

Over the past 15 years or so Europe's Information Society policy discourses have stressed the potential of Information and Communication Technologies (ICTs) and media-enabled services to promote economic growth and social inclusion, transform public service delivery and improve the quality of life (EC 2005). Communication and information access are increasingly mediated by digital technologies to the point where those unable to use these technologies are at risk of being disadvantaged in a range of areas, including e-government information, ICT-enabled public services, and the more familiar public electronic communications.

Almost ten years after the launch of eEurope (EC 2000) the European Union (EU) is facing the reality of low levels of Internet access by disadvantaged groups who are core users of public services. There is a growing sense of concern in policy-making circles that some sections of the population which do not use digital ICTs and are key customer groups of public services are at risk of social exclusion: *'There is still evidence of a digital divide with some groups largely excluded from benefiting from access to the Internet'* (Cabinet Office 2005b, 7). The halving of the gap in Internet usage by 2010 for older people, people with disabilities, and unemployed persons is set as a key target for policy action in the 2006 Riga Declaration on eInclusion in order to address issues in the fields of active ageing, accessibility, digital literacy and competence (EU & EFTA 2006, 2). Policy thinking is subsequently taking a user-centric view, shifting attention to individuals and groups who do not use today's new ICTs. At national level, the UK has announced that a better understanding of customer needs and behaviours especially 'the needs of key groups – such as older people' is to become a priority at central level (Cabinet Office 2005a, 7-8).

As digital networks and services are in place, low levels of new media use can be seen as mirroring the lack of skills and competencies required to use digital, online ICTs. Expressing concern about the inequities characterising access to and use of new ICTs the European Commission has now prioritised the development of media literacy in all sections of society. In December 2007 the first Communication on media literacy was published at EU level announcing a study to be launched in 2008 on how to assess media literacy in the EU population (EC

2007a). According to the Commission (EC 2007b, 6) *'media-literate people will be able to exercise informed choices ... and take advantage of the full range of opportunities offered by new communications technologies'*. The public policy questions behind media literacy initiatives are about the promotion of access to and use of digital, interactive ICTs and the content and services available through them.

This paper looks into how those people who do not use today's new media are addressed in policy discourses. Any answers to questions regarding (non-) use, and the policy initiatives that may ensue can largely be defined by the way in which those 'non-users' are framed and positioned. As Braman (2004) reminds us, how a policy issue is defined can be seen to determine, among other things, the modes or argument used, who is considered as a relevant actor and the resources and goals considered pertinent. The positioning of non-users of new ICTs can therefore be expected to have a bearing on public policy initiatives to promote the literacies required to access and use new ICTs. More specifically, this paper examines the situation of older adults, commonly defined as those 'over the age of 65', who are customarily taken as the typical category of non-users of new media. Even though the policy research data used here mainly refer to older adults in the UK, the paper engages in a discussion and critique of broader trends in policy and popular explanations of phenomena of ICT (non-) use.

New media and older (non-) users in policy discourses:
Disabling representations

Although Internet use is growing steadily, take-up and use levels remain lowest amongst older people. According to the UK Office of National Statistics, there remains a large divide between the young and the old, with 83 percent of the 16 to 24 age group accessing the Internet in 2006 compared with 15 percent of the 65 plus age group, and with 10 percent of the 16 to 24 age group never having used the Internet, compared with 82 percent of the 65 plus age group (ONS 2006, 4.) Numbers fall dramatically across the EU where, according to the *Eurostat* survey, just over 10 percent of Europeans aged 65 or over accessed the Internet in 2005 against 68 percent of individuals aged 18-24[1] (EU & EFTA 2006). Not surprisingly, similar findings were reported in the first national audit of media literacy in the UK, undertaken by the Office of Communications (Ofcom) in 2005-06. The

---

1 In 2005 57% of individuals living in the EU did not regularly use the Internet; only 24% of persons with a low education used the Internet against 73% of those with a high education; only 32% of unemployed persons used the Internet against 54% of employed persons. There are, of course, sharp distinctions across the EU with pensioners living in Nordic countries being more likely to use the Internet.

research found that people who are 65 years of age or older have significantly lower levels of media literacy and show lower levels of interest in and perceived need for various aspects of digital media technologies than other age groups. The ownership and use of networked computers was also lowest among respondents aged 65 or over as it reached 20 percent of households against a national average of 54 percent (Ofcom 2006a).

Older adults are a problem for public policy and so is their relationship with new electronic media technologies and services. People who are 75 years of age or older are a key category of 'heavy users' of welfare support such as social care and health services and could be major beneficiaries of ICT-enabled public services (e-public services). The use of new ICTs is supposed to benefit many of the isolated, home-centred individuals who use social welfare services. Benefits accruing from Internet access include enhanced opportunities regarding outreach services, convenient access to health care information, opportunities for interpersonal communication and lifelong learning. In the context of e-government initiatives to support the electronic delivery of government information and services and to increase the take-up of Internet access, explicit mention has been made to the use of ICTs in social care provision to make information about the range of services available more accessible to older customers and to thereby support active ageing and independent living (see Curry et al. 2002). However, as most older people do not use new ICTs they cannot benefit from them and are at a risk of 'digital exclusion', along with other disadvantaged groups.

How individuals relate to new media technologies is commonly discussed by reference to their chronological age. New media are viewed as the domain of younger generations. Ofcom's audit of media literacy concluded that age features as 'the single most significant defining factor in levels of media literacy' (Ofcom 2006b, 11). Older people's (non-) engagement with new ICTs has been explained in terms of their cognitive, mental and physical decline. In light of early human-computer interaction research, older people have been understood as being physically and psychologically disadvantaged when learning to use computer technologies (Trocchia & Janda 2000). Accounts of barriers typically mention changes associated with the physiological process of ageing, such as a decline in vision and a slowing down of movement that make it difficult to use technological artefacts designed for younger, able-bodied users. Also, learning to use new ICTs is taken to be further impeded by declines in perceptual and cognitive abilities.

More recently, policy thinking has tended to interpret take-up and use figures in terms of attitudinal barriers. Again, this line of interpretation sees attitudes to new media technologies as being strongly associated with age. A survey by Ofcom's Consumer Panel (2006a) identified a lack of confidence in learning to use ICTs, a perceived lack of interest and a perception that new ICTs are not needed as factors deterring older people from developing new media literacies. According to this survey, 56 percent of adults aged 65 and over 'voluntarily excluded themselves' compared to the national average of 22 percent (ibid, 37). The survey reached the familiar conclusion that 'age remains one of the most significant factors' affecting how people engage with new media technologies (ibid, 1).

At the same time, there is a newer and growing perception of older people who are new media savvy, the so-called 'Silver Surfers'. The concept of Silver Surfers, referring to confident and competent older consumers of new ICTs, is becoming a metaphor of choice in policy publicity[2]. Silver Surfer discourses can be seen to reinforce popular claims about older people and new media. For instance, that older adults 'stand to benefit from ICT in various ways', that the ability to make use of new technology is 'a ready means through which to "bridge the generation gap"' (Selwyn et al 2003, 262) and that those who have not joined the information-rich 'haves' of society 'have failed to do so out of choice, or stodginess' (Riggs 2004, 82). Old age as the inescapable destination of 'have nots', 'can nots' or indeed 'are nots' (young and included) can thus be regressed into youth through the consumption of new ICTs. These kinds of claims do not challenge some stereotypical representations of older people[3].

Individual-centred, age-based, static and binary notions of media access

In short, older people are commonly taken to be missing out on the opportunities presented in digital, online communications as they are inhibited from using new media mainly because of their individual circumstances and deficiencies experienced as a result of their chronological age[4]. Two quite contradictory explanations of media (non-) use can be distinguished here. First, older people are unable to obtain the literacies they need to use new media and, second, they choose not to use new ICTs which are more or less widely available in Western societies, thus voluntarily excluding themselves, *because* they are old. Both explanations are

---

2 Over the past couple of years Silver Surfer news have featured regularly in Ofcom's Media Literacy Bulletins, published online at: www.ofcom.org.uk/advice/media_literacy/medlitpub/bulletins/ (see, for example, issues 7, 9 and 10).
3 Here older age as decay and peril is calling attention to itself as something that can be reversed to 'youth' through consumption. The 'silver surfer' concept does not challenge ageist attitudes of the kind manifested in the growing trend for newer generations of older people to be seen to act as consumers in the growing market for 'eternal youth' with regard to their physical appearance and tastes. On cultural attitudes to ageing and consumption, see Harkin and Huber (2004, 30-37).
4 'Chronological age' refers to the number of years people have lived, in contrast to the stage they have reached in their physical or emotional development.

characterised by a tendency to strip older (and young) people of social relations.[5] Older non-users are positioned here as isolated individuals who do not engage in relationships with other individuals. Their age, which becomes their defining property, is not situated as a lived experience of interacting human beings, one that unfolds within different domains of life in the home, the community, the market and civil society[6]. Here, (non-)engagement with new ICTs is a feature of generalised, aged individuals.

The idea of age-based blanket rejection/acceptance goes hand-in-hand with an understanding of media access as a matter of absolutes. Prevailing views about the relationship of older people with new media draw on static and binary concepts of media access and use, differentiating between individuals who have access to the Internet and those who do not. However, Internet access is not a matter of a one-off act of providing a connection to the network and learning skills in using computers and browsers. Access rests on a dynamic and social process. It encompasses network capabilities, equipment and software as well as social infrastructure, skills and competencies. Using the Internet entails the continuous development of user knowledge, along with the updating and upgrading hardware and software (Livingstone 2003).

Not just individuals alone

Policy questions around the ability of older people to use new ICTs meaningfully and beneficially, and more generally around the 'digitally excluded' groups, are better considered if we abandon age-based generalisations as well as static, dualistic and individualistic notions of media access and use.

First, homogenising generalisations do not capture age(ing) as a lived experience. For one thing, as Riggs (2004, 228-9) comments, widespread generalisations about older age and new technologies are not sufficiently nuanced to acknowledge cultural differences in experience along axes such as education and social class. Older Internet users are today more likely to come from the relatively affluent, educated middle classes. In the UK, for instance, Internet access among older adults has been stratified by socio-economic status and educational background (Selwyn et al. 2003). The situation in the UK reflects similar trends in the US

---

5 The blanket labelling young people as 'Internet experts' simply reproduces the popular perception of engagement with new ICTs in terms of a generation gap.
6 Dominant discourses on older non-users of new ICTs can be seen as a deeper substratum of ageist dichotomies that position older and younger generations as being polarised from each other and at times disengaged by the community as a whole (cf. Age Concern 2007).

where class, ethnicity, income and educational level 'help to predict on which side of the Digital Divide elders are positioned' (Riggs 2004, 226). Advanced age then cannot be seen to determine whether or not older people are using the Internet. A recent study by Ofcom's Consumer Panel looked into older people's feelings and attitudes to new media technologies and found that 'digitally engaged' older pensioners had developed new media literacies primarily as a result of their experience in the workplace and that exposure to and engagement with media technologies led to the further development of media literacies (Ofcom Consumer Panel 2006b, 1-3). Thus, (non-) use of today's new media is not just a matter of an individual's personal circumstances but is also subject to uneven opportunities to access formal and informal learning and support. With this in mind, Selwyn et al. (2005, 20) point out '*it is not being an older adult ... per se which makes you an internet non-user, but the opportunities, needs, motivations, material circumstances and lived experiences of being an older adult*'.

Second, explanations that focus on individuals alone fail to acknowledge the relational nature of media use. Interactionist perspectives have shown that practices of ICT use are grounded in existing relations of social interaction. As put by Bakardjieva (2005, 190), the user of a media technology '*is not facing the technology and the content and activities accessible through it as an isolated individual.*' Relationships of warmth and knowledge sharing play an important role in introducing someone to a new technology. Many people first encounter the idea of engaging with new media through their family and close friends (Haddon 2000). For many older people, it can be their grandchildren, for example, who show them how they can use the email to send and receive photographs.

Qualitative research has highlighted how significant others can mediate between the specialised knowledge and skills necessary to use new ICTs and the situation and needs of new users. Bakardjieva's concept of the 'warm expert' describes personal contacts of friends and relatives who help non-users understand the relevance of a new ICT and what is accessible through it to their own situation. Warm experts help 'novices' learn not only how to use this technology but also what this technology can do for them (Bakardjieva 2005; Bakardjieva & Smith 2001). Verhaegh (2007) proposes the related concept of 'warm user' to describe someone who does not come from one's immediate environment but plays this role as a volunteer in community settings by helping residential end-user[7] collectivities.

---

[7] The term 'end user' may not be the most appropriate to use with reference to Web 2.0 technologies which allow 'users' to take on more or less active roles in the value creation process (cf. Slot and Frissen 2007).

Third, as mentioned in the previous section, popular age-based explanations draw on binary and absolute concepts of access and use. They fail to acknowledge that individuals engage with new, interactive ICTs in complex and varied ways. Engagement with interactive media is not necessarily on a 'self-service' basis. Qualitative research has identified a mode of mediated access through personal contacts, again usually relatives or friends, who act as 'proxy' users with regard to contacting others electronically, obtaining information or transacting online (Selwyn et al., 2005). The Oxford Internet Survey (OxIS 2005, 6) reported that the practice of 'use by proxy' increases the likelihood of those with a basic knowledge of the capabilities of online ICT (of what the technologies can do for us) to use its benefits.

Use by proxy can be a relevant practice of media use which spans the domestic and the institutional space/time. The 'local expert' concept can be borrowed from the community informatics literature (Clement & Shade 2000) to describe supporting relationships of warmth that extend/are formed outside of one's immediate environment of family and friends. Building on the notions of 'local expertise' and 'warm user' this paper suggests that use by proxy can be an enabling practice that is not divorced from a consideration of the conditions of an older person's life. Older people's activities of seeking information, contacting others and accessing services can be embedded in adverse everyday situations. Dealing with these can involve relationships of care provision. Older (non-) users of new ICTs may be homebound as a result of suffering from an isolating illness and may depend on community care services. Experienced community support workers can act as intermediaries not only with regard to learning about new media technologies[8] but also by contacting people electronically and accessing information and services on behalf of a non-user.

Implications for policy-making and analysis

Conceptualisations of media literacy and use as a feature of generalised and isolated individuals do not help articulate policy visions or develop programmes to promote equitable opportunities to use digital, interactive ICTs and the content and services available through them. The different forms that engagement with interactive digital media technologies can take, and the relational character of this engagement, are important to consider in order to assess situations of (non-) use. As use of today's new media becomes more widespread, caring relationships of warmth are increasingly appreciated in the research community as an infrastructure of support available

---

8   Ofcom's media literacy audit found that younger adults with mobility impairments are the least likely to have experience of learning about new media and are less likely to be interested in learning, compared with people who do not have this disability.

to and accessible by individuals. This perspective can be radically different from the dominant thinking that constructs older people who do not use the Internet as incapable of showing interest in, and learning to use new ICTs due to properties they (do not) possess as a result of their chronological ageing. The emphasis here is on the profoundly social character of ICT use. As put by Verhaegh (2007, 176), 'the unit of analysis is not the individual user'.

Following Tuomi's (2005, 28) proposition to reconstruct our categories for studying 'the user' of ICTs in order to make visible the social basis of meaningful use, the intended uses of new, interactive media – what are these ICTs for in terms of social practice – are also important to consider. The use of new ICT-enabled services such as health care information delivered via the Internet becomes a question of either matching the service to a given form of activity, for instance, obtaining information in public libraries or providing social care services to older people, or social learning where older customers and professionals working in local libraries or care provision have to learn how to use this service to develop new practices. I have argued a similar point elsewhere (Sourbati 2008) specifically in relation to the situation in Sheltered Homes for older people where a lack of engagement with a new networked computer facility and an inability to use the health care information available online characterised the everyday routines of both young care professionals and older residents.

What this paper understands as an anthropocentric perspective on policy questions of media use – one that centres on human beings – introduces a requirement to think beyond isolated individuals. Social practices of access to information, public services and voice/expression which are increasingly mediated by digital technologies have a collective dimension. Almost a decade after the launch of e-Europe, policy-making efforts have not been attuned to the need for inclusive practices that promote access to online connectivity for different cohorts of older adults and other 'non-users'. In the UK, a member state with relatively high Internet penetration rates, there has been little evidence of a sustained commitment to support the use of new ICTs for older citizens and carers.[9] The recent shift in policy attention towards issues of non-use carries a promise for a user-centred

---

9 Government-sponsored training to encourage older people to learn using networked computers has been available as short, half-hour sessions, dubbed 'Silver Surfer' events. These are marketed as opportunities for older people who are unfamiliar with networked computers to join 'tester sessions', to experience the use of online ICTs. Between 2002 and 2004 Silver Surfer events were run as part of the UK Online programme which established a network of 6,000 community Internet access points in museums, public libraries and other community learning centres. Following the completion of the UK Online programme, such initiatives are today run mainly by the charitable and voluntary sector and are supported by corporate sponsorship.

perspective, one that puts the social aspects of ICT use at its very centre. However, if we place the focus exclusively on individual (non-) users and how they (do not) fit new ICTs into their everyday routines we may lose sight of policy matters concerning the redistribution of resources and capabilities which make technologies usable.

In light of this analysis media, use must be conceptualised by reference to social and material infrastructure, keeping in mind the role of relationships of warmth and the non-human aspects of ICT use.[10] How social and material infrastructures are made available and how much they cost to use must be addressed in public policy if universal access to new ICTs is to be promoted. The latter would involve investing in human capital in order to make available mediated forms of engagement to those who are not able to interact with the systems on their own. Where applicable, the literacies required to access and use e-public services and information could be made available through proxy users.

Concluding remarks

This paper started with a review of dominant policy discourses on older people in the information society. Older people, supposedly major beneficiaries of major public policy initiatives in e-public services, e-government and the digitalisation of public electronic communications, are commonly perceived as being incapable of obtaining the literacies required to use new ICTs due to their old age. Consequently, they are positioned as deficient and excluded. The paper proceeded with a discussion of the assumptions behind these conventional understandings of older 'non-users' of new ICTs, and of their consequences for policy development. A number of conclusions emerge from this discussion.

First, age-determined explanations have consequences regarding future policy development. To allow conventional representations of old age to influence the provision of e-services to future generations may be to disadvantage them and to misdirect government resources. The implicit assumption that the newly old (today's younger generations) will be uniformly media literate is misplaced and could lead to other types of disadvantage. As new ICT services develop fast and the skills and literacies required to use them become more complex and network capacity requirements increase, many of today's 'included' users may be tomorrow's excluded.

Looking into the position of older people can reveal how fundamentally flawed are certain sets of assumptions that underlie popular perceptions about new media

---

10 The material, technological aspects of ICT use including network connectivity, equipment and software.

technologies and their (non-) use(rs). In exploring these dichotomous and individualistic understandings of media access and use, this paper has argued that, methodologically, perspectives that focus on individuals alone are limited. Individualistic conceptions of interactive ICT use fail to capture the relational character of engagement with information and communication media. Drawing on a body of broadly interactionist research media use can be conceived of more fruitfully in terms of individuals who interact with other individuals in their interface with technologies[11] in order to do things.

This approach to policy issues of media literacy and use entails a reconceptualisation of 'users' and their relationship with media technologies. When it comes to public policy, especially social policy matters of distributional equity, mediated forms of ICT use are important to bear in mind and provide for. Caring relations of warmth in the community can mediate access to digital systems and services for people who may need assistance in doing so. After all, the real challenge for public policy may not be today's unconnected individuals, the 'non-users' and their non-possession of adequate levels of media skills and competencies, but the social practices of access to information, voice/expression and public services.

References

Age Concern 'Introduction to intergenerational practice' Information Leaflet (2007) URL: http://www.silversurfers.org/AgeConcern/Documents/Intergenerational_Prac-tice.pdf (accessed April 2007)
Bakardjieva M. Internet Society. The internet in everyday life London: Sage (2005)
Bakardjieva M., Smith R. 'The internet in everyday life: Computer networking from the standpoint of the domestic user' New Media and Society 3: 1 (2001) pp. 67-83
Braman S. 'Where has media policy gone? Defining the field in the twentieth first century' Communication Law and Policy 9: 2 (2004) pp. 153-82
Cabinet Office Transformational government enabled by technology. The Cabinet Office, November 2005 Cm6683 (2005a) URL: http://www.cio.gov.uk/documents /pdf/transgov/transgov-strategy.pdf (accessed April 2007)
Cabinet Office Connecting the UK. The Digital Strategy Cabinet Office. A Joint Report with the Department of Trade and Industry (2005b) URL: http://www.cabinetoffice.gov.uk/strategy/work_areas/digital_strategy/index.asp (accessed April 2007)
Clement A., Shade L. 'The access rainbow: conceptualising universal access to the information/communication infrastructure' ed. Gurstein M. Community Informatics Hershey PA: Idea Publishing (2000) pp. 32-51.

---

11   This point was not developed at any length here.

Curry R.G., Trejo Tinoco M., Wardle D. The use of information and communication technology (ICT) to support independent living for older and disabled people A report for the Department of Health. October 2002 URL: http://www.icesdoh.org/downloads/ICT-Report-R-Curry-Oct02.pdf (accessed April 2007)

European Commission (EC), 'eEurope 2002. An Information Society for all.' Action Plan prepared by the Council and the European Commission for the Feira European Council, 19-20 June 2000, June 14, Brussels: European Commission URL: http://europa.eu.int/information_society/eeurope/2002/action_plan/pdf/actionplan_en.pdf (accessed April 2007)

EC 'i2010 – A European Information Society for growth and employment.' Communication from the Commission to the Council, the European Parliament, the European Economic and Social Committee and the Committee of the Regions, COM (2005) 229 Final, Brussels, 1/6/2005, (2005).

EC 'Communication from the Commission to the European Parliament, the Council, the European Economic and Social Committee and the Committee of the Regions. A European Approach to Media Literacy in the Digital Environment' COM (2007) 833 final. Brussels 20/12/2007 URL: http://ec.europa.eu/avpolicy/media_literacy/docs /com20070833final.pdf (2007a) (accessed December 2007)

EC 'Amended proposal for a Directive of the European Parliament and of the Council amending Council Directive' 89/552/EEC. COM (2007) 170 final. Brussels 20/3/2007 URL: http://ec.europa.eu/avpolicy/docs/reg/modernisation/proposal_2005/com_2007_170_en.pdf (2007b) (accessed October 2007)

European Union (EU) and European Free Trade Area (EFTA) 'Ministerial Declaration on e Inclusion', Riga, Latvia, 11-13 June 2006 URL: http://ec.europa.eu/ information_society/events/ict_riga_2006/doc/declaration_riga.pdf (2006) (accessed April 2007)

Haddon L. 'Social Exclusion and Information and Communication Technology. Lessons from studies of single parents and the young elderly' New Media and Society 2:4 (2000) pp 387-406

Harkin J., Huber J. Eternal Youths. How the baby boomers are having their time again. Demos (2004)

Livingstone S. 'What is media literacy', Media@LSE Department of Media and Communications URL: http://www.lse.ac.uk/collections/media@lse/whosWho/sonia Livingstone. htm#medialiteracy (2003) (accessed April 2007)

Office of Communications (Ofcom) Media Literacy Audit: Report on Adult Media Literacy Ofcom, 2 March 2006 URL: http://www.ofcom.org.uk/advice/media_literacy/medlitpub/medlitpubrss/medialit_audit/medialit_audit.pdf (2006a) (accessed April 2007)

Ofcom Media Literacy Audit: Report on media literacy amongst older people Ofcom (April 2006) URL: http://www.ofcom.orgk/advice/media_literacy/medlitpub/ medlitpubrss/older/older.pdf (2006b) (accessed April 2007)
Ofcom Consumer Panel Consumers and the communications market: 2006 Ofcom (June 2006) URL:http://www.ofcomconsumerpanel.org.uk/publications/ Older_People_and_Comms_FINAL.pdf (2006a) (accessed April 2007)
Ofcom Consumer Panel Older People and Communications Technology. An attitudinal study into older people and their engagement with communications technology Ofcom (July 2006) URL: http://www.ofcomconsumerpanel.org.uk/ publications/Older_People_and_Comms_FINAL.pdf (2006b) (accessed April 2007)
Office of National Statistics (ONS) 'Internet Access. Households and Individuals' 23 (August 2006) URL: http://www.statistics.gov.uk/pdfdir/inta0806.pdf (accessed April 2007)
Oxford Internet Survey (OxIS) The internet in Britain. Oxford Internet Institute (May 2005) URL: www.oii.ox.ac.uk/research/oxis/oxis2005_report.pdf (accessed May 2006)
Riggs K.E. Granny@Work: Aging and new technology on the job in America New York: Routledge (2004)
Selwyn N., Gorard S., Furlong J., Madden L. 'Older Adults' Use of Information and Communications Technology in Everyday Life' Ageing and Society 23: 5 (2003) pp. 561-582
Selwyn N., Gorard S., Furlong, J. 'Whose Internet is it Anyway?' European Journal of Communication 20: 1 (2005) pp. 5-26
Slot M., Frissen V. 'Users in the 'golden' age of the information society', Observatorio (OBS*) Journal 3 (2007) pp. 201-224 URL: http://obs.obercom. pt/index. php/obs/article/viewFile/153/110 (accessed December 2007)
Sourbati M. 'On older people, internet access and electronic service delivery. A study of sheltered homes' eds. Mante-Meijer E., Haddon L., Loos E. The Social Dynamics of Information and Communication Technology. Aldershot, Hants: Ashgate (2008) pp. 95-104
Trocchia P.J., Janda S. 'A phenomenological investigation of Internet usage among older individuals' Journal of Consumer Marketing 17: 7 (2000) pp. 605-16
Tuomi I. 'Beyond user-centric models of product creation' eds. Haddon L., Mante E., Sapio B. Kommonen K-H., Fortunati L., Kant A. Everyday Innovators. Researching the Role of Users in Shaping ICTs Dordrect: Springer (2005)
Verhaegh S. 'From Simple Customer to Warm User: Who Cares about the Maintenance of Community Innovations?' Observatorio (OBS*) Journal 3 (2007) pp. 155-84 URL: http://obs.obercom.pt/index.php/obs/article/view/149/108 (accessed December 2007)

Theme III:
ICT use and sustainable development

Inge Røpke, Kirsten Gram-Hanssen and Jesper Ole Jensen
Households' ICT Use in an Energy Perspective

Introduction

The development of the information society has been and still is accompanied by enthusiasm and a strong sense of necessity, and the challenge for political and administrative institutions at all levels is to increase the pace of the development and remove all hindrances. The necessity springs from the drive for competitiveness and the emergence of new business opportunities in the so-called "experience economy". At the same time, other parts of the political and administrative system are concerned about environmental issues, not least, due to the prospects of global warming. Information and communication technologies (ICTs) offer both potential for energy savings and increasing demand for energy use, so there are good reasons to bring together these two agendas. In the early 1990s, the first studies on the positive environmental prospects of ICT emerged (Freeman 1992), and the first steps were taken towards regulating ICT energy use. Since then, the importance of ICT in relation to energy consumption has had some interest, but still the two agendas tend to develop in relative isolation, and there is still a long way to go before they are really brought together (Alakeson & Wilsdon 2003, 10).

This chapter is intended as a contribution to considering ICT in an energy perspective. ICTs have many other environmental impacts than those related to energy, but they are only included in so far as they influence the energy impacts. The point of departure is the integration of ICTs in households, and the energy impacts of changing household practices are discussed. Most studies of ICT and energy have concentrated on macro scenarios or the prospects seen from the production side, so households have not received much attention. In this context, the chapter has an explorative character, and it is based on a combination of literature studies, discussions with experts, and a visit to the "digital home" in Taastrup, Denmark. The data used in this chapter mainly refer to Denmark. The main interest is to provide a basis for further in-depth studies of households, and for more proactive political approaches dealing with the energy impacts of ICT. The intention is not, however, to quantify the complex relations between household ICT use and the related energy impacts, outline scenarios for future developments, or to assess whether ICT development in households is good or bad in an energy perspective. The integration of ICT in household practices is a fact; thus, it is less important whether the net energy impact is positive or negative than it is to find ways to avoid the negative impacts and encourage the positive. The purpose of the chapter thus fits into the discussion of humans as e-actors: On the one hand, the ICT-related environmental impacts influence the quality of human life, and on the other hand, the activities and behaviour of humans as e-actors co-produce these impacts. As e-actors, we influence whether the positive or negative impacts on energy consumption become dominant; therefore, it is important to discuss ICT-use in an energy perspective to find out what we can do, individually and collectively.

In the following, some of the previous studies on ICT and energy are briefly mentioned, and the consumption approach is related to these. Secondly, the integration of ICT in everyday practices and the dynamics behind the changes are outlined, inspired by a historical perspective. Thirdly, a figure illustrating the relationships between everyday practices and the related energy impacts is presented, followed by descriptions of energy impacts directly related to ICT in households, indirect impacts outside households, and derived impacts both within and outside households. The chapter concludes with some remarks on political implications and questions for further research.

Previous studies and the consumption perspective

Early studies on the emergence of the information society tended to emphasize the positive potentials related to ICTs, such as the possibilities for increased production efficiency in most sectors (Freeman 1992); this is still central to more recent studies, although rebound effects come much more to the fore (Berkhout & Hertin 2001; Hilty et al. 2005; Jørgensen et al. 2006). Furthermore, it is emphasized that the Internet opens opportunities for information sharing in business and academia with regard to environmental issues (Richards et al. 2001, see also a European series of conferences under the heading Informatics for Environmental Protection), and corresponding positive effects are identified in relation to consumers and environmental NGOs (Reisch 2001).

Gradually, the enthusiasm was supplemented with more discussion on the problematic environmental impacts of ICT. Before the entry of ICTs, offices were usually considered less important when energy requirements were calculated, but since the late 1980s, offices were seen as energy consuming places. Both for economic reasons and in consideration of the environment, more attention turned towards energy savings (e.g. in 1992, the U.S. EPA introduced the Energy Star labelling for office equipment). In the late 1990s and early 2000s, a heated discussion took place in the U.S. in the wake of some provocative statements concerning the high electricity consumption of ICT equipment, titled *Dig more coal – the PCs are coming* (Huber & Mills 1999). The statements were repudiated by many other researchers, as can be seen from the summary of the debate at http://enduse.lbl. gov/projects infotech.html, where links can be found to the many contributions; short summaries can be found in Laitner (2003) and Cole (2003).

Other studies go beyond electricity and include both direct and indirect environmental effects of ICT use, including various categories of rebound effects, for instance Erdmann et al. (2004), Hilty et al. (2005) and Plepys (2002). In Berkhout and Hertin's study for the OECD on the environmental impacts of ICT (Berkhout & Hertin 2001, summarized in Berkhout & Hertin 2004), they distinguish between direct effects, indirect effects, and structural and behavioural effects of ICT. Direct effects stem from the production, use and disposal of hardware; indirect effects concern efficiency improvements in production processes and in design and operation of products and services; whereas structural and behavioural effects are a mixture of rebound effects and effects related to increased consumer information. Berkhout and Hertin argue that the direct effects are mostly negative, whereas the indirect efficiency effects are largely positive, and the structural effects (including rebound effects) are highly contested. Related categorizations are used in other studies, e.g. in the foresight study by Jørgensen et al. (2006) and in Hilty et al. (2005).

In most macro studies on ICT and environment, consumers play a very minor role. This role is mostly related to the indirect, structural level where the positive potential related to behavioural change is emphasized. In particular, teleshopping and teleworking are pointed out as having a potential for energy savings related to transport (just as business travel is expected to decrease because of videoconferencing). However, in studies focusing on electricity, consumers are becoming more visible (Aebischer & Huser 2000; Aebischer & Varone 2001; Cremer et al. 2003; Roth et al. 2006), and small sections on ICT emerge in reports on consumption and environment (European Environment Agency 2005).

Consumers have been most visible in relation to the discussion of standby electricity use, beginning in the early 1990s (Sandberg 1993). Since then, the energy efficiency conferences ACEEE (www.aceee.org), ECEEE (www.eceee.org) and EEDAL (http://re.jrc.ec.europa.eu/ energyefficiency/events/eedal2006.htm) have had workshop sessions on standby con-sumption. Papers have focused on measurements of the size of ICT-related energy consumption in households (Harrington et al. 2006; Roth 2006) and have discussed how to agree on standards, which can be useful for energy labelling and other types of product regulation (Jones 2006; Murakoshi et al. 2005). However, standby consumption in households has increased steadily, and internationally, it is estimated to represent 4-11% of the total electricity consumption (Meier 2005). Standby consumption can be reduced by encouraging producers to develop appliances using less energy, or by getting users to turn off the appliances instead of leaving them on standby. Internationally, the former has received by far the most attention, and this would also be the most efficient if it were successful. In 2005, however, only Japan had compulsory programmes concerning standby, whereas both Europe and USA worked with voluntary agreements (Meier 2005). Although progress is seen, regulation and standardization is difficult because of the rapid technological development (IEA 2001).

Nationally, there have also been campaigns targeting consumer behaviour. A Danish study (Gram-Hanssen & Gudbjerg 2006) indicates that some households quite easily change routines and are able to eliminate the majority of their standby consumption, while others find it more difficult as they have expectations of being online all the time and their appliances are connected to each other.

In this chapter, the intention is to go beyond the relatively narrow roles assigned to consumers in studies on ICT and energy. There is a need for paying more attention to consumers, first of all because ICT is increasingly integrated in everyday life. Furthermore, a consumption perspective can highlight aspects that complement the aspects brought forth when focusing mainly on production, thus also opening up new opportunities for managing the energy impacts. In general, when a production perspective is the point of departure in environmental studies, technological changes tend to be perceived in terms of solutions, because technology can contribute to efficiency improvements. In spite of the increasing awareness of rebound effects, the perspective tends to be mostly optimistic. This differs from the consumption perspective, where new technologies are only in exceptional cases introduced to improve, for instance, the energy efficiency of household activities. New technologies serve as drivers behind consumption growth and will as such contribute to increasing environmental impacts (Røpke 2001; Røpke 2003). From this perspective, efficiency improvements become a modification of the main effect. The consumption perspective thus tends to bring the more problematic aspects of technological change more directly into focus – since they are not relegated to the position of rebound effects.

The organization of the paper is inspired by the studies mentioned above and considers different levels of effects (Berkhout & Hertin 2004; Jørgensen et al. 2006). As the perspective of this chapter is more narrow than those studies, the same categories are not directly applicable, but a related way of thinking is reflected in a three level categorization of the energy impacts related to ICT use in households. The impacts are thus grouped as follows:

– *Direct energy consumption* (mostly electricity) related to the use of ICT equipment in household practices, both in the dwelling and on the move.
– *Indirect energy consumption* related to the provision of households' electricity consumption, the production and disposal of ICT equipment for household use, and the running of the infrastructure, such as sending masts and servers.

The term "indirect" is thus used here as it is usually used in the energy literature, rather than in the way used in ICT studies.
– *Derived energy impacts* relate to changes in the composition of consumption and in behavioural patterns influencing households' energy consumption as well as systemic energy consumption.

The two first categories of energy consumption tend to increase when the amount of equipment is increased, although this can be counteracted by increased efficiency of new equipment. In the third category, more positive impacts can be expected to dominate, such as those related to equipment installed to manage heating and lighting in the dwelling in an energy-saving way – however, the outcomes in this category will be highly contested. This category also covers the effects of teleshopping and teleworking for energy consumption of both households and the wider system. The term rebound effect is not used in this categorization, because the term is attached to the indirect effects of a change that is motivated by environmental concerns (rebound effects in consumption are discussed by Hertwich 2005). In relation to a few cases, it could be relevant here to talk about rebound effects – for instance, in the case of energy-saving heat regulation, which might save money that can be used for more energy-consuming purposes – but few of the ICT acquisitions are motivated by environmental concerns, so this is omitted here.

The integration of ICT in everyday life

As a basis for dealing with the energy impacts of household ICT use, this section focuses on the ongoing process in which ICTs gain access to everyday life. The process is seen in the perspective of the history of technology, as this indicates the sweeping character of the changes.

In some respects, the integration of the computer in everyday life can be compared to the integration of the small electromotor. When the electromotor was introduced, it became integrated in a wide range of domestic appliances and tools – vacuum cleaner, mixer, refrigerator, washing machine, dishwasher, air conditioning, drilling machine, and tooth brush. The electromotor could replace muscular strength and transmit energy for heating and cooling, and innovators searched for all conceivable possibilities for developing devices applying this new technology. The motor became part of the thorough transformation of household work, the near disappearance of domestic servants, and the increasing participation of women in the labour force (Cowan 1983; Olesen & Thorndahl 2004). The point is not that the electromotor was driving all these changes, but it became integrated in the ongoing social processes and was put to uses formed by the social dynamics. Thus, Cowan emphasizes how the technology could have been used in other ways with different social outcomes, such as collective solutions to household chores, if the social and cultural dynamics had been different. The computer has a general applicability comparable to the electromotor and can be integrated in practically all everyday activities. The computer replaces or enhances brain capacity – the ability to calculate, manage, communicate, and regulate – a quality that can be used everywhere. Presently, innovators are searching all conceivable possibilities for applying this new technology in appliances, tools, and devices that can be tempting for consumers and fit into their topical concerns and desires.

The computer is not only connected to the electricity net (directly or indirectly through batteries), like the electromotor, but can also be connected to networks of communication, including the Internet, the so-called motorway of information. The Internet introduces a new infrastructure that calls for comparisons with the introduction of electricity, tele-communication, broadcasting, and even the water supply and sewerage systems. When developing these large technological systems, many actors and interests are involved and contribute to the co-evolution of technologies and use patterns. When such a system is stabilized, it becomes an unacknowledged basis of everyday life – one more system that we are served by and serve on a daily basis (Otnes 1988). The Internet has not yet acquired this status of unacknowledged basis of everyday life, but the new possibilities for acquiring information and entertainment and for communication are increasingly being integrated in all conceivable activities, driven by both commercial and political-administrative interests and by users themselves.

Furthermore, the present co-evolution of technologies and everyday life is characterized by increasing mobility. This trend can be seen as a continuation of previous efforts to make all sorts of equipment available for activities on the move, such as the portable gramophone, the portable typewriter, the transistor radio and all sorts of equipment for the car and the camping trip. The mobile phone is probably the most successful innovation ever in this line of mobile appliances, and Levinson (2004, 13) argues that this follows from the basic human need to talk and walk. Since in large geographical areas the mobile phone is combined with wireless access to the Internet, then the mobile encyclopaedia, mobile library, and mobile entertainment centre are available as well. The development of wireless connections and better batteries permit more and more activities to be carried out on the move, gradually reducing the difference between what can be done at home and on the move.

These general observations are reflected in the ongoing integration of computer, Internet, and mobile phones in numerous everyday practices. The pervasiveness of these technologies can be illustrated with examples from the different spheres of everyday life. The use of computer and Internet is increasingly integrated in:

- *Work and education:* Telework, e-learning, ordinary school work, well-equipped home offices, video conferences.
- *Reproductive work:* Shopping, banking, public services, health monitoring, the intelligent home (regulation of heating, lighting, security systems), security, child care (entertainment, monitoring), cooking (find the recipe), do-it-yourself (exchange experiences, find information). Computer and Internet also add a new task to the list of reproductive activities, namely ICT maintenance, just as the car once added the task of car wash.
- *Leisure:* Social communication, entertainment, games, creativity, documentation, hobbies, gambling, sex.
- *Civil society:* Organizations, political activities.

Theories concerning the formation of practices in everyday life point out three constituent aspects of a social practice: The competences needed to carry out the practice, the material devices used for the activity, and the meaning attached to it (Shove & Pantzar 2005; Warde 2005). This theoretical framework has been used to discuss the formation and change of specific practices, but it can also be used to illustrate more general dynamics cutting across many practices. ICT is an example of generic technological change – a change of basic technologies influencing all sorts of applied technologies – which provides a supply of renewed material devices for many different practices. Simultaneously, these practices are influenced by changes in the other two constituent aspects, as technological change co-develops with changing discourses that offer new meanings to various practices, and with the development of training in the use of the new technologies. In Figure 1, the three constituent aspects are illustrated in the top part of the figure, surrounding everyday practices. For all three aspects, government regulation, subsidies, campaigns, and other activities play a decisive role alongside the governance enacted by the firms and organizations involved – for instance, in the provision of safety, standards, business models, and training, as well as in influencing the discourses through reports on the need for keeping up in the competitive race, the prospects for experience economy, and the potential for using ICT in various sectors.

In the formation of everyday practices, the ICT-related dynamics meet with other social dynamics related to dominant social concerns and trends of the time. Examples are the long-term trend towards individualization and personal independence, the discourse on busyness, stress and the balance between work and family life, and the preoccupation with body and health. In Figure 1, these cross-cutting trends are mentioned within the box of everyday practices. In relation to each specific practice, many other, more detailed concerns will be important.

Direct energy consumption

The most immediate energy impacts of the integration of ICT in everyday practices are visible in household electricity consumption. Still this impact is not large compared to other categories of energy consumption in households, but it is increasing. Denmark has been particularly successful with regard to decoupling household energy consumption from economic growth. From 1990 to 2005, household energy consumption increased only 4.4%, but electricity consumption for lighting and appliances increased 18% (Energistyrelsen 2006). Most electricity is used for white goods, but the importance of media technologies, including TV, video, computers and related equipment, is increasing. Presently, approximately 20% of electricity consumption is used for media equipment, and about half of this is used for standby (Gram-Hanssen 2005).

As illustrated in Figure 1, energy consumption related to the use of ICT depends on the quantity of ICT equipment, the energy efficiency of this equipment, and the patterns of use, that is, the number hours of use, the time on standby, and the intensity of use (the energy consumption of some appliances depends on the kind of use). In the following, some of the present trends influencing electricity consumption will be highlighted.

Presently, television and video weigh more heavily than computers, and in the near future, a particular burst of energy consumption can be expected in relation to the digitization of television and the diffusion of HDTV, (High Definition TeleVision). The increasing energy consumption is related to the need for set-top boxes that can be combined with existing TV sets or are integrated in new sets. In spite of increasing interest in keeping down energy consumption of TV sets, little interest has been directed towards set-top boxes, and many models are rather ineffective. Since the stock of TV sets is large – nearly one set per person (Energistyrelsen 2006) – and since many people will have to acquire digital capability if they want to watch television (except for a large group connected to cable TV who can carry on as usual), the impact can be expected to be considerable. Of course, digitization can be an opportunity to replace older energy-consuming models with newer and more energy-effective models (LCD (Liquid Crystal Display) flat screens are more efficient than the old CRT (Cathode Ray Tube) screens); however, replacements are often combined with increasing screen size, counterbalancing the efficiency improvements. The interest in so-called home cinema equipment has increased, including acquirement of plasma screens, which are particularly energy-consuming. TV sets prepared for receiving HDTV are also more energy-consuming, because of the higher resolution. Instead of following the trend towards increasing average efficiency exhibited by white goods, the average efficiency of TV sets has been relatively stable and even decreased a little (Energistyrelsen 2006). As mentioned, the number of TV sets is already very high, but the diffusion of flat screens might increase the number further, as these screens are easy to place everywhere, bringing TV into kitchen and bathroom and adding to the use of TV as a kind of "background" for other activities.

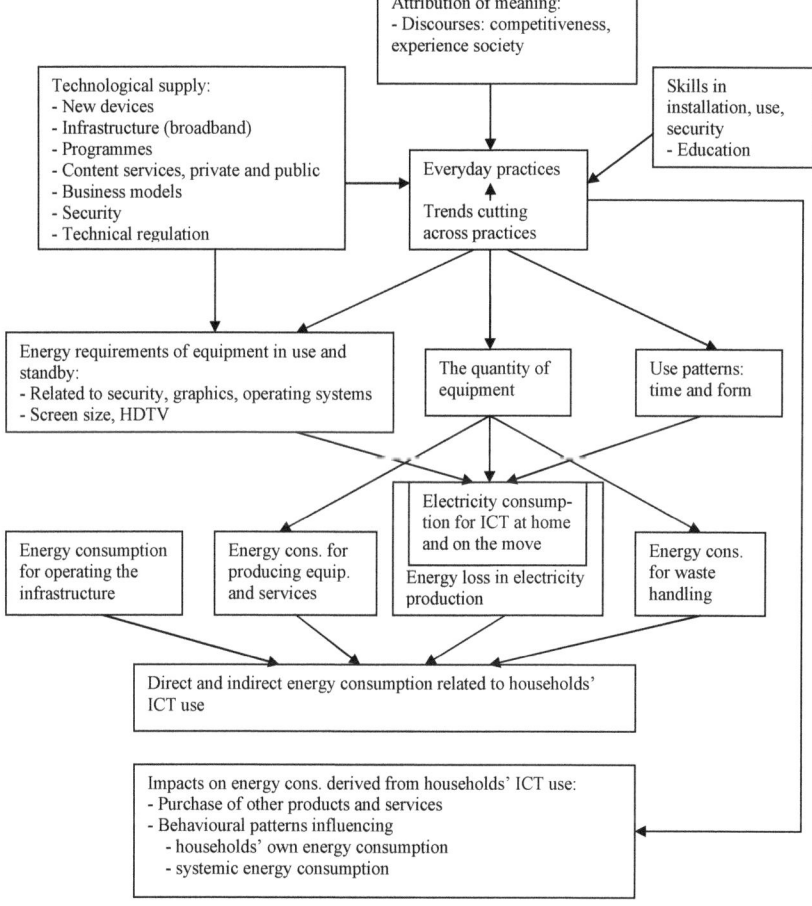

Figure 1: Relations between ICT-related changes of everyday practices and the ensuing impacts on energy consumption.

Digitization of television does not seem to be directly related to any profound changes in the practice of watching television. The quality of the picture improves, and it is possible to turn on subtitles in various languages. When digitization is combined with the use of media centres/hard disk recorders, the opportunities for flexibility are increased, as programmes can be shifted in time more easily than with the use of video and DVD. Visions regarding interactive television are discussed (Jensen & Toscan 1999), but it still remains to be seen whether practices change more profoundly.

While television is bound to a particular practice, computers and Internet are integrated in a wide variety of practices. The increasing energy consumption related to computer and Internet springs from the integration in an increasing number of practices and the ensuing increase in time use and amounts of equipment. When time use at the computer increases, household members increasingly demand their own computer so they do not have to wait for their turn. The demand for individual independence that is well-known from the acquisition of TV sets now makes itself felt for computers – that each person should have his or her computer seems obvious for younger generations. A less developed trend – which might become more important in the future – is the emergence of activity-specific or room-specific computers – for instance, specially equipped computers for use in the kitchen, the bathroom, or in the garage, where conditions may be tough.

Due to rapid technological change and ever more advanced applications, there is not only a demand for more computers, but also for ever more powerful computers and other ICT equipment. Demand thus increases for:

- higher quality, such as larger screens with better resolution
- more processing power, needed e.g. to run the latest versions of operating and security systems and the advanced graphics in games
- more data storage capacity, needed for the increasing amounts of photos, videos, sound files, mails
- larger bandwidth, needed for video-streaming and for upstream P2P (peer to peer) file-sharing of videos and music.

These changes constitute a strong force counterbalancing improvements in energy efficiency. Seen over a long period, various factors have influenced the energy efficiency of computers (based on Cole 2003). To increase the processing power of computers without increasing the size, heat reduction was necessary, and this stimulated efficiency improvements. With the introduction of laptop computers energy-saving was encouraged because of the desire to increase battery life, and the advances for laptops were later brought into desktop computers; this was the case, for instance, for built-in power management, which was brought from laptops to desktop computers in the early 1990s. The U.S. conservation programme, Energy Star, strongly encouraged further improvements, so from the mid-1990s, standby con-sumption decreased drastically, and impressive savings were achieved in business offices in the U.S. However, the power levels in operation did not change much, because the efficiency improvements were co-developed with more powerful microprocessors, more memory, and more disk storage. The monitor part of the computer became more energy-intensive in the 1990s, because of the almost universal shift to colour screens and larger screens with higher resolution. However, over a more extended period of time, the shift from CRTs to LCDs saves energy.

Since modern computers are very diverse due to consumer-specified features, the power requirements vary so much that it can be difficult to assess the general trend (Cole 2003, 138). Danish data indicates that the average new desktop computer does not require less energy in operation than computers a few generations older (T. Fjordbak Larsen, personal communication). However, an increasing number of new computers are laptops, and they are more energy-effective than desktop computers. In 2006, for the first time, the number of laptops sold in Denmark exceeded the number of desktop computers. This can be an energy-saving trend, if the laptops replace the desktop computers, but it is difficult to assess to which extent the laptops are additions rather than replacements. Desktop computers are still cheaper in terms of processing power per dollar, so a person interested in playing games or carrying out other demanding graphical activities will often prefer a desktop. Furthermore, it is easier to extend a desktop computer with supplementary graphics cards or other peripherals. Power management functions offer good opportunities for energy savings, but they have to be activated. This is not always done, either because of lack of knowledge or because of technical difficulties related, for instance, to network connections and coupling to other equipment.

The question of complementarity versus substitution in the case of laptops and desktops can be raised in a more general context. In many cases, ICT equipment incorporates a variety of functions and can, in principle, replace other, more specialized appliances. An example is the camera phone, which can render the camera superfluous. However, the camera in the mobile phone cannot provide the same quality and capacity as the dedicated camera; therefore, the camera phone may become part of a diversification process rather than part of a rationalization of the number of appliances. Another example is the combined printer-scanner-copy machine, which can reduce the number of appliances attached to the computer. However, it is expensive to run a scanner because of the need for colour cartridges, so it can be cheaper to invest in a supplementary laser printer for printing texts.

The trend towards diversification of equipment seems to be strong, as reflected in the wide variety of available devices advertised in magazines. Not the least in regard to mobile devices, the supply is widening as more mobile functions become available. Rapid technological change implies that multiple generations of equipment co-exist (such as tape recorders – CD players – MP3 players, and video – DVD – hard disk recorders). Consumers thus tend to have an increasing number of small and/or supplementary devices, often related in various ways to the core products – the computer and the TV set. The direct energy consumption of each of these devices in the use phase is usually not large (except for standby consumption that can be high for some products), but the sum of the small contributions may be significant. Adding to this is the phenomenon that less attention is focused on the energy consumption of the peripheral devices than on the energy-efficiency of the computer and the TV set. One reason may be the quick renewal rate, which does not allow producers to pay much attention to optimizing energy-efficiency; and another reason may be the lack of regulatory attention, partly due to the difficulties related to regulating products that are changing so quickly.

A particular trend adding to ICT-related energy consumption emerges from the phenomenon of multi-tasking. Especially young people are able to manage computer, television, music centre, mobile phone, and the electric guitar – all at the same time. A Danish study thus demonstrates the high electricity consumption by teenagers (Gram-Hanssen et al. 2004). Older generations may be less able to multi-task, but they are able to install systems that use electricity without anybody being present, such as surveillance cameras and other security systems. One of the visions related to the "intelligent home" is the possibility of communicating with the security systems at a distance (for instance, opening the door for the postman bringing a parcel or the plumber coming to repair an installation in the house).

The "intelligent home" is based on a network infrastructure in the house and a central server (sometimes more than one) with Internet connection. Running the central infrastructure can be very energy-demanding, as an early study indicates (Huser & Aebischer 2002). Presently, few people have realized this idea, but the increasing number of servers, routers, wireless networks etc. in homes illustrate that a pro-active approach would be highly relevant to avoid large increases in energy consumption. As part of the trend towards so-called pervasive computing, electronics is increasingly added to manage such electric equipment as white goods, cookers, and cooker hoods, and RFID tags are about to be integrated in many other goods. This will add to the problems with electronic waste, but it is difficult to assess the energy impacts. Finally, it is worth mentioning that the search for new ways of using ICT has resulted in more functions using energy in the use phase – functions which were previously carried out without energy consumption in the use phase. Examples are the electronic diary and shopping list, maps for navigation, photo frames showing digital pictures, and surveillance.

Summing up, the increasing direct energy consumption related to ICT equipment has many sources. The effect of increasing quantities of equipment and of more time spent on activities using ICT is difficult to counterbalance with efficiency improvements, especially because the equipment in itself becomes more powerful, and because in some cases the attention on energy-efficiency is limited.

Indirect energy consumption

Relatively few data are available for elucidating the indirect energy consumption related to household use of ICT, but it is possible to give a broad outline.

The first component of the indirect energy consumption relates to the provision of the electricity used for operating the household equipment. This component differs between countries in accordance with the efficiency achieved in electricity production. Due to a high degree of combined power and heat supply, this efficiency is relatively high in Denmark. This component of the indirect energy consumption is thus only about the same size as the direct electricity consumption.

The second component relates to the energy used for the production of ICT equipment. For desktop computers used at home, Kuehr, Velasquez and Williams (2003, 4) estimate that more energy is needed to produce the machine than to power it during the use phase – contrasting sharply with other durable goods like refrigerators, where relatively much more energy is needed in the use phase. Later estimates (e.g. Jönbrink & Zackrisson 2007) suggest that energy consumption in the use phase for computers is about two to three times the energy needed for manufacturing (the different results are probably related to both increased use time per computer and increased production efficiency), but this is still far from the proportions that are characteristic for other durable goods. For mobile phones, the economic life is very short (the average service life for mobile phones in Europe is estimated to be one year), and this makes the relative importance of the energy consumption in the production phase even greater (Jönbrink & Zackrisson 2007; Legarth et al. 2002). In general, the rapid rate of renewal for ICT equipment implies that energy use for production is a very important category.

The third component relates to waste handling. The high-tech parts of computers and other electronic equipment are difficult to recycle, while the bulk materials like steel and aluminium are easier to handle (Klatt 2003). Recycling processes require energy, but as they provide materials that can substitute virgin materials requiring more energy to extract, the net result is usually positive. Overall, the energy aspect of waste handling is negligible, whereas the problems with toxins and working environment are huge (Hilty et al. 2006; Jönbrink & Zackrisson 2007).

Finally, the fourth component relates to the operation of the ICT infrastructure. Few studies are available, but they indicate that the issue is important (e.g. Hille et al. 2007). A recent report from IDC illustrates the enormous growth of digital information and the need for storage capacity, not only at user level but also for service providers such as Google (Gantz et al. 2007). Some service providers run large parks of servers, so services that appear to be virtual – immaterial – from a user perspective can be based on quite extensive material investments. The virtual world of "Second Life" thus has a material basis in the servers of Linden Lab. Running the base stations in the UMTS-network for mobile phones also requires much electricity (Emmenegger et al. 2006), and in general, the increasing number of mobile devices with Internet access will add to the energy consumption of the infrastructure.

Derived energy impacts

While both direct and indirect energy consumption tend to increase when the number of appliances and the time spent using them are increased, the derived energy impacts are more likely to be positive. Most obviously, ICT can be used directly for energy savings. Thus, ICT can be used for managing heating and lighting in the dwelling (lowering of the temperature at night, sensors turning off the light when nobody is in the room), and ICT can also make it easier for households to monitor their energy consumption and thus encourage savings. The Danish Electricity Saving Trust estimates a potential for electricity savings from 10 to 30% in households by using intelligent building systems to control the electric equipment. For instance, in summer cottages, heated by electricity and only used occasionally, using such systems has a large potential for reducing consumption; however, today, existing systems are too expensive due to a lack of competition, and also the standards are closed, meaning that they cannot communicate with the electronic equipment of existing systems (Ingeniøren newsletter 21.04.2006).

Also, the Internet can be used for making available relevant information on energy savings, as can be seen, for instance, at the homepage of The Danish Electricity Saving Trust http://www.elsparefonden.org/ and the recently initiated public campaign to encourage people to help save one ton of CO_2. While these impacts are positive in an energy perspective, it should not be overlooked that the Internet, in an analogous way, can encourage energy-intensive consumption – for instance, by making available new options for booking cheap flights and finding exotic travel destinations (Reisch 2001).

While it is relatively simple to see that ICT can be used for energy-saving purposes, it is far more complex to consider the effect on the various practices into which the use of ICT becomes integrated. In some cases, the use of ICT is just an "add on", where more equipment is added to well-known activities that are not much changed. An example can be the use of a "running computer" for monitoring one's training efforts; such an addition does not change the practice of running in ways that has an impact on energy consumption. The same goes for quality improvements, such as larger screens, HDTV, and better graphics in game consoles.

In other cases, practices are changed more profoundly by the integration of ICT. Environmental improvements, including energy savings, have been expected from such changes, especially in relation to teleshopping, teleworking, and the replacement of material products such as newspapers and CDs by Internet-based services. Jørgensen et al. (2006) summarize a number of studies on telework and transport. Whereas some of the early studies were very optimistic with regard to the potential for energy savings, more recent studies emphasize that a substantial part of the transport savings are counterbalanced by increased transport for other purposes and increased transport by other family members. In general, the results regarding structural impacts are highly sensitive to system boundaries, and are dependent on behavioural assumptions. Studies are often inconclusive, because it is difficult to know, for instance, whether people will continue to shop in stores, even though they buy some things via the Internet, and whether they will move further away from their workplace to take advantage of lower property prices when they work at home part of the week.

Supplementary to the discussion on derived impacts in relation to individual practices, it is possible to raise the issue from a more general perspective: If consumers tie their money and their time to the acquirement and use of ICT, then less money and time are available for other purposes – and the question is, whether these other purposes are more or less energy-intensive per monetary unit and/or per unit of time. It may seem surprising that the question is raised in terms of both money and time, as one of these two perspectives could appear to be sufficient, particularly if an economic maximization model is applied (Linder 1970). However, in practice, both time and money constitute limitations on consumption, and institutional constraints imply that the two factors cannot be reduced to the one or the other. To start with the monetary perspective, the acquirement of ICT equipment and services takes up an increasing share of consumers' income. In general, competition on hardware keeps prices down and energy intensities high. In some cases, service providers have succeeded in keeping high prices due to monopolistic or oligopolistic market conditions, which implies relatively low energy intensity per monetary unit (examples are charges for telephoning, Internet access, and packages of television programmes). However, public regulation is quite active with regard to breaking the monopolistic tendencies, not only because of the general wish to promote competition, but also because of the particular interest in developing the information society. A recent project thus demonstrates that the energy intensity of ICT-based leisure activities is relatively high (Hille et al. 2007, 166-67).

From the perspective of time, it is worth considering whether the integration of ICT tends to take up time that could have been used for other purposes, or whether, on the contrary, time is freed for other purposes. If, for instance, reproductive activities, such as paying the bills, shopping, and contacting the taxing authorities, can be carried out in a shorter time by using the Internet, then time is freed for either working more (and earning more money) or having more leisure time (where money can be spent). Also, activities usually considered to be leisure, such as planning holiday travels, can be accomplished more effectively, thus freeing time. Multi-tasking and accomplishing tasks on the move can add to the productivity increase. On the other hand, the Internet is known to be time-consuming. One can become absorbed in surfing and sidetracks, thus reducing the time available for other activities and related consumption.

It is difficult to conclude anything regarding the consequences of the changing composition of time use and consumption in the wake of ICT integration in various practices. But it can be argued with more certainty that the supply of ever-changing ICT and the integration of ICT in a wide variety of products and practices serve as part of the motor driving consumption growth. It is difficult to imagine the achievement of any kind of satiety in this dynamic setting.

Concluding remarks

As emphasized in the introduction, the intention of this chapter is not to assess whether the integration of ICT in household practices is good or bad in an energy perspective. In any case, the issue is so complex that even very elaborate studies would hardly be able to lead to any decisive conclusions. It is more important to find ways to avoid the negative energy impacts of ICT development, and to encourage the positive impacts. The issues dealt with in this chapter suggest various ways in which the net result can be improved:

– The indirect energy consumption, especially that related to the production of ICT equipment, carries great weight. Therefore, "The simplest and most effective way to reduce environmental burden may be to ensure that users need fewer new PCs in the first place", as Kuehr, Velasquez and Williams (2003, 14) argue. In chapters 8, 10 and 13 in the anthology edited by Kuehr and Williams

(2003) it is discussed how the lifespan of computers can be extended through more effective used-computer markets, smooth transfer of software licenses to secondary users, and easier ways to upgrade computers. The issue of lifespan extension is highly relevant, also for other ICT equipment and not least for mobile phones.
- Power management functions are important for electricity consumption in the use phase, and it is still highly relevant to focus on the reduction of standby consumption, both by technical means and through changed patterns of behaviour.
- Digitization of television should be complemented with intense campaigns for the choice of energy-efficient replacements.
- The focus on the energy use of the core products, the computer and television, should be broadened to also include the wider range of ICT equipment.
- Economic considerations have not been the focus of this chapter, but it should be mentioned that the net energy impact of ICT use is influenced by the price of energy. For instance, there is a potential in using ICT for energy savings, and the realization of this potential depends, at least partly, on energy prices. The price of energy for transport is also decisive with regard to the derived impacts – for instance, whether people decide to move further away from their workplace when they have the opportunity to telework part of the week. In short, price incentives, as well as other incentives not directly related to the technology, influence the net energy impact of ICT use.

The above suggestions relate to direct and indirect energy consumption, whereas it is much more difficult to consider how positive energy impacts can be encouraged and negative impacts prevented when focus is turned to the derived impacts. To improve the basis for elaborating suggestions for a pro-active approach to ICT-related energy consumption, further in-depth studies of household ICT use could be useful. Such studies could deal with questions such as:

- In which practices are ICT becoming integrated? For which household members?
- In which cases does the ICT integration serve as an add-on to previous ways of carrying out the activities, and in which cases do the activities change more profoundly?
- Does the use of ICT save time, for instance, in relation to shopping, banking transactions, and enquiries to public authorities?
- Does the use of ICT save transport in relation to the same activities?
- What does social communication via ICT imply for people's wish to meet socially?
- Is ICT applied for the purpose of saving energy?

- How often are various appliances replaced?
- Do several generations of appliances co-exist?
- Which functions are served by diversified equipment?
- Which functions are merged in rationalized equipment?
- What do households do with equipment they want to discard?

Hopefully, such studies on households' ICT use in an energy perspective can encourage the increased integration of the agendas related to the information society and to climate change, respectively.

References

Aebischer B., Huser A. Networking in Private Households. Impacts on Electricity Consumption, Swiss Federal Office of Energy (2000)

Aebischer B., Varone F. 'The Internet: the Most Important Driver for Future Electricity Demand in Households'Proceedings of ECEEE Summer Study (2001) pp. 394-403

Alakeson V., Wilsdon J. 'Digital Sustainability in Europe' Journal of Industrial Ecology 6 (2003) pp. 10-12

Berkhout F., Hertin J. Impacts of Information and Communication Technologies on Environmental Sustainability: Speculations and Evidence. A report to the OECD, Science Policy Research Unit, Brighton, UK: University of Sussex (2001)

Berkhout F., Hertin J.'De-materialising and Re-materialising: Digital Technologies and the Environment' Futures 36 (2004) pp. 903-920

Cole D. 'Energy Consumption and Personal Computers' eds. Kuehr R., Williams E. Computers and the Environment. Understanding and Managing their Impacts Dordrecht: Kluwer Academic Publishers and United Nations University (2003)

Cowan R.S. More Work for Mother: The Ironies of Household Technology from the Open Hearth to the Microwave New York: Basic Books (1983)

Cremer C., Eichhammer W., Friedewald M., Georgieff P., Rieth-Hoerst S., Barbara Schlomann B., Zoche P. Energy Consumption of Information and Communication Technology (ICT) in Germany Up to 2010. Summary of the Final Report to the German Federal Ministry of Economics and Labour, Frauenhofer ISI and CEPE Zurich: Swiss Federal Institutes of Technology (2003)

Emmenegger M. F., Frischknecht R., Stutz S., Guggisberg M., Witschi R., Otto T. 'Life Cycle Assessment of the Mobile Communication System UMTS. Towards

Eco-efficient Systems' The International Journal of Life Cycle Assessment 11 (2006) pp. 265-276

Energistyrelsen Energistatistik 2005 København: Energistyrelsen (2006)

Erdmann L., Hilty L., Goodman J., Arnfalk P. The Future Impact of ICTs on Environmental Sustainability Brussels: European Commission. Joint Research Centre IPTS (2004)

European Environment Agency Household Consumption and the Environment Copenhagen: European Environment Agency (2005)

Freeman C. The Economics of Hope: Essays on Technical Change, Economic Growth and the Environment London: Pinter Publishers (1992)

Gantz J. F., Chute C., Manfrediz A., Minton S., Reinsel D., Schlichting W., Toncheva A. The Expanding Digital Universe: A Forecast of Worldwide Information Growth through 2010. An IDC White Paper – sponsored by EMC, IDC (2007)

Gram-Hanssen K. 'Husholdningers elforbrug – hvem bruger hvor meget, til hvad og hvorfor?' Statens Byggeforskningsinstitut, SBi 2005: 12 (2005)

Gram-Hanssen K., Gudbjerg E. Reduktion af standbyforbrug i husholdninger – hvad virker? Viby: Lokal Energi (2006)

Gram-Hanssen K., Kofod C., Nærvig Petersen K. 'Different Everyday Lives Different Patterns of Electricity Use' Proceedings of ACEEE Summer Study on Energy Efficiency in Buildings (2004)

Harrington L., Jones K., Harrison B. 'Trends in Television Energy Use: Where It Is and Where It's Going: En Route to Zero Energy Buildings' Proceedings of ACEEE Summer Study on Energy Efficiency in Buildings (2006)

Hertwich E. G. 'Consumption and the Rebound Effect. An Industrial Ecology Perspective' Journal of Industrial Ecology 9 (2005) pp. 85-98

Hille J., Aall C., Klepp I. G. Miljøbelastninger fra norsk fritidsforbruk – en kartlegging Norge: Vestlandsforsking & SIFO (2007)

Hilty L. M., Behrendt S., Binswanger M., Bruinink A., Erdmann L., Fröhlich J., Andreas Köhler A., Kuster N., Som C., Würtenberger F. The Precautionary Principle in the Information Society. Effects of Pervasive Computing on Health and Environment Berne: TA-SWISS, Center for Technology Assessment (2005)

Hilty L. M., Köhler A., Von Schéele F., Zah R., Ruddy T. 'Rebound Effects of Progress in Information Technology' Poiesis Prax 4 (2006) pp. 19-38

Huber P. W., Mills M. P. 'Dig More Coal – The PCs Are Coming' Forbes no. 31 May (1999)

Huser A., Aebischer B. Energieanalyse FutureLife-Haus, EnergieSchweiz (2002)

IEA Things That Go Blip in the Night. Paris: International Energy Agency (2001)

Jensen J. F., Toscan C. eds. Interactive Television. TV of the Future or the Future of TV? Aalborg Aalborg University Press (1999)

Jönbrink A. K., Zackrisson M. Lot 3. Personal Computers (Desktops and Laptops) and Computer Monitors Second draft final report (Task 1-7) European Commission DG TREN (2007)

Jones K. 'Australian Mandatory Standards for Consumer Electronic Equipment' Proceedings of the International Conference on Energy Efficiency in Domestic Appliances and Lighting (2006)

Jørgensen M. S., Andersen M. M., Hansen A., Wenzel H., Pedersen T. T., Jørgensen U., Falch M., Rasmussen B., Olsen S. I., Willum O. Green Technology Foresight about Environmentally Friendly Products and Materials – The Challenges from Nanotechnology, Biotechnology and ICT Danish Ministry of the Environment, EPA, 34 (2006)

Klatt S. 'Recycling Personal Computers' eds. Kuehr R., Williams E. Computers and the Environment: Understanding and Managing their Impacts Dordrecht: Kluwer Academic Publishers and United Nations University (2003)

Kuehr R., Williams E. eds. Computers and the Environment: Understanding and Managing their Impacts", Series : Eco-Efficiency in Industry and Science Dordrecht: Kluwer Academic Publishers and United Nations University (2003)

Kuehr R., Velasquez G. T., Williams E. 'Computers and the Environment – An Introduction to Understanding and Managing their Impacts' eds. Kuehr R., Williams E. Computers and the Environment: Understanding and Managing their Impacts Dordrecht: Kluwer Academic Publishers and United Nations University (2003)

Laitner J. A. S. 'Information Technology and U.S. Energy Consumption. Energy Hog, Productivity Tool, or Both?' Journal of Industrial Ecology 6 (2003) pp. 13-24

Legarth J. B., Willum O., Gregersen J. C. Miljøkonsekvenser af levetidsforlængelse af elektronikprodukter, Miljøstyrelsen, København, Arbejdsrapport fra Miljøstyrelsen nr. 18 (2002)

Levinson P. Cellphone. The Story of the World's Most Mobile Medium and How It Has Transformed Everything! New York: Palgrave Macmillan (2004)

Linder S. B. The Harried Leisure Class New York: Columbia University Press (1970)

Meier A. 'Standby: Where Are We Now?' Proceedings of ECEEE 2005 Summer Study (2005)

Murakoshi, C. et al. 'New Challenges of Japanese Energy Efficiency Program by Top Runner Approach' Proceedings of ECEEE Summer Study (2005)

Olesen B., Thorndahl J. Da Danske Hjem Blev Elektriske 1900-2000 Århus: Kvindemuseets Forlag (2004)

Otnes P. 'Housing Consumption: Collective Systems Service' ed. Otnes P. The Sociology of Consumption: An Anthology Oslo: Solum Forlag A.S. (1988)

Plepys A. 'The Grey Side of ICT' Environmental Impact Assessment Review 22 (2002) pp. 509-523

Reisch L. A. 'The Internet and Sustainable Consumption: Perspectives on a Janus Face' Journal of Consumer Policy 24 (2001) pp. 251-286

Richards D. J., Allenby B. R., Compton, W. D. eds. Information Systems and the Environment Washington, D.C.: National Academy Press (2001)

Røpke I. New Technology in Everyday Life – Social Processes and Environmental Impact', Ecological Economics 38 (2001) pp. 403-422

Røpke I. 'Consumption Dynamics and Technological Change – Exemplified by the Mobile Phone and Related Technologies' Ecological Economics 45 (2003) pp. 171-188

Roth K. 'Residential IT Energy Consumption in the U.S.' Proceedings of EEDAL (2006)

Roth K. W., Ponoum R., Goldstein, F. U.S. Residential Information Technology Energy Consumption in 2005 and 2010, TIAX LLC for U.S. Department of Energy, Cambridge, MA, D0295 (2006)

Sandberg E. 'Electronic Home Equipment – Leaking Electricity' Proceedings of ECEEE Summer Study (1993)

Shove E., Pantzar M. 'Consumers, Producers and Practices. Understanding the Invention and Reinvention of Nordic Walking' Journal of Consumer Culture 5 (2005) pp. 43-64

Warde A. 'Consumption and Theories of Practice' Journal of Consumer Culture 5 (2005) pp. 131-153

Kerstin Wüstner

Attitudes towards mobile phone communication technology[1]

Introduction

Mobile phone communication is of great economic importance in Germany and the vast majority of people possess and use mobile phones. Although mobile phones are part of everyday life, a rising number of people share critical attitudes and express a fear of what they perceive to be the possible harmful effects, mainly of masts. Within this discussion about these possible effects attitudes are often polarized. On the one hand, people are convinced that the limits of the various measurements and values which have been set are safe, whilst on the other hand, some people are sure about the effects of electromagnetic fields (EMF) damaging their health In this chapter I explore how mobile phone communication is quite differently socially represented in both groups of opinion. This chapter will look more closely at attitudes towards this technology which is so established in everyday life. Which concerns do people express? Are there gender differences? How is the impact of people's values? The chapter focuses mainly on the results of the underlying empirical study.

Mobile phone technology in Germany

Mobile phone technology has greatly influenced everyday life, bringing with it a lot of comfort. About three quarters of all German people possess a mobile phone and there is no longer hardly any place in Germany, where there is no mobile phone reception (BfS 2003).

Mobile phone technology is of great economic importance; the former government had sold UMTS-licences for about 51 billions Euro. Thus, companies and politics are interested in the establishment of this technology. Many people share a positive evaluation of mobile phone communication, yet there is also a noticeable number, who are concerned about possible negative effects of living close to masts or of using mobile phones. To prevent people from any harm, Germany has enacted a law -Article 26 BImSchV[2] – that refers to recommendations by the IC-

---

1 I would like to thank the referees for their most valuable comments.
2 BImSchV: Bundesimmissionsschutzverordnung.

NIRP (International Commission on Non-Ionizing Radiation Protection). Despite this the limit values set in Germany are higher than in some other countries, such as Italy, Switzerland, Poland or China (Wiedemann et al. 2001).

Attitudes towards mobile phone technology in Germany

Attitudes can be derived from publications and the public discourse on this technology, and in turn they are influenced by them. Publications on mobile phone technology are quite polarised (Ruddat et al. 2005). On the one hand, companies and politicians in particular state that there are no proven negative effects at all and that the limits set are sufficient. On the other hand, environmental organisations, citizen's groups and some physicians warn of negative effects of the exposition to EMF.

There are also studies that do not find any proof for negative health effects (e.g. Takebayashi et al. 2006) as well as studies that hint that EMF could lead to health problems (e.g. the European Reflex project, or Oktay & Dasdag 2006). In general, studies mostly analyse either physiological effects of EMF or they try to figure out the percentage of people who are labelled to be "hypersensitive" because they "pretend" to be affected negatively by mobile phone communication technology (Kheifets et al. 2005, Schütz et al. 2005). Overall, the assessment also results from risk perception on the individual or on a societal level.

An increased demand for mobile phone communication has lead to the rising number of base stations (Siegrist et al. 2005). Yet, Siegrist and Cousin state that there are noticeable differences in the risk perception of mobile phones on the one hand and base stations on the other hand, while the latter arouses a lot of suspicion and fears. The authors also point to differences in the knowledge between experts and laypeople. It could be argued that high risk perception of laypeople (in contrast to experts) could be due to missing knowledge. Yet, in this study Siegrist & Cousin, demonstrate a higher level of knowledge among those who hold a critical view of masts. Nevertheless, knowledge "gaps" could be detected with respect to some topics on which people were less well informed, e.g. interaction patterns between cell phones and base stations, regulations and radiation in general. The study underlines how complex the relationship between knowledge and anxieties could be. Besides knowledge, another quite important factor is trust. Siegrist and others (2003) show that trust and confidence greatly influence whether people accept base stations in their neighbourhood. Generally, risk perception depends on associations aroused by a topic (and vice versa, Siegrist et al. 2005). It can be formed by time and experience (Lima 2004). Some studies describe how experiences with risks can lead to normalization, especially in the case of voluntary risks (Twigger-Ross & Berakwell 1999) and less-visible consequences (Barnett

& Breakwell 2001). Yet, the latter could also provide space for speculation and interpretation. Further, the frequency of construction of technical systems can influence risk perception, too. Siegrist and others (2005) suppose the relatively low risk perception of high-voltage transmission lines in Switzerland and the high risk perception of masts is due to the different intensity of visible construction activities.

In the case of Germany, there is a special effect to be noted. In the past, several cases have become public where masts had been hidden in churches or by other means (www.umweltinstitut.org). This can arouse noticeable suspicion and mistrust.

Which of these attitudes can be found among the German population? In general, about 30% are (very) concerned about mobile phone communication technology, and 28% are (very) concerned about mobile phones (wik 2005, Infas 2004, I+G Gesundheitsforschung 2002). How people develop attitudes towards mobile phone communication technology is a question of their *subjective evaluation* process. Studies show that several factors could influence this process (Siegrist et al. 2005, wik 2005, Infas 2004, I+G Gesundheitsforschung 2001), e.g.

- Importance of mobile phone communication in every day's life,
- Knowledge on mobile phone technology,
- Belief that a transmitter station is close to home,
- Sources of information,
- Trust and confidence,
- Concerns about other risk factors,
- Participation in citizen's groups,
- Suffering from particular health problems,
- Socioeconomic status.

Taking these results into consideration, our study aims to gather a deeper understanding of the construction of attitudes towards mobile phone communication technology. It includes most of the listed facets found in other studies to be relevant and it is extended for values. This aspect is sometimes analysed with reference to general risk perception (e.g. BMU 2004), yet no study is known in which the importance of values for attitudes towards mobile phone communication technology was analysed. Further, we will have a closer look at gender differences. In several studies on attitudes towards technology and risk perception gender differences are described (BMU 2004): Women care more for the environment, feel more affected by environmental problems and show more emotional reactions (e.g. anger) about it. Figure 1 illustrates the factors that will be included in our further analysis.

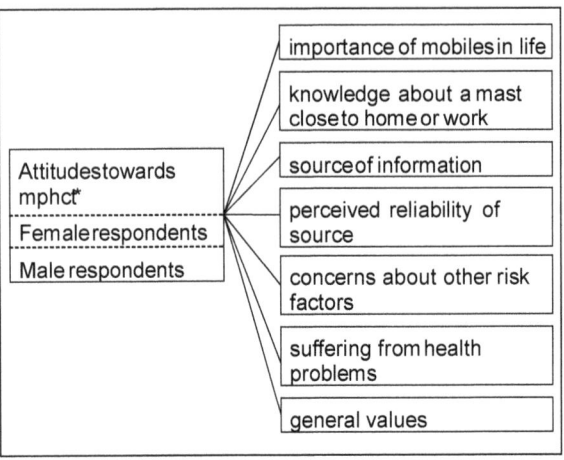

*mphct: mobile phone communication technology

Figure 1: Attitudes towards mobile phone communication technology: included facets

Study design

We conducted an online-survey on attitudes towards mobile phone communication. The following questions were included:

- Where do people search for information about possible effects on mobile phone communication?
- How do they perceive the reliability of these sources?
- Do they know about any mast close to home or work?
- How do they assess general statements on possible health effects of mobile phone communication?
- Are people afraid of mobile phone technology?
- How do they assess other factors with respect to their possible risks?
- Do respondents suffer from any health problems?
- To which causes do they attribute them?
- Which values are important in their lives?

The questionnaire embraced 218 items in total and in most instances a six point scale was used, from 1 = "not at all" or "never" to 6 = "definitely" or "always".

Respondents

During a six week period, 526 people filled out the online-questionnaire completely. Compared to other online surveys, this number of participants a reasonable response rate (Schütz et al. 2005).
62% of our respondents were male, 38% were female. Further characteristics of our sample can be drawn from table 1:

Age	%	Education	%
- 20	1.5	none	0.4
21-30	13.5	primary and secondary school ("Volks- u. Hauptschule")	6.4
31-40	22.9	secondary modern school level 1 certificate ("Mittlere Reife")	15.4
41-50	32.1	vocational baccalaureat diploma ("Fachabitur, Fachhochschulreife")	12.1
51-60	20.2	university-entrance diploma ("Abitur/Hochschulreife")	16.6
61-70	9.2	university degree	41.6
71 -	0.6	conferral of a doctorate	7.5

Table 1: Age and education of the respondents

As confirmed in another study (INFAS 2004), in our study most of those people who took part, were interested in possible effects of EMF. These were men, people at the age of 40-51 and with high formal education. Thus, this was a special selection effect which meant that the case study only represented this group of highly interested people. Of course, the results presented are not representative and this is further limited due to the mode of data collection via the Internet.

Subjective assessment of mobile phone communication

Our analysis concentrates on different attitudes towards mobile phone communication technology. We include cognitive as well as affective attitude components. Behavioural components are left out, because it has proved to be very difficult to master the gap between the intention to behave and actual behaviour in studies with a quantitative design similar to ours. An additional point is that we also added values. Values and attitudes differ in the way that values are more abstract, general orientation lines in life whereas attitudes are always addressed to something or somebody. Table 2 presents some information about study variables.

	No. of items	Range	Mean	SD	Coeff. α*
Gender (1: male, 2: female)	1	1-2	1.38	0.48	-
importance of mobile phones in life					
necessity to use mobile phone because of work	1	1-6	2.64	1.98	-
necessity to use mobile phone because of private reasons	1	1-6	1.75	1.34	-
knowledge about masts closed to					
home (1: no, 2: yes, 3: do not know)	1	1/2/3	-	-	-
work (1: no, 2: yes, 3: do not know)	1	1/2/3	-	-	-
source of information					
scholarly literature	1	1-6	4.27	1.82	-
TV	1	1-6	3.44	1.81	-
Internet	1	1-6	5.03	1.44	-
Radio	1	1-6	3.14	1.77	-
Newspapers	1	1-6	3.99	1.73	-
Physicians	1	1-6	3.65	1.80	-
citizen's groups	1	1-6	4.27	1.82	-
Friends	1	1-6	3.86	1.68	-
Church	1	1-6	1.38	0.97	-
Politicians	1	1-6	1.79	1.34	-
environmental organizations	1	1-6	3.81	1.82	-
Companies	1	1-6	2.18	1.56	-
Scientists	1	1-6	4.52	1.55	-
Perceived reliability					
Physicians	1	1-6	3.82	1.44	-
citizen's groups	1	1-6	4.20	1.65	-
Friends	1	1-6	3.84	1.36	-
Church	1	1-6	2.19	1.30	-
Politicians	1	1-6	1.67	0.96	-
environmental organizations	1	1-6	4.30	1.47	-
Companies	1	1-6	1.85	1.19	-
Scientists	1	1-6	4.01	1.31	-
Concerns about other risks					
risk trait[3]	22	1-6	4.35	0.79	0.90
health problems					
index of all health problems	33	1-6	1.53	0.82	0.86
Values					
social acceptance	6	1-6	3.67	0.84	0.69
social commitment	3	1-6	4.28	0.95	0.67
Religion	2	1-6	2.61	1.61	0.67
health orientation	3	1-6	4.74	0.97	0.62
family orientation	2	1-6	5.33	0.93	0.48
individualistic orientation	3	1-6	4.53	0.89	0.52
attitudes towards mobile phone communication technology					
pro mobile phone technology	7	1-6	1.84	1.09	0.84
Neglect	4	1-6	2.45	1.22	0.60
Anxiety	4	1-6	3.26	1.73	0.84
convinced about harms	3	1-6	3.32	1.70	0.73

* in case of two items, the correlation coefficient is displayed

Table 2: Psychometric data and study variables

First of all, we will have a look at the mentioned factors that could influence attitudes towards mobile phone communication technology.

3 Trait to perceive various environmental factors to be risky.

Importance of mobile phones in life

88% of all respondents have at least one mobile phone in their household. This number is comparable to the German average, although the official number is a bit lower. As stated before, about three-quarters of the population possess a mobile phone, yet the question was not addressed to the household. Two items were included from which it is possible to cautiously deduce the importance of mobile phones in life. The first of these was: "I would be willing to refrain from using a mobile phone, but I cannot, because I do need it due to professional reasons", the second was "I would be willing to refrain from using a mobile phone, but I cannot, because I do need it due to private reasons". More people need a mobile phone for work than because of private reasons. There is no gender difference for the first facet, but a significant difference for the second one. Women need it more for private reasons than men (mean women: 2.07, men: 1.57). This is probably due to the (typical) role of women to care for the children and thus they might use it mainly for the purpose to be able to communicate with them flexibly. This, however, is just a supposition that cannot, however, be proved by our data.

Knowledge about masts closed to work or home

Nearly 83% of our respondents knew about at least one mast close to home, 8% were sure that no mast was close and 9% do not know whether there is any. The same was asked for the workplace. Here 72% stated that there was at least one mast, 9% were sure that there was no mast and about 19% could not answer this question. There were no differences between female and male respondents.

Source of information and perceived reliability

Further, we asked from which sources people obtain their information about mobile phone communication technology (see figure 2).

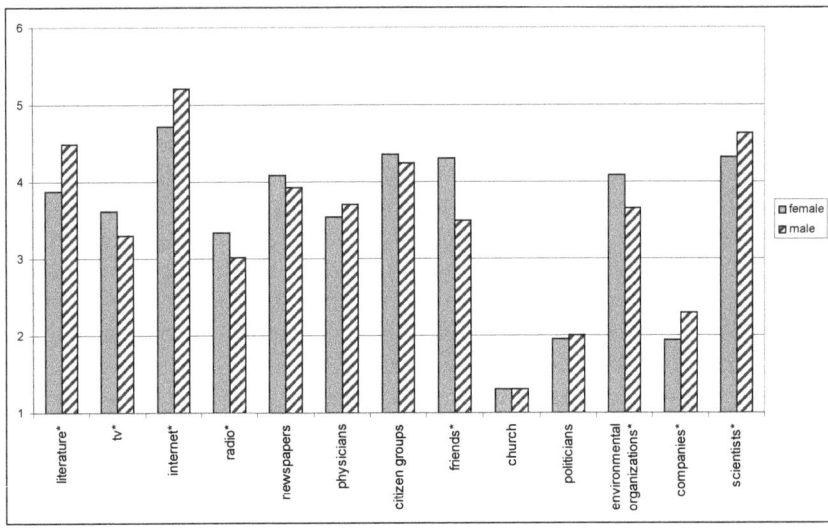

significant differences are marked with *

Figure 2: Gender differences for the different use of sources of information

It can be demonstrated from the data in Figure 2 that most respondents used the internet to gather information, but here we need to take into account the way of data collection via the internet. Thus, our respondents are used to accessing it for different purposes. Further, a lot of respondents try to get information from scientists, scholarly literature and social organisations (citizen's groups or environmental organisations). Comparably few use information provided by companies or the church.[4]

How the respondents tried to get information differs between men and women: male respondents use the internet, read scholarly literature, gather information from scientists or companies significantly more; Women, on the other hand, use conventional media, like TV or radio. They also talk more to friends or consult environmental organizations.

The next aspect we focus on is the perceived reliability of most of the sources (see figure 3). Our respondents tend to trust social organizations (environmental organizations, citizen's groups), scientists, physicians and friends but they do not trust information provided by churches, companies and politicians. Interestingly, the low level of trust addressed to churches is even comparable to the trust ad-

---

4   Some churches publish reports on topics address health aspects or respond to anxieties among people.

dressed to companies. Politicians are perceived not be very trustworthy. There are remarkable gender differences for the trust given to physicians, citizen's groups, friends and environmental organizations. In all cases women trust these sources slightly more than men. Maybe this results from their wish to reduce anxieties and to receive reliable information, either to establish positive, negative or neutral attitudes.

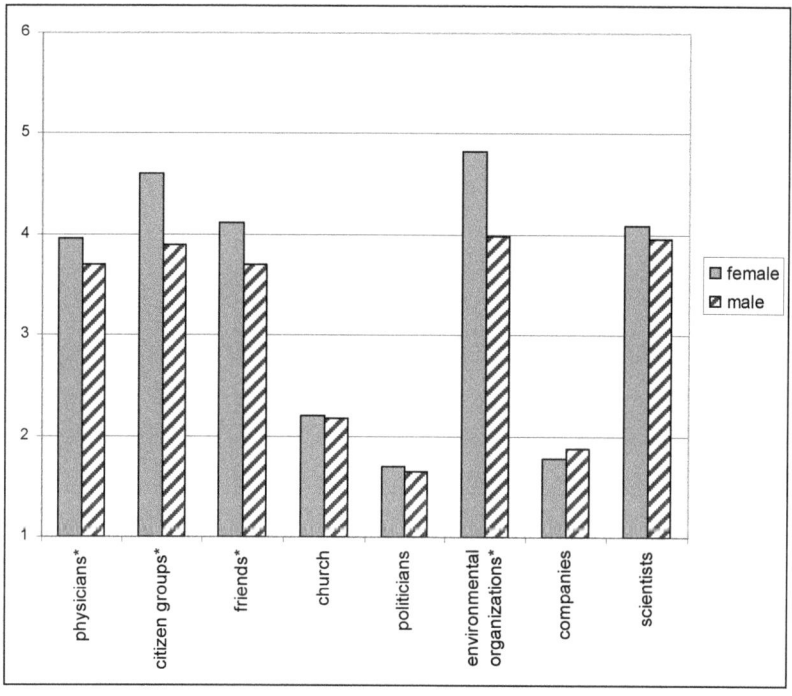

significant differences are marked with *

Figure 3: Gender differences for the perceived reliability of different sources of information

Concerns about other risk factors and health problems

Concerns about other risk factors, such as nuclear power stations, air or water pollution, are significantly more prevalent among women than among men (mean for women 4.56, men 4.20). This tendency has also been demonstrated in other studies (BMU 2004).

Further, we asked about health problems of our respondents. Women report slightly more health problems than men (mean women 1.61, men 1.49), but this small difference is not significant.

We can conclude, with some caution, that men and women of our sample do not differ with respect to their health in general, but in their environmental awareness.

Values

In this next section we explore how much each value is important for people[5]. Here we differentiate between women and men again (figure 4).

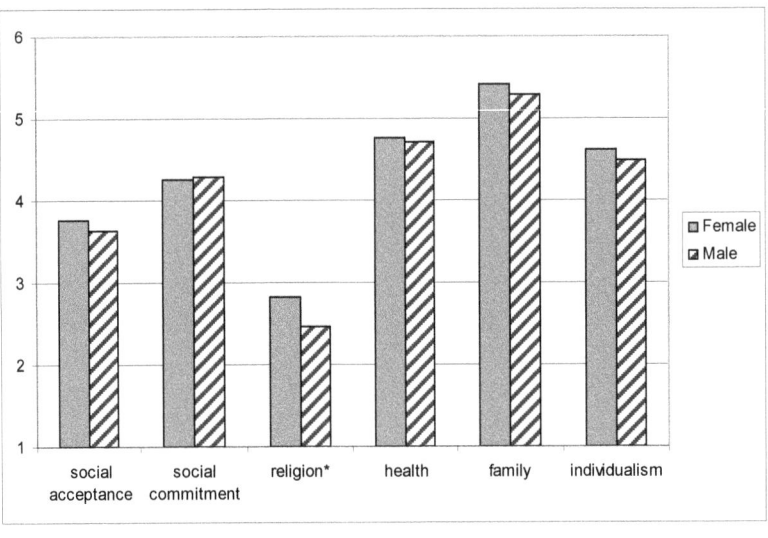

Figure 4: Gender differences for values

---

5   The factors result from the question: "In your life, how important is it for you to..." The mentioned dimensions consist of the following items: factor *family orientation*: have a successful partnership, have or start a family; factor *health orientation*: be healthy and fit, play sport on a regular basis, to value a healthy environment; factor *individualism*: to be independent, have as much leisure as possible, to have lots of fun; factor social *commitment*: be engaged politically, engaged in activities supporting people in need, help others, factor *social acceptance*: be accepted/acknowledged by others, be attractive to others, have a career, be able to afford all those things one likes to have, job security and have a lot of friends; factor *religious orientation*: pray on a regular basis, be engaged in church/religious activities.

The most important value is family orientation, followed by health orientation and individualism. The next important value is social commitment. Social acceptance and religion are the least important values. There are not many gender differences with only religion showing a slight but significant difference.

Following on from this description of gender differences with regard to these general aspects we can now turn to the analysis of concrete attitudes towards mobile phone communication technology.

Attitudes towards mobile phone communication technology: positive assessment

About 15% of our sample shares a rather positive view of mobile phone communication. 17% say this technology is important for a high standard of living. 22% are sure that companies do not only react to what is legally mandatory, but care for people's health. 16% are convinced that the limits set by the German government will protect health sufficiently. Social cognition can be lead by representativeness heuristic (Nisbett & Ross 1980). This means that people refer to a group they think are knowledgable and believe that this group is representative. In our study 14% believe that mobile phone communication has no harmful effects, because they know only a few people who are convinced they have developed health problems due to exposure to EMF. Also 14% think that the critical discussion about possible harming effects only takes place because of hysteria of just a few people. Another factor which could influence attitudes is the overconfidence phenomenon (McKenna 1993, Weinstein 1987): According to this concept people tend to underestimate the probability they may be affected by negative incidents – it can happen to others but not to themselves. Optimism is especially high if they have not had any experience of the possibly hazardous source, if they assess the rate of occurrence low and their own ability to control the situation to be high. In our study, 12% are sure they are immune to negative effects of masts, even if others fall ill. Finally, we found that causal attribution is important. Information which can be easily brought together with existing knowledge will be adapted more easily. Causal attribution can also be used in order to avoid cognitive dissonance. In general, people tend to assess risks more according to their own plausibility assumptions than because of statistical data (Versteegen 1992, Nisbett & Ross 1980). 15% reported they suffered from health problems, but they are sure, that these do not have to do anything with an exposition to EMF. We also examined if there any gender differences in our study. Figure 5 compares the mean of women and of men, while it presents all mentioned items that will be brought together as factor 1 in our further analysis.

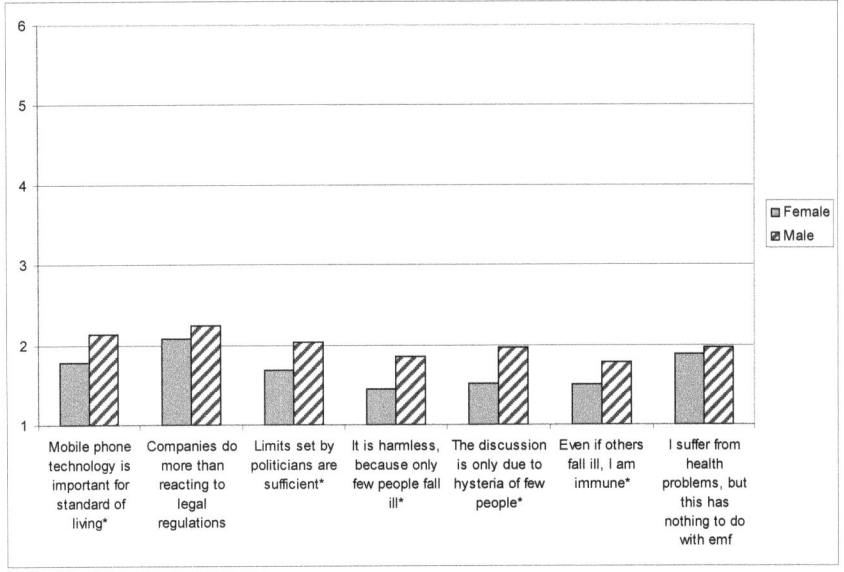

emf: electromagnetic fields, significant differences are marked with *

Figure 5: Gender differences for items of factor 1

It is evident that more men than women share a positive view of mobile phone communication. Men assess the impact of this technology on the standard of living to be higher and have more trust in politics. Further, they are more convinced that the discussion about possible negative effects on health has been kicked off only because of extreme emotional reactions of a couple of people and that the technology is harmless as only very few fall ill. There are no significant differences for trust in economy nor in the statement they have health problems which are not attributed to EMF.

Discussion

We now turn to attitudes of women and analyse possible relationships with the aspects mentioned above and displayed in figure 1. It can be seen that women who report they have at least one mobile phone in their household share only slightly but significant more positive attitudes towards this technology (mean 1.69) than the minority who do not possess a mobile (mean 1.34). For those who use mobiles there exists no significant relationship between the importance of mobile phones in everyday life (work and private) and a positive evaluation of it (factor 1).

Positive attitudes differ according to the knowledge about masts located close to people. If women do not know whether there is a mast close to home or work a positive evaluation of mobile phone communication technology is highest (means in both cases 2.00) and it is lowest among those, who know about at least one mast (means 1.56 and 1.49). This could be explained easily: People who share pro arguments might not perceive masts because of selective perception or missing interest – they are not important for them. Or the other way round: Critical attitudes enhance the wish to get more information about possible harming sources in the vicinity.

There are also several significant correlations between factor 1 and the sources women resort to in order to gather information. Women who are in favour of the technology do not inform themselves via the internet ($r = -0.38**$)[6], scholarly literature (-0.36**) or newspapers (-0.18*). They also do not talk with friends about this topic (-0.36**) or try to get information from physicians (-0.19*), scientists (-0.23**), citizen's groups (-0.46**) or environmental organisations (-0.28**). Further, it is important how women perceive the reliability of these sources. Women who have higher values in factor 1 tend to trust companies (0.28**), scientists (0.20**) and politicians (0.20**) and they mistrust citizen's groups (-0.52**), environmental organizations (-0.40**), and even their friends (-0.28**).

At the same time, women with positive attitudes towards mobile phone communication technology do assess other risks rather low (-0.24**). There is no significant correlation with their health.

The analysis of the relationship between values and this attitude reveals a significant positive correlation with the value of social acceptance (0.21**), and negative correlations with social commitment (-0.30**) and religion (-0.20**). There are no significant correlations for the other values.

The same analysis for men the following results: There is again a slight but significant difference between men who have at least one mobile in their households (mean 2.05) and those who do not (mean 1.40). There is a tendency for pro arguments to be found more among men than among women. A positive evaluation of this technology shows a positive correlation with the importance of mobile phones due to private reasons (0.19**). It seems to be independent from occupational needs.

In contrast to the results for women, it is not important whether there are masts close to home or work.

---

6 If not stated differently, Pearson's correlation coefficient r is displayed in brackets.

In addition there are a lot of correlations of factor 1 and the sources used for information as well as their perceived reliability. In general it can be said that men who share positive views of mobile phone communication technology rely on information provided by politicians (0.15*) and companies (0.27**). They do not consult environmental groups (-0.28**), citizen's groups (-0.50**), physicians (-0.26**) or even friends (-0.31**). The same tendencies can be noticed for the perceived reliability of these sources.

Like for our female respondents, men who share positive attitudes towards the technology tend to also have a relaxed view of other risk factors (-0.23**). On the other hand, mainly healthy men rate high on factor 1, while suffering from an illness could also lead to a weaker support of mobile phone communication technology (-0.23**). This tendency is also reflected in the correlation between the value of health orientation and factor 1 (-0.26**). Social acceptance correlates positively (0.22**), while social commitment shows a negative correlation (-0.13*) with a positive assessment of the mobile phone communication technology. Factor 1 shows a noticeable and highly significant correlation of 0.35** with the next factor, which is called "neglect".

Attitudes towards mobile phone communication technology: neglect

People can share the view that is not only difficult to find out what effects this technology might have, but also that it would be better not to bother too much about this question. About 40% state that one cannot escape all environmental hazards possibly that might cause possible harm anyway. 18% do not know what to believe because there were too many controversial study results. 12% agreed that it would be better not to think about possible negative effects of mobile phone communication technology in order to enjoy life. Again the answers of our female and male respondents are compared (figure 6).

Feelings of powerlessness and uncertainty are higher among women. This is in line with the abovementioned results: Women are more sceptical about possible negative effects of mobile phone communication technology and henceforth they do not support it as much as men.

For women, there is no difference with respect to the possession of a mobile or the importance of mobile phones in everyday life. Those who do not know about a mast close to home or work have also highest means in factor 2 (means 3.28, 3.22) in contrast to those who know about a mast (means 2.52, 2.42). This is again a consonant result.

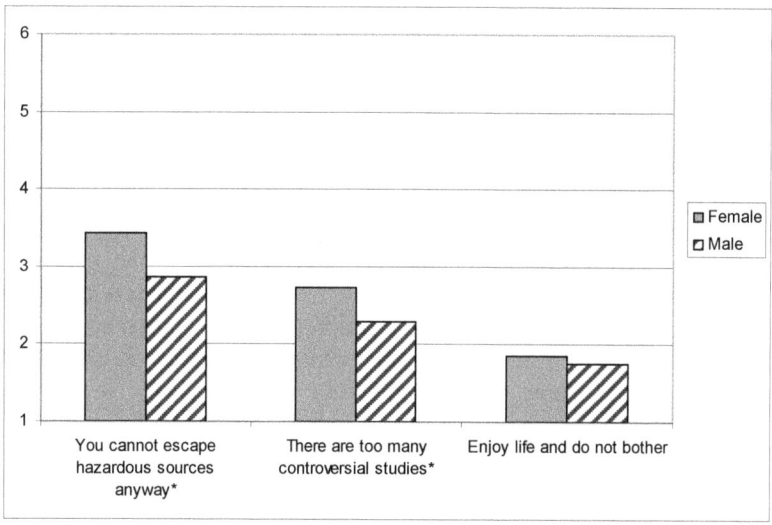

significant differences are marked with *

Figure 6: Gender differences for items of factor 2

The correlations with sources for information are similar to those for factor 1, but they are noticeably higher for neglect. Women with high values on factor 2 do not resort to scholarly literature (-0.43**) or information provided in the internet (-0.38**) or by newspapers (-0.18*). They also do not consult citizen's groups (-0.38**), environmental organisations (-0.26**), scientists (-0.25**), physicians (-0.25**) nor friends (-0.27**). Women who share the above mentioned attitudes again rely on scientists and companies (both 0.21**) or politicians (0.16*), while they mistrust citizen's groups (-0.40**), environmental organizations (-0.26**) and friends (-0.24**). Again, there is a negative correlation between concerns about other risks and neglect, of course (-0.24**), and no significant relationship with health problems. Above, the correlations between attitudes combined in factor 2 and values are quite similar to those with factor 1. Women who strive for social acceptance (0.17*), but not for social commitment (-0.27**), religion (-0.23**) or who care not so much for health (-0.16*) show higher values on factor 2.

As concerns men in general there is no difference between those who have a mobile and those who do not. But it does matter for what reason they use a mobile. The more they feel forced to use it for private reasons the higher is the tendency of neglect (0.23**).

Similar to women the highest values for factor 2 could be found among those men who do not know about any masts close to their home or workplace (means 3.30, 3.01) – in comparison to those who know one (means 2.28, 2.29). Men who have high values on factor 2 do not use scholarly literature for information so much (-0.31**) or information in the internet (-0.29**) or newspapers (-0.12*), or provided by citizen's groups (-0.36**), environmental organisations (-0.27**), scientists (-0.21**), physicians (-0.17**) or friends (-0.18**). Men with high values in neglect consider information provided by companies to be trustworthy (0.20**), while the sources citizen's groups (-0.31**), environmental organizations (-0.26**) and friends (-0.26**) are perceived to be untrustworthy. Further, neglect is higher among healthy men (-0.14*) with lower concerns about other risks (-0.17**). Similar to the results of women, socially engaged men who care for their health (both -.23**) have lower values in factor 2, while men who strive for social acceptance or who share individualistic values tend towards neglect (0.13*, 0.12*).

Attitudes towards mobile phone communication technology: anxieties

While the last factor described uncertainty and a tendency towards neglect, this next one focusses concisely on anxieties. The anxiety factor does not show a significant correlation with neglect (0.05), but a negative correlation with the first factor (-0.35**) and a positive one with the fourth factor (0.27**) – this will be described later in the chapter.

The questions refer to being afraid of masts. 52% expressed to be afraid of them because one cannot see the radiation. 47% are afraid because they do not know what effects EMF might have. For 46% the source of anxiety is not knowing how to protect themselves. 40% are afraid because they are convinced that they cannot do anything against it. The analysis of gender differences brings along very interesting results (figure 7).

Women are more afraid of mobile phone communication masts in all four dimensions. The analysis of possible relationships with the aspects included reveal interesting details: Anxieties seem to develop irrespective of possessing a mobile or of the possible importance of mobile phone communication technology in everyday life, or the knowledge about or sight of masts or of values.

In contrast, it is again relevant from which sources women gather information: Information presented by newspapers (0.17*), environmental organisations (0.22**) or friends (0.23**) seem to aggravate anxieties, while information by companies could reduce them (-0.26**). Women who are afraid of mobile phone communication technology trust environmental organisations (0.34**), citizen's groups (0.33**) and their friends (0.17*). They also express more concerns about other risk factors (0.36**) and if they have health problems their anxiety level tends to be higher, too (0.21**).

For men the importance of mobile phones also has no influence on experiencing anxieties. Yet, it depends again on sources of information: TV or radio reports (both 0.20**), articles in newspapers or the internet (both 0.13*), information provided by citizen's groups (0.30**), environmental organizations (0.26**) and friends (0.21**) increase anxieties, (or anxious men seek information especially from these sources.) They do not trust politicians (-0.13*), scientists (-0.12*) or companies (-0.22**), but rely on physicians (0.18*), environmental organizations (0.35**), citizen's groups (0.34**) and friends (0.14*). The more they perceive other factors to be risky or the worse they suffer from health problems, the more they develop anxieties (0.26**, 0.22**). While there were no significant correlations between anxieties and values for women, there are weak ones for men, in the case of religion (0.12*) and health orientation (0.15**).

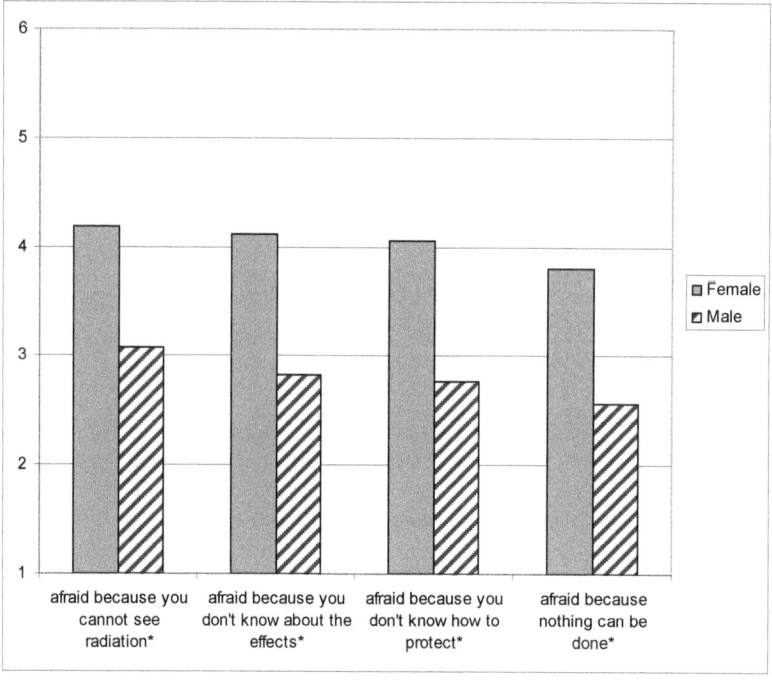

significant differences are marked with *

Figure 7: Gender differences for items of factor 3

Attitudes towards mobile phone communication technology: conviction that mobile phone communication damages health

This factor correlates negatively with the first factor (-0.59**) and the anxiety factor (-0.34**). Again, different factors which could influence social cognition were included. The first one looked at personal involvement. 40% are convinced that EMF caused by masts damages health, because they have felt ill themselves. 52% know somebody, who fell ill because of the exposition of a mast, and are hence convinced that EMF caused by masts damages people's health. Again, the two modi of causal attribution and representativeness can shape attitudes. The weakest direct personal involvement is the case for those, who have heard that EMF caused by masts can damage people's health. 51% share this view. Gender differences are illustrated in figure 8.

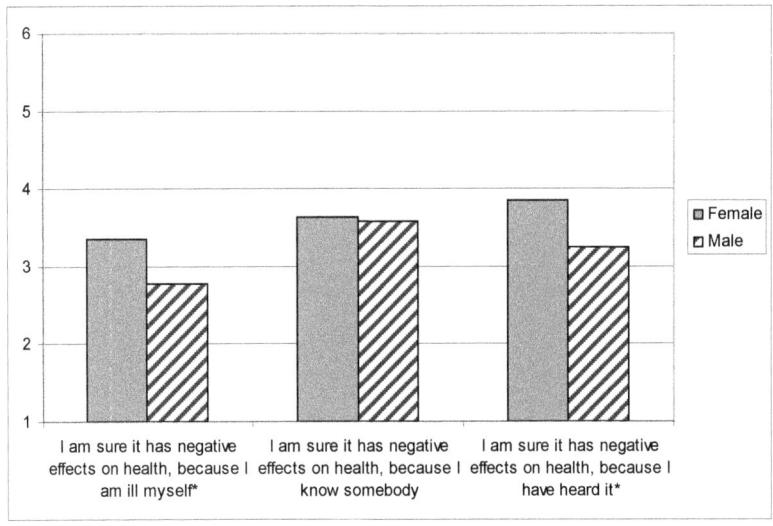

significant differences are marked with *

Figure 8: Gender differences for items of factor 4

Women are significantly more convinced about harming effects of mobile phone communication technology in circumstances where they are affected by health problems themselves or if they have heard about it. There is no significant difference for the third item which is addressed to the health problems of other people.

Critical attitudes of women do not depend on the importance of mobile phones in their lives. Women with high values on factor 4 gather information especially from scholarly literature (0.44**), provided in the internet (0.45**), TV (0.20*) or newspapers (0.25**). They consult physicians (0.24**), environmental organizations (0.30**), citizen's groups (0.55**) and ask their friends (0.46**). They trust environmental organisations (0.41**), citizen's groups (0.54**), their friends (0.46**), but mistrust politicians (-0.32**) and companies (-0.25**). Interestingly, they gather information from scientists (0.31**), but they also mistrust them (-0.17*). If women have health problems, they also tend to exhibit critical attitudes towards mobile phone communication technology (0.21**). Further, this correlates with concerns about other risk factors (0.26**). Socially committed or religious women have higher values on factor 4 (0.30**, 0.17*).

For men, there is no influence of the importance of mobile phones. There is also no difference with respect to the knowledge of a mast at work, but only about the knowledge of one close to their homes. Men who know about a mast there, have significantly higher values on factor 4 (mean 3.27 – in comparison to those who do not know about any masts 2.00). Again, there are a lot of significant correlations for sources of information and their perceived reliability. Critical attitudes go hand in hand with the utilization of scholarly literature (0.32**), the internet (0.42**), TV (0.25*), radio (0.20**) or newspapers (0.23**). Men who share these attitudes try to get information from physicians (0.24**, whom they trust 0.24**), scientists (0.21**, whom they – like their female counterparts – mistrust, -0.30**), environmental organizations (0.25** – trust 0.47**), citizen's groups (0.53** – trust 0.66**) and their friends (0.34** – trust 0.38**). They are not interested in information presented by politicians (-0.16*) or companies (-0.14*) whom they mistrust (-0.28**, -0.38**). Also for men there are positive correlations between general tendency to perceive different factors to be risky (0.31**) as well as for health problems (0.32**) and factor 4. At last, socially committed, religious and health oriented men tend to share critical views on mobile phone communication technology.

Attitudes towards mobile phone communication technology in the broadband society

The broadband society tries to use new technologies in order to enhance communication, to make it easier, faster and provide more quality – or in general – to be beneficial for people (Sapio 2006). Although mobile phone communication is widely accepted and appreciated the accompanying technology, the construction of masts, is still heavily discussed. In order to assess risks people can resort to another element of the broadband society: the internet. This is especially demonstrated by our study. All in all, people find themselves in a situation where they would like to use technologies without taking possible negative side effects.

Our study demonstrated that there are not many differences in attitudes of people who possess a mobile phone and those who do not. Rather the reasons they (feel forced to) use it seem to be more important. . Thus, our study points out that it might be necessary not only to ask for mobile use, but also for the context (work-private).

In our study critical attitudes dominate. It also reveals some interesting gender differences in attitudes towards mobile phone communication technology with slightly more positive attitudes among men.

The rising number of masts could lead to normalisation (this would be in line with results by Lima et al. 2005), or it could enhance anxieties because people are constantly reminded of hazards (see e.g. Siegrist et al. 2005). Societal risk perception could also be explained by the diffusion rate of technologies. The faster the growth rate the higher risk perception can be described as a societal sensitivity effect (Lima et al. 2005). Maybe risk perception will decrease if masts become more familiar to people or if the diffusion rate slows down. Yet this is only a possibility as other examples provide different effects, like nuclear power which although established in the sixties, still attracts very controversial discussion.

If our respondents know that there is a mast close to home or work, they also tend to share critical attitudes towards this technology. Of course, it could be the other way round and it is the people who are afraid of EMF who search for information about masts. In contrast to the study by Siegrist and others (2005) there is a significant difference in risk perception between those who believed they live close to a base station and those who do not know about any. In our study, this knowledge (or belief) only influences critical statements on masts, but it does not influence anxieties, the emotional component of attitudes. Thus, if normalisation really prevailed, we could expect a decrease in critical cognitive assessment, but not necessarily a reduction of anxieties.

Our study underlines the social dimension of mobile phone communication in several ways:

1. It becomes obvious how information about this technology seems to be socially represented (Moscovici 2001). There are certain patterns with some sources associated with mainly critical information and some s with mainly pro-technology information. The same can be said for the perceived reliability of the sources. Scholarly literature and information provided in the internet are used for a critical reflection of this technology. Information provided by physicians, environmental organizations, citizen's groups and friends seem to confirm criti-

cal attitudes towards mobile phone communication technology. As demonstrated above this is also partly the case for information provided by scientists. While information provided by citizen's groups, environment organisations and friends are perceived mostly to be trustworthy, mainly by those who share critical attitudes about the technology in question, it is labelled as untrustworthy by the supporters or those who tend to neglect. In turn, supporters (and those with high values on factor 2 – neglect) assess information provided by politicians, companies and scientists to be trustworthy. Yet, as we demonstrated above, information by scientists is often gathered by our respondents, even if they assume it not to be trustworthy.

These results could underline that knowledge about and attitudes towards mobile phone communication technology are socially represented differently depending on the social system from which people gather information and depending on the observing groups, too.

Generally, women and men show different ways and intensities to search for information via different media or from different institutions or persons. Women refer more communication oriented sources. Further, they tend to trust their sources more, while men seem to be a bit more suspicious.

Our study supports the importance of trust and confidence as demonstrated by Siegrist and others (2005), but it reveals quite a complex construct. It depends on whom people trust and whom they do not trust. Further, it was shown that people could also have an ambivalent relationship to some social groups like scientists.

2. Especially socially oriented values seem to be correlated with attitudes towards mobile phone communication technology. While other values do not show many significant correlations with the given attitudes, we find some significant correlations for social acceptance with the positive assessment of mobile phone communication technology and with neglect. This is the case for women and men. On the other hand: People who exhibit social commitment do not value mobile phone communication technology so positively nor do they tend to neglect. At the same time they are more convinced about the possible harming effects of this technology. Only for anxieties is there no correlation with this value. As social acceptance and social commitment are the main important values, it can be carefully concluded that social cognition of mobile phone communication is, above all, socially driven.

Our analysis delivers some quite interesting results concerning attitudes towards mobile phone technology and a more differentiated and detailed gender comparison than most of the other studies stated above. Apart from this, it also provided a clear picture of various socially represented information about mobile phone communication technology.

Yet, these results can only be used as a starting point for further studies. Our results are neither representative nor can they reveal causalities. Although the description of our results suggested sometimes to read them in a particular way, this is not proved by the data. All in all, it seems to be worthy to investigate attitudes under a broader perspective like in our study with different facets of attitudes. Further, it should be extended to include a representative sample while other ways of data collection should be applied, too. The best solution would be to undertake a longitudinal study.

Although it is sometimes discussed only to involve experts when it comes up to regulating technology (Nilsson 2004), it could turn out to be difficult to enhance a technological development without recognizing what is happening in some social subsystems. Thus, also lay people's perceptions should be taken into account (Stirling & Gee 2003).

References

Barnett J., Breakwell G. M. 'Risk perception and experience' Risk Analysis 21:1 (2001) pp. 171-177
BfS, Ergebnisse der bundesweiten repräsentativen Umfrage im Jahr 2003 zur Wahrnehmung des Mobilfunks Bonn (2003)
BMU, Umweltbewusstsein 2004 Berlin (2004)
I+G, Gesundheitsforschung Stakeholder-Perspektiven zur Novellierung der 26. BImSchV. Ergebnisse der bundesweiten Telefonumfrage im Auftrag des BfS. München (2002)
Infas, Ermittlung der Befürchtungen und Ängste der breiten Öffentlichkeit hinsichtlich möglicher Gefahren der hochfrequenten elektromagnetischen Felder Mobilfunks – jährliche Umfragen. Abschlußbericht für das BfS. Bonn (2004)
Kheifets L., Repacholi M., Saunders R., van Deventer E. 'The Sensitivity of Children to Electromagnetic Fields. Paediatrics' 116 (2005) pp. 303-313
Lima M. L. 'On the influence of risk perception on mental health'. Journal of Environmental Psychology 24:1 (2004) pp. 71-84
Lima M. L., Barnett J., Vala J. 'Risk Perception and Technological Development at a Societal Level' Risk Analysis 25:5 (2005) pp. 1229-1239
McKenna F. P. 'It won't happen to me' British Journal of Psychology 84:1 (1993) pp. 39-50
Moscovici S. Social Representations. New York: University Press (2001)
Nilsson R. 'Control of chemicals in Sweden: an example of misuse of the "precautionary principle"' Ecotoxicology and Environmental Safety 57:2 (2004) pp. 107-117

Nisbett R. E., Ross L. Human Inference: Strategies and Shortcomings of Social Judgment Englewood Cliffs, NJ: Prentice-Hall (1980)
Oktay M. F., 'Dasdag S. Effects of intensive and moderate cellular phone use on hearing fuction' Electromagnetic Biology and Medicine 25: 1 (2006) pp. 13-21
Ruddat M., Sautter A. et al. Statistische Metaanalyse zu Mobilfunkstudien und Medienanalyse zum Risikodiskurs des Mobilfunk im Rahmen des Forschungsprojekts „Untersuchung der Kenntnis und Wirkungen von Informationsmaßnahmen im Bereich Mobilfunk und Ermittlung weiterer Ansatzpunkte zur Verbesserung der Information verschiedener Bevölkerungsgruppen" Stuttgart (2005)
Sapio B. 'Participation in the Broadband Society' Medijksa istrazivanja 12: 2 (2006) pp. 121-131
Schütz J., Vollrath L., Egle T. U. et al. Abschlußbericht „Mainzer EMF-Wachhund". http://www.mainzer-emf-wachhund.de/wachhund-doc/wachhund/EMF-Bericht.pdf, (2005)
Siegrist M. & Cousin M.-E. Laypeople's Knowledge about Mobile Communication. EHT Zurich. URL: www.mobile-research.ethz.ch/var/pub_siegrist_ref20.pdf
Siegrist M., Earle T. C., Gutscher H. 'Test of a trust and confidence model in the applied context of electromagnetic filed (EMF) risks' Risk Analysis 23 (2003) pp. 705-716
Siegrist M., Earle T. C., Gutscher H., Keller C. 'Perception of Mobile Phone and Base Station Risks' Risk Analysis 25: 5 (2005) pp. 1253-1264
Stirling A., Gee D. 'Science, precaution, and practice' Public Health Reports 117 (2003) pp. 521-533
Takebayashi T., Akiba S., Kikuchi Y. (all the surnames of authors must be reported) 'Mobile phone use and acoustic neuroma risk in Japan' Journal of Occupational and Environmental Medicine, 15 (2006) pp. 802-807
Twigger-Ross C. L., Berakwell G. M. 'Relating risk experience, venturesomeness and risk perception' Journal of Risk Research 2:1 (1999) pp. 73-83
Versteegen U. ‚Risikowahrnehmung und Gesundheit' Zeitschrift für Klinische Psychologie XXI: 1(1992) pp. 28-35
Weinstein N. D. 'The precaution adoption process' Health Psychology 7 (1987) pp. 355-386
Wiedemann P. M. Risikopotenziale elektromagnetischer Felder' Forschungszentrum Jülich: Jülich (2001)
wik-Consult Zielgruppenanalyse zur differenzierten Information über Mobilfunk und Gesundheit Bad Honnef: WIK (2005)

Theme IV:
New technologies, new challenges

Sharon Baurley, Erik Geelhoed, Philippa Brock and Andrew Moore

Communication-Wear: User Feedback as Part of a Co-design Process

Introduction

With the downscaling of traditional textile industry in the European Union (EU), it is envisaged that, in Europe, a high-tech clothing sector will soon emerge (Euratex 2004). First applications have already surfaced in the area of sports and health (Paradiso et al. 2004). Looking further out into the future, it may only be a matter of time before some of these wearable and smart textile technologies are adopted within the fashion industry. However, as yet it is unclear what kind of compelling applications might accelerate the uptake of smart materials in the consumer market (Photopoulos 2006). Fashion is uniquely placed as a future mediator of technology, in particular within the relatively new "experience economy"; a culture where the human senses, experiences, and emotions are more and more of commercial interest. The *Communication-Wear* concept seeks to operate within, and contribute to, the emergence of a new genre in clothing and fashion, where fashion and ICT converge. This research is multi-disciplinary, drawing on expertise from fashion and textile design, electronics, wearable computing, and user research.

Communication-Wear proposes to marry conventions and cultures of fashion, as being an expressive medium that connects people with the social world, with principles of nonverbal communication as well as with current cultures of mobile communications. Fashion/clothing and mediated communication technologies have common attributes in terms of how they enable people to construct an identity, to be expressive, to differentiate themselves, and declare their uniqueness, and which enables communication between people allowing them to form communities. People do this through their consumption of these commodities and services. The communication of identity through fashion can be to one's self, or from self to others, the meanings behind which are often ambiguous and open to (mis)interpretation (Barnard 1996). A large percentage of face-to-face communication takes place via nonverbal means, i.e., through facial expressions, touch, and bodily gestures (Argyle 2001) and the links between expression and nonverbal communication through body movement and touch in human communication have long been identified (Ekman & Friesen 1969; Jones & Yarborough 1985). Morris (2002) for example distinguishes: Affect displays, movements of the body and face to show emotion; illustrators, gestures which help to reinforce verbal messages; and auto-contact behaviour or 'self-intimacies', which are 'touching actions we direct towards ourselves that provide comfort because they are unconsciously mimed acts of being touched by someone else'. Mobile phones are already 'affective technologies – that is, objects which mediate the expression and exchange of feelings and emotions' (Lasen 2002). 'However, a significant amount of human expression and interaction information is never captured, transmitted, or expressed with current computer mediated communication.' (Paulos 2003) The design framework for Communication-Wear (Baurley 2005) is informed by these diverse strands of research.

In the way that Rheingold (2002) states that 'The killer applications of tomorrow's mobile infocom industry won't be hardware devices or software programmes, but social practices', so our research locates potential youth groups at the centre of the development of fashion/clothing prototypes by engaging them as co-developers and evaluators using design-led techniques, in order to determine what and how people might communicate through augmented clothing, and how this might fit in with, and support people's everyday communications.

We developed a smart textile system integrated into prototype garments that provides a *menu* of touch gestures that the garment can sense and actuate. In a way we used the prototypes as research probes as a means to create conditions in which participants could experience, play and dream, possibly gauging a deeper level of knowledge or tacit knowledge about user's desires, preferences and behaviours. Our approach aims to gain insight into what some catalysts and drivers of future consumer fashion wearable technology might be, and to explore methods to design *smart* clothing that is active and dynamically changeable. In order to do this we have conducted iterative studies using probes to gain insight into how people might appropriate the functionality and create their own meanings through visual, aesthetic, and/or tactile codes. One aim was to determine whether established sensory associations people have with the tactile qualities of textiles could be used as signs and metaphors for experiences, moods, social interactions and gestures, related to interpersonal touch. This is the second study in the series.

Related work

Work in the area of remote communication through touch includes 'ComTouch' (Chang et al. 2002), a vibrotactile communication device, which augments remote voice communication with touch. The 'Lumitouch' (Chang et al. 2002) system consists of a pair of interactive picture frames. When one user touches their picture frame, the other picture frame lights up. 'InTouch' (Brave & Dahley 1997) is an internet-based concept that aims to create the illusion that two people, separated by distance, are interacting with a shared physical object. *CuteCircuit* is developing its 'F+R Hugs' (www.cutecircuit.com) into a commercial offering. 'TapTap' (Bonanni 2006) is a wearable haptic system that allows human touch to be recorded, broadcast and played back for emotional therapy. There is also much literature on the effects of new technologies on human beings (Gemperle et al. 2003; Fortunati et al 2003; Rettie 2005).

'Communication-Wear' design framework

We have taken a design-led approach in this research, as we are proposing artefacts for consumption. Design is at the interface between technology or material and the consumer. As we are dealing specifically with wearable technology, fashion and textile design methods play a key role in our process.

The point of departure for most studies of dress and fashion is the consumer culture, a cultural system of making meaning, and of making meaning through what we consume. Consumer culture is, what Raymond Williams (Williams 1981) and other writers have called, the *"bricks and mortar of everyday life"*, the music you listen to, the clothes you wear, etc. These are aspects of material culture, which we use to map out identities for ourselves. Those identities are often equivocal and unclear in their signals. *"Fashion, clothing and dress constitute signifying systems in which a social order is constructed and communicated"* (Barnard 1996). Meanings can also be generated as a result of negotiations between people resulting from their joint actions, e.g., communication as social interaction through messages (Fiske & O'Sullivan 1994). In the Semiotic (or Structuralist) model of communication as identified by Fisk, *"it is the process of communication that produces or generates meanings"* (Barnard 1996), in which both sender and receiver are constituted. The designer can be the source of the meaning of the garment, "a product of the designer's intentions, where intentions are defined as a person's thoughts, feelings, beliefs, desires about the world and the things in it" (Barnard 1996). Similarly, wearers can attribute their own meanings to the garment, thereby expressing their own beliefs, hopes and fears "through their use of the garment" (Barnard 1996).

Textiles have a range of tactile qualities, which textile and fashion designers have always exploited as part of their design method to engineer a look, concept, mood. There are well-established descriptors for the sensory associations and *hand* qualities of textiles used in the fashion and textile industry when choosing a textile for a clothing application. There is an industry-standard set of polar opposite attributes for fabric hand, e.g., smooth-rough, soft-crisp, cool-warm, delicate-coarse, hard-soft, etc. There are also surface attributes that include sticky, slippery smooth, greasy, fluffy, granulous, scratchy, hairy, etc. These have been de-veloped through using subjective assessment tests by experts. The descriptors along with other attributes, such as colour, shape, and pattern, are used by fashion designers as a legitimate design method to develop seasonal design collections. The collections can then become trends or genres, which are generally understood in terms of their meanings, as they are a result of fashion production and other forms of cultural production, e.g., media and graphics.

In the same way that youth groups create new languages using SMS, so *smart* clothing will need a design palette or *language*, which users can co-opt, adapt and assign their own meanings to, or make their own meanings with. A range of textile actuation types such as shape change, light-emitting, and tactility, has been designed during the course of this research. The aim of the user studies is to determine whether established sensory associations people have with the tactile qualities of textiles could be used as signs and metaphors for experiences, moods, social interactions and gestures, related to interpersonal touch. By enabling users to feel or experience these sensations, they will be engaged in deeper levels of discussion about their associations, thereby revealing insights into how they would make their own meanings, develop their own language to communicate and express using this sensory textile language.

The team designed the garments and their textiles according to these sensory associations and design principles, as well as drawing upon their own experiences and associations. Designers often draw from their own experiences. In a first iteration, the touch actuation consisted of heatable textiles, textiles that change from being cool to warm upon receipt of touch communication. A fabric that has a warm handle is generally understood to have comforting associations; synonyms include having or displaying warmth or affection, passionate and psychologically warm, friendly and responsive, caring, fond, tender. If a designer were devising a fashion collection, he/she would start with a concept board that communicated the mood on a visual and tactile level. If a key component of the collection was a *warm* mood, the designer would include in his/her concept board swatches of fabric that were warm to the touch, a warm colour palette, as well as images or photographs which communicated a sense of warm. The selection of swatches and images would be informed by established cultural understandings of them, as well as the designer's experience of these cultural associations. The author employed a heatable textile as a means to engender these feelings in a person when receiving touch messages. The placement of touch actuators, i.e., heatable textiles, is informed by a 'vocabulary of touch' as devised by Argyle (Argyle 2001) The actuators were placed on the upper back, and front of left and right arms.

Prototype technology platform

In a first exploratory study aimed at mobilising participants' tacit knowledge and their associations of touch and gesture with respect to codes of our material culture, in this instance, textiles and clothing. We generated insights and inspiration for new design ideas around touch communication, and representation, simulation of touch gestures. The main concepts of the study were: A broader range of sensory capability, i.e., the ability to sense and exchange more sensations; to explore the idea of tactile change to represent touch, not just warming sensations; and a visual representation of touch to include colour and/or light. These findings have been used to generate a new conceptual design for the next iteration of *Communication-Wear*, used in the study reported here.

The initial stages of development of the technology platform of the prototype have been reported in a separate article (Randell 2005). In short: Each garment is twinned with a mobile phone via Bluetooth. Communication between garments takes place as follows: Both the sender and the receiver (wearer of the garment) carry a mobile phone. A text message from the sender's mobile phone sends an instruction to the receiver's Bluetooth-enabled mobile phone. This then sends an instruction to the recipient's garment. Users can also send touch messages by gesturing them, as opposed to using text. Textile gesture (mechanical stretch) sensors were located on the upper back where the arm joins the trunk of the body, and touch sensors were situated on the lower parts of the sleeves (Randell 2005). Galvanic Skin Response (GSR) sensors were also introduced, which were integrated into the lining of the garment looping around the index and second finger on the left hand. Woven textile circuits carried power and data signals.

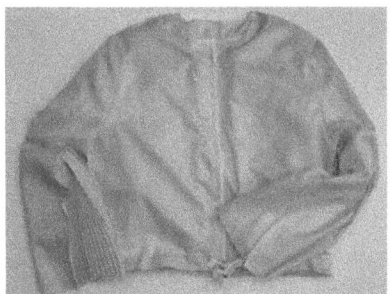 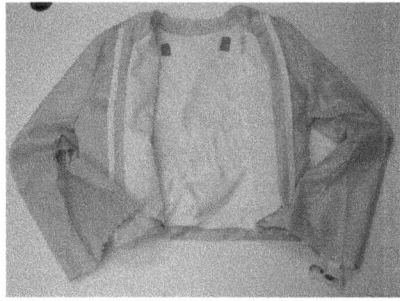

Figure 1: Prototype jacket (left), inside the jacket, showing the heat pads (right)

Actuation of *hug* messages took place via the generation of a warming sensation using heatable textiles, symbolising the warming sensation felt when touched by another person. The heat pads were located in the upper back of the jacket (on the shoulder blades, Figure 1). When a hug or embrace gesture is sent, the heat pads in the back of the jacket heat up.

A tactile actuator that attempted to simulate a *stroking* sensation was engineered using shape memory alloy wire and a pleated fabric insert. This pleated insert was located on the inside of the lower part of the sleeve so that it would slide against the topside of the lower part of the arm (see Figure 2). The placement of these actuators is informed by Argyle's 'vocabulary of touch' (Argyle 2001).

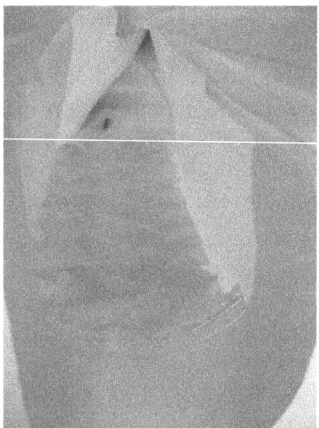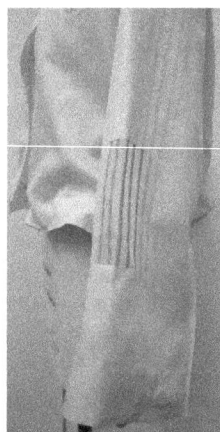

Figure 2: Stroke actuator inside sleeve (left), detail of touch sensor integrated into the sleeve (right)

Fibre-optics (see Figure 3) were engineered into the garment on the underside of the sleeves. Thus, a subjects by hugging themselves and stretching the mechanical stretch sensors able to deliver a warming sensation to the upper back of the partner. An arm stroke by the sender was received as pleated fabric being drawn up the arm. The recipient receives the touch message through actuation, as well as an SMS confirmation, saying 'hug shared', or 'left touch shared', etc. In addition, physiological arousal, as detected by the GSR sensors, was relayed to the partner by light being emitted from the fibre-optic section. The GSR took the form of textile electrodes integrated into a semi-glove configuration at the end of the sleeve in the garment, which wrapped around the index and second finger. GSR can detect levels of arousal; it cannot detect emotion on its own, but would need to be complemented with other sensor readings such as respiration, heart rate, etc. Using the GSR fits in well with the aims of the user study, in that we are not conducting a scientific experiment on the functionality of the GSR, but we are trying to create conditions in which participants can experience and *feel* the functionality afforded by the technology.

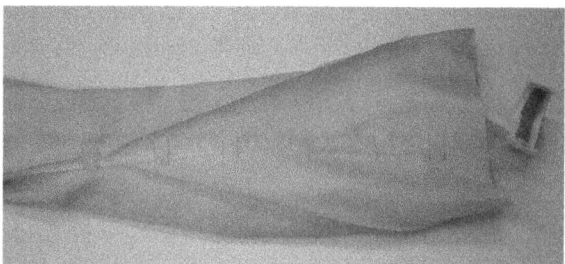

Figure 3: Light-emitting fibres integrated into the sleeve with GSR sensor at the end of the sleeve

User feedback

Four pairs of participants took part, a total of seven women and one man (aged between twenty and twenty-five), who were recruited locally (in Bristol). The pairs of participants were briefed on the functionality of the garments, which was also demonstrated to them. The participants then spent a period of time exchanging sensory messages or touch communication. Participants were not able to see each other, as they were separated by a partition in the lab. Afterwards pairs were interviewed together. All sessions were video-recorded and transcribed.

The aim of the study was to try to elicit from participants how they made sense of and interpreted the tactile sensations, in relation to their own perceptions of touch. Through having experienced the tactile sensation in relation to its given meaning, participants were asked to describe and articulate the particular qualities the sensation engendered, and compare those with their own experiences and associations. Participants were also asked to relate their experience with the prototype to their current mobile phone communication practices. During the interview we gauged how users experienced the sense of touch or presence, how they related this type of communication to their current communication practices. In addition we asked them to think of other tactile actuation types that would engender such a touch or presence.

Sensations of touch or presence

Some participants thought that the stroke actuator was 'creepy', saying that the creepiness was due to there being a feeling of the presence of someone, even though no one was there: *"When you feel something, and you know the other person is doing something, it does feel quite nice." "It felt like I was making a connection with someone near me." "Felt a bit creepy ... felt quite pleasant, but creepy because you felt someone but was there, but there was no one present."*

A couple said that the feeling was akin to a spider or insect: *"It (sleeve actuator) did not feel like someone was stroking my arm, it was more like a spider."*

And some thought it was too subtle to make a judgement upon: *"... was very close to a real brushing sensation. It was quite weird." "... it gave me a feeling of electricity going through me ... a warm and tingly feeling."*

The heat pads as metaphor for an embrace touch worked for some: *"The heat worked as a literal, and an abstract. You would of got the idea that someone is doing it to you ... the heat on the back." "The heat thing I liked, a bit like a hug; I felt my whole body heat up."*

The heat pads as metaphor for an embrace touch was thought to be largely dependent upon the location in the garment; with some subjects stating that it would be more effective if located on sensitive areas of the body. The feelings these sensations engender are largely socially constructed: *"I know that I'm not the only one that feels consoled by a hand on my lower back ... everyone that knows me well, would know that that means more to me."*

"If there were heat pads on my lower back then I would feel an embrace; that would be something that I would respond to." "... something that could be quite intimate, heat travelling up/down your spine ..."

The majority of participants had a clear preference for the light-emitting fibres. The GSR sensors linked to light-emitting fibres represented an interesting difference between doing something that is intentional (touch), and doing something that is unintentional. They liked the concept of knowing how the other person was feeling though the GSR sensors, a kind of subliminal messaging and mood sensing: *'What was most intriguing was the fact that she's having a reaction; maybe it's not to me, that doesn't matter, it's the fact that it is very personal to see someone's sweat represented by light. It is a personal or intimate thing." "The reason why I like the lights is because it's about how someone is feeling."*

There were comments indicating that the light-emitting fibres were preferable to other types of actuation as it is not something we would normally have access to, whilst the other types of sensing and actuating are trying to replace something we do have access to when face-to-face: *"... it's because it's something that you would never know; you can't read people's reactions in that way; you would never know someone's personal reaction* (under normal circumstances), *and then suddenly you can read it, it lights up, it's really in your face, the glow. I think it's that contrast between not knowing and then suddenly knowing; and you are the only one who knows." "What intrigues me is that it's* (GSR and fibre optics) *not trying to replace something else, because it's something unique."*

Most thought that seeing what was happening to the other person, *"communicating through your body"*, would make them feel closer to that person: *"I like the idea of people's feelings being communicated."*

The majority of participants stated that they would like to choose the location of actuators in the garment, as well as type of actuator. This was expressed from both a sender's and a recipient's point of view, as it might be a good mechanism for maintaining control and ensuring privacy by being able to make their own meanings. *"The absence of a meaning of what that* (the light-emitting fibres) *meant would be difficult for me."* For example, one respondent said they would like to be able to choose the location depending upon their knowledge of the recipient, or pressure points. This would enable users to express a shared understanding of each other, which would not be unintelligible to onlookers: *"I thought the location (of the fibre optics on the underside of the sleeve) was good, because this is the most emotional part ... this is something that is connected to my body, and it's not visible, it is private, for me." "You would want certain key words, like you could put your phone on 'flirt' mode and certain words or actions would trigger a 'hug' .... To have words that triggered emotions, feelings. You could assign certain key words to the function in the garment."*

Even though there is a limited range of actuator types, some subjects suggested that people might simply "re-programme" themselves and adapt. Similarly, a number of subjects thought the actuation strange at first, and stated that once they knew what to expect, such communication may become an accepted part of people's communications practices: *"I think that you develop your own language. You would re-programme yourselves to make associations with the different types of actuation ... you would end up knowing that that feeling would be someone sending you some love." "....people would think 'oh you are wearing a funny interactive broche', but actually you have just sent something to your friend and they got really excited"*, as it wouldn't mean anything to people outside of their group.

With regard to issues of privacy, the majority of subjects said they would like to be in control in relation to the people they are exchanging messages: *"If you were on the phone you could see a physical reaction of what someone just said. I don't think that would be too intrusive ... that would be a good option on the phone ... but I would only want to communicate with certain people."*

Relating this type of communication to communication practices

Comments indicated that it could be used in a similar way to text, or used to augment text. Participants related the use of emoticons in text messaging with tactile communication in on-going conversations, as *"in a text message you can't really read into emotions"* *"... the fibre optics in conjunction with words or texts would definitely work for me, because it is such an intimate thing; I can imagine doing that. ...but it would have to be used in a similar way to text, where you always know you might be wrong, you might misunderstand this person... words can be used in so many different ways."* *"... if my partner says "I look forward to seeing you", I send him a 'face', I don't say "yes, I'll meet you at blah, blah", I send him a 'face'. "It would be nice if, at the end of a text, you would get a hug."* One participant suggested that touch communication might work for her as *"I am a very tactile person"*, text is cold and impersonal: *"When you are speaking you have tone of voice, whereas in a text you can't really read into emotions."*

The majority of participants thought that it would be something they would use remotely, over distance, and not with people who are in the vicinity: *"If it was discretely telling you that you had a phone call, like as if there was something pulling on you ... a subtle signal as opposed to your phone vibrating."* *"Say you both are going into a similar situation, for example, shopping – and you get separated, you could communicate to each other and send each other messages about how you are feeling."* You can express yourself, you can touch the people you're with: *"What is attractive about this, is that you are doing your normal day stuff and suddenly you get something which is of a different nature than what you would expect, because it has been sent by somebody who is somewhere else."*

Participants thought that simply being able to sense someone's presence would have significant value: *"Just the fact that you are linked, you are communicating through several senses. When you are facing someone you have visual, tactile, spoken word, etc. And when you are remote you can't see that person all you have is text, spoken word, but if you can see things are happening to this person at the other end, you feel closer to that person.".* *"If you did it in a certain situation, when you know they would need support."* *"I think distance would be a good context in which to use it. It would be an emotional thing ..."* *"Family, friends – they do like to know that you are all right ... easy way to say 'hi, love you'."*

The difference between doing something intentional (touch) and unintentional or uncontrollable (GSR), that this clothing concept encompasses, was discussed, and in relation to that the issue of context awareness and a system that had the ability to learn about someone's patterns of behaviour: *"It would be good if you could move it around, depending upon what you're doing."* *"... when you are watching films."*

One or two participants said they might use it when the person with whom they are communicating is in the same space, or nearby, a kind of *"wink, wink, nudge, nudge"* communication: *"If you see your partner on the other side of the room, you can communicate what you are feeling ..."*

One participant suggested that they wouldn't use it in conjunction with text or voice communication: *"I would use it more after I hang up to show that I was still thinking about them. I am acknowledging about what we just talked about."*

Conversely, most thought they would use this communication as a means to console or support someone in a way they would when face-to-face, and/or in conjunction with voice communication: *"That (touching) is something you do automatically when someone is upset. So it would be nice to be able to do that to someone when you can't be with him or her" "When you feel very low or happy – important to receive that signal, that you know you are not alone."*

The study pairs were fairly evenly split on the issue of the people with whom they would communicate in this way. All participants stated that they would want to be in control over whom they had this kind of communication with. Approximately fifty percent of the pairs said they would only communicate in this way with partners or close friends, and not close family, i.e., parents or children. This group suggested that it would be with people with whom they have an intimate relationship such as a close friend; and maybe for people who don't have an established level of intimacy with their partner, but are aspiring to it: *"Someone that I had an intimate relationship with, and it was quite new, that might work, or a very good girlfriend, or male friend; someone who you are close to, but not as intimate as with your partner." "It would feel wrong if it was with someone in my immediate family." "My kids would use this for sure, more so the girls than the boys. They are very touchy amongst their girlfriends."*

Whilst the other half stated the exact opposite: *"The problem is that I am separated from my family; it would be great to feel that someone is close to me."*

A number of participants thought that this type of communication was a natural progression for the mobile phone. However, participants generally said they wouldn't want this type of communication all of the time, suggesting that it would be strange at first, but they could imagine that that perception might change. They equated this view with the mobile phone phenomenon, and the resulting impact on social norms, suggesting that if this concept becomes an established part of people's communication practices, then their frequency of use might change. It was largely thought that this concept would be a novelty unless it was widely accepted: *"(The mobile phone is not a gadget to me) ... anymore; it was at the start, and that's because it would be if only a few people had them; but obviously, everyone has got them now; it's become a necessity". "It was strange at first; don't know what you are going to feel ... once you got use to it, it is ok. I didn't know what I was going to be feeling, the not knowing ..."* "*You would sort of re-programme yourself to make associations with the different types of actuation ... you would end up knowing that that feeling would be someone sending you some love."*

Participants were asked if they would feel conspicuous gesturing to send messages in public spaces, which was discussed in relation to current cultures of self-touching, and nonverbal communication: *"Depends, I mean everyone is talking into headsets now, before I thought it looked odd. The more widespread it is, and then it becomes normal. Perhaps we will see everyone doing this in the supermarket."*

Other tactile actuation types engendering touch or presence

One study pair talked about the 'goose bump' effect, saying that touch should arouse the user in some way, whilst another talked about tickling sensations, suggesting that sensitive parts of the body could be targeted: *"Goose bumps, that's what I'm always after; you know when your mum brushes your hair, or when you're trying on different clothes, a piece of music .... it's kind of intimate, but it's kind of nice ... it's like a tickling feeling." "Stroking would be the nicest, if it generated a tickling sensation ... then it's a real touch."*

One or two participants said they would like to receive visual messages that communicated someone's mood: "If you could tell through what you were wearing how your friends were feeling. Like it would come up they were feeling anxious so you could send them a hug." "I think a mood thing ... a colour spectrum maybe ... of whether someone is anxious or happy."

Participants suggested that it would be valuable to build-up a repertoire of possible complements that might be used in particular situations, which was related to text messaging, where there are *"endless combinations"* of words available to us that make it *"a universal thing"*: *"... we have such high expectations of technology now; I think we are so spoiled with so much technology that I think the key to success with this project is its multiplicity. It would have to have a wealth of combinations, almost like words ... as many different levels or levels of intensity, or combinations, that you could possibly imagine." "Would be interesting if you combined the stroke with the heat, like a real hand, touching ... that would be my preference versus something that is changing colour, light."*

The participants were asked whether they favoured literal representations, where actuators could yield a pressing or contracting sensation, or more metaphoric ones. They were also asked what came to mind when they thought of touch: *"The feeling you get from someone you love, you get instantly – literal would be better. Abstract is very personal, more difficult ..." "The pressure with the 'hug'.*

Handholding – pressure and presence. Squeezing, reassuring feeling. A hand on your shoulder, a sort of 'stop', calm down, you're 'ok' feeling." "Pressure is an important thing."

Discussion

This study elicited user feedback to determine whether established sensory associations people have with the tactile qualities of textiles could be used as signs and metaphors for technology mediated experiences, moods, social interactions and gestures, related to interpersonal touch. We generated insights and inspiration for new design ideas around touch communication, and representation, simulation of touch gestures. In an iterative design exercise, we integrated design recommendations from a first study into the prototype used in the current study. We included a number of new textile sensors in the second iteration, namely galvanic skin response (GSR), touch, and gesture sensors. The touch and gesture sensors would enable users to exchange messages through self-touching. GSR can detect levels of arousal, which yielded interesting results as a kind of *subliminal* messaging, in comparison to the apparent *control* of touch and gesture sensors. The GSR sensor linked to a light-emitting textile actuator was undoubtedly favoured by most of the study pairs, as they liked the idea of feelings being communicated. The GSR was not viewed as trying to replace something we have when face-to-face, such as touch; it provides information we might never gain *even when* fact-to-face. The GSR represented an interesting difference to the touch and gesture sensors to participants, in that it is automatic and uncontrollable. Even though people can engage in self-touching, which is also unconscious (and can be viewed as mimed acts of being touched by someone else, and possibly indicating a desire or need to be touched), perhaps participants were not aware that the other sensors could be just as subliminal.

In response to the issue of a physical pressing or vibration sensation being *"more like something real"* from the first study, we included a shape-shifting textile actuator that moved up and down the arm, to represent a stroking action. We, again, based the design of these actuators on textile sensory descriptors, namely a silky-soft textile. It was interesting to see how participants compared the warming actuation with this shape-change/shifting actuation. It was largely felt the stroke actuator was too subtle, *"like an insect, barely touching"*, and the frequency of movement was too sudden to reflect an empathetic touch. Only one participant said that this actuator was like a real brushing sensation. Participants were equally divided on the issue of the heat actuator, with one half saying that they liked it and that it engendered a feeling of touch, and the other half saying that it was weird, strange and unusual.

In response to the suggestion that colour or a visual display might be a *"bridging"* step between voice and text communication and communication of physical sensations, we included photonic textiles as a symbol or metaphor for a participant's arousal, sensed by the GSR described above. This is a very different actuation compared with the touch actuations, one being intimate and invisible, and the other being visual and public. It is difficult to decouple the apparent meaning of the GSR sensor from the light-emitting textile, so it cannot be said whether or not participants liked the aesthetic of this or not. Only one study pair articulated that they would like clothing that glowed or flashed. The issue of textiles in clothing emitting light or colour for all to see did not trouble participants; only one participant stated that she would not like to show her emotions on her clothing, but there was a shared understanding amongst everyone that such concern can be offset through personalisation.

During discussions with most study pairs, comparisons were made between text messaging and this type of touch communication. It was largely thought that this product should *"embody a wealth of combinations, almost like words"*; to engender multiplicity and universality to allow for personalisation. Touch communication is *"a more primitive way of communicating"*, whereas words are more *"sophisticated"*. Hand-written letters can embody rich qualities, in terms of smell, and the handwriting, which might alter as the letter progresses. In terms of this clothing concept, if technology permitted, it would be interesting to introduce actuation that could change in frequency to convey a sense of intensity in a tactile message. There is an important issue of keeping *"spontaneity alive"*, as one participant commented, *"otherwise it becomes another emoticon"*. Therefore, using this type communication in certain contexts would be key, otherwise the 'hug' would become just a textile warming-up, as users become *"de-sensitised"*. Participants suggested that they would like to move the actuation around the garment, depending upon what they are doing, or upon their knowledge of the recipient, e.g., targeting sensitive parts of the body. One participant suggested that tactile communication could augment text messaging, where key words trigger certain types of actuation, thereby building up a repertoire of possible complements over time and through on-going conversations; this way meanings of such complements would be personally encoded. Conversely, about a third of the study pairs suggested that if sensations received were not what the user expected, you would *"re-programme yourself to make associations with the different types of actuation"*, thereby fostering a common under-standing of their meanings.

To summarise, participants generally liked the idea of being able to communicate feelings, particularly through GSR. Many of them suggested that this type of communication seemed like a natural progression. The heatable textiles were understood and seemed to correlate with about half of the participants' perceptions of touch. As in the first study, the tactile sensation of pressure corresponded with people's associations of touch. But we have gained some insights into the potential use of the sensory qualities of textiles in representing intimate communication. What we can conclude is that communication is personal, but just like writing, there is a need for a universal language of sensations that people can configure to make multiple meanings. It cannot be underestimated that we are at the beginning of exploration in designing for smart clothing. As textile technology progresses, more options will become available with which to fashion new types of sensations and aesthetics.

Conclusion and future work

In this chapter we have highlighted some of the related research around affective communication and wearable technology. There are many different approaches within this space, which perhaps suggests that it is an emerging area of interest. The findings from this exploratory study should be taken as a start to try to gain insights and understandings around this kind of communication using consumer fashion wearable technology, as part of an on-going iterative and participatory design process in the *Communication-Wear* programme. We adopted an experimental design approach in that we're using prototypes as research *probes,* and using the language of our material culture, namely fashion and textiles, as the focus for this research. We were conscious that if this concept is to support their daily lives, then it must look like it would. We have generated data that suggests how people might use this kind of touch communication to support or complement their current communication practices. We have also started to explore people's sensory associations of touch, and to relate those to textile attributes in order to gain inspiration for new designs for the actuation of touch communication. We used a relatively small test sample, because we wanted to carry out an in-depth exploration, rather than general perceptions from a larger body. The analysed findings from this study have been used to design and produce a third iteration, which is now being tested in a field-based study, during which we will explore the social aspects of this communication.

Acknowledgments

This research is supported by the Arts and Humanities Research Council through the AHRC's Fellowships in the Creative and Performing Arts scheme, UK.

References

Argyle M. Bodily Communication London: Routledge (2001)
Barnard M. Fashion as Communication London: Routledge (1996)
Baurley S. 'Interaction Design in Smart Textiles Clothing and Applications' ed. Tao X. Wearable Electronics and Photonics Cambridge: Woodhead (2005)
Bonanni L., Lieberman J, Vaucelle C., Zuckerman O., 'TapTap: A Haptic Wearable for Asynchronous Distributed Touch Therapy', Conference on Human-Computer Interaction. ACM Press: New York (2006), pp. 580-585
Brave S., Dahley A., 'inTouch: A Medium for Haptic Interpersonal Communication, Conference On Human Factors in Computing Systems (CHI '97), ACM Press: New York (1997), pp. 363-364 URL: http://www.cutecircuit.com/now/projects/wearables/fr-hugs (accessed January 2009)
Chang A., O'Modhrain S., Jacob R., Gunther E., Ishii H., 'ComTouch: Design of a Vibrotactile Communication Device' Proceedings of the conference on Designing Interactive Systems: Processes, Practices, Methods, and Techniques. ACM: New York (2002), pp. 312-320
Chang A., Koerner B., Resner B., Wang X., 'LumiTouch: An Emotional Communication Device. Extended abstracts of Conf. On Human Factors in Computing Systems' (CHI '01) New York: ACM Press (2001), pp. 313-314
Ekman P., Friesen W. 'The Repertoire of Non-Verbal Behaviour: Categories, Origins, Usage, and Coding' Semiotica 1 (1969) pp. 49-98
Euratex 'European Technology Platform for the Future of Textiles and Clothing: A Vision for 2020'. The European Apparel and Textile Organisation report (2004)
Fiske J., O'Sullivan T., Key Concepts in Communication and Cultural Studies London: Routledge (1994)
Fortunati L., Katz J. E., Riccini R. eds. Mediating the Human Body: Technology, Communication, and Fashion Mahwah, New Jersey: Lawrence Erlbaum Associates (2003)
Gemperle F., Di Salvo C., Forlizzi J., Yonkers W. 'The Hug: a new form for communication' Proceedings of Designing for user experiences. ACM Press: New York (2003), pp. 1-4
Jones S. E., Yarborough, A. E. 'A Naturalistic Study of the Meanings of Touch' Communication Monographs 52 (1985) pp. 19–56
Lasen A. A Comparative Study of Mobile Phone Use in Public Spaces in London, Madrid and Paris Vodafone (2002)
Morris D. People Watching London: Vintage (2002)
Paradiso R., Loriga G., Taccini N. 'Wearable Health-Care System for Vital Signs Monitoring' IFMBE Proceedings of Health Telematics 2004 6 (2004)

Paulos E. 'Connexus: A Communal Interface' New York: ACM (2003)
Photopoulos S., 'Smart Fabrics and Interactive Textiles: OEM and End-User Requirements, Preferences and Solution Analysis', USA, VDC, (2006)
Randell C., Baurley S., Anderson I., Müller H., P. Brock P. 'The Sensor Sleeve: Sensing Affective Gestures' Workshop Proceedings of 9th IEEE International Symposium on Wearable Computers (2005)
Rettie R. M. 'Presence and Embodiment in Mobile Phone Communication' PsychNology Journal 3 (2005) pp. 16–34
Rheingold H. Smart Mobs: The Next Social Revolution Cambridge, MA: Basic Books (2002)
Williams R. Culture. Fontana New Sociology Series, Glasgow: Collins (1981)

Larissa Hjorth

Beyond the Frame: The Place of Mobile and Immobile Media

Introduction

Over the last couple of years we have become customized to the global media informing us of the revolutionary and democratic possibilities of mobile media. In one way, the rise of mobile media parallels the rise of the webcam (Koskela 2004) by enabling everyday users to document and edit their stories. However, mobile media promises more to become the portal to new arising forms of distribution such as MySpace, Facebook, Cyworld mini-hompy, YouTube etc. These new modes of sharing and context perform new modes of mobility. However, in the excitement to document Web 2.0 convergence, some dimensions of mobile media – most notably its oscillation between forms of mobilism and immobility, delay and immediacy – are being overlooked. So how can we conceptualize the types of visual, aural and more importantly, haptic economies that are occurring around mobile media convergence?

One of the dominant features of mobile media is noted by what Ilpo Koskinen (2007) characterizes as 'the aesthetics of banality'. Much work has been conducted around the mobile media practices in terms of camera phone visual and distribution characteristics; however, it seems that the haptic economies, so particular to mobile media, are in need of re-evaluation. Mobile media can encompass a multitude of practices from camera phone imagery, SMS, mobile movies and mobile gaming. Whilst Mizuko Ito and Daisuke Okabe's 3 S's (2003) – sharing, storing and saving – noted some of the particular features of mobile media, we need to examine the politics of 'waiting for immediacy' just outside the frame. Mobile media challenges the ocular-centricism of 20th century screen cultures, de-focusing the primacy for the visual in favour of effectual economies such as the haptic. But if the *flâneur*'s 'frame-centrism' has been surpassed by the phoneur's (Luke 2005) 'beyond the frame' practices, how do we develop paradigms to account for the haptic workouts occurring just outside the frame that undoubtedly affect inside the frame? How do we account and document the increasingly art of documenting? What is this 'waiting for immediacy' backlash so prevalent in a diversity of everyday practices?

Waiting for immediacy: locating mobile media

The birth of mobile media could be viewed as nascent. However such a belief, propagated in global media's lauding of the new mobile revolution in consumer agency – in the form of a reworked Alvin Toffler's (1980) prosumer (consumer as part of the production proess) and Web 2.0 – neglects to address the dynamic dimensions of technology. In the rise of the ubiquitous rubric of mobile media, many forms of practices have emerged – from micro-movies (that is, movies made for the mobile devices) and pocket films (movies made by the mobile device to be screened either on the mobile device or other screens including the cinema) to casual and hybrid games that involve cross platforming techniques including Social Networking Systems (SNS). In this emergence of mobile media, the prosumer has transformed into the producer/user conflation of 'produser' (Bruns 2007) as part of a broader global trend towards 'full-time intimacy'.

From social intimacy to creative user content, labor has taken on various immaterial and material guises. These new forms of labor and intimacies are what has been termed as the technics of mobility (Murphie 2007). Technics of mobility, in the context of mobility, refer to expressive forms of mobility and immobility across socio-emotive, psychological, economic, political and geographic terrains. They produce localized imaging communities characterized by camera phone images and vernacular text messages as well as new commodity forms such as mobile novels.

As mobile communication and new media industries converge, the all-pervasive futurist rhetoric becomes stifling. And yet, if the twin histories of new media and mobile communication have taught us anything, the 'new' is always mediated and remediated. This cuts to the core of all communication and cultural practices implicated in intimacy. For Jay Bolter and Richard Grusin (1999) new media is remediated with older media into a dynamic ongoing process that disrupts any causal or linear notion of old and new technologies. As Margaret Morse (1998) concisely notes in the case of the Internet, all forms of intimacy are mediated – by language, gestures, and memories. Emerging forms of visual, textual and haptic mobile genres such as SMS and camera phone practices – re-enacting earlier rituals such as 19th century letter writing, postcards (Hjorth 2005) and gift-giving customs (Taylor & Harper 2002) – have only served to highlight the remediated nature of the rise of mobile media.

As I have argued elsewhere (Hjorth 2007a), there is much to be learnt from understanding the parallels between new media theory on remediation and mobile communication's usage of the domestic technologies approach. In order to fully understand such projects as location-aware mobile gaming, we need to draw from both new media remediation and mobile communication domestic technologies approach. Like the domestic technologies approach (Silverstone & Hirsch 1992; Miller 1987), the study of new media through the lens of remediation echoes a similar philosophical stance. As influential theorist in the field of media-archaeology, Erkki Huhtamo has argued, the cyclical phenomena of media tends to transcend historical contexts, often placating a process of paradoxical re-enactment and re-enchantment with what is deemed as 'new' (1997).

According to Timo Kopoma, the mobile phone is an extension of 19th century media (2000). For Kopoma, mobile media creates a new 'third' space in between public and private space. On the one hand, the project of examining mobile media entails observing the remediated nature of new technologies and thus conceptualizing them in terms of media archaeologies (Huhtamo 1997). On the other hand, mobile media's re-enactment of earlier technologies is indicative of its domestic technologies tradition that extends and rehearses the processes of precursors such as radio and TV.

Both traditions emphasize the cyclic and dynamic process of media technologies that cannot be simplistically divided between old and new. Rather, the cartography of mobile media is one imbued by paradoxes. In the case of camera phone practices – whether still or moving – mobile media demonstrates two distinctive paradoxes, that of the reel in the real, and the inherent poetics of delay in the practice of immediacy. As Lev Manovich (2003) identified, contemporary new media and digital practice is all consumed by fetishising the 'real' through the lens of the reel – that is, texture and skin of the analogue as a process embroiled in the haptic as much as the visual.

Camera phone practices, as an extension of photography and snapshots, are about performing normality (Gye 2005; Lee 2005). This can be done by re-enacting 'reel' techniques, that is, analogue representational codes. Contemporary digital media is obsessed with the analogue that can be seen from its software (Photoshop, final cut) to the fact that it tries to resemble the reel rather than the actual (Manovich 2003). Through the rise of mobile media, and attendant forms of frames from SMS, MMS to SNS the 'banal' reel is rendered 'newsworthy' and relevant to the receiver (Koskinen 2007, 51). In this way, contextualizing is central to the content of mobile media and in the case of MMS it is a process akin to that of the postcard (Hjorth 2005).

As with the postcard, there are archetypical "tourist" samples provided which then need to be contextualized in terms of the sender's experiences and voice otherwise the image is just rendered banal. Often camera phone practices re-enact older images and genres in the act of the reel as an ode to the gestures, rather than spectacle, of analogue. One of the significant features of the postcard is that it bears the markings of place, both in the form of actual stamp and also the damage occurred whilst in transit. The postcard is not a visual experience and to vindicate it to visual aesthetics misses the point. Thus the co-presence and intimacy actually occurs on a haptic level, with the receiver feeling the texture of place in the postcard's grain. This is highlighted by the need of readers to hold the postcard in the hand, rather than just look at it vicariously. Stroking the postcards, seeing if you can feel the sender's touch, if feeling the images.

Although MMS images need to be contextualized to give them meaning beyond the banality of the everyday, postcards need to be contextualized from symbols of tourist clichés into the sender's "ordinary" interpretation and experience. But both involve the haptic. In particular, as my research (Hjorth 2009) on camera phone practices in Seoul, Tokyo, Hong Kong and Melbourne has noted, many respondents prefer to show and view camera phone images on the mobile phone while sitting with friends. It becomes a way to reflect and a site for confession. The phone is passed back and forth, the gesture of touch and perpetual symbolic gift-giving (Taylor & Harper 2002) heightens the experience.

As the practice of analogue diminishes with the turn of the century, one of the key fallacies of the 20th century becomes apparent – the tyranny of visuality. However, what renders the analogue as such a significant practice had less to do with the visual end products and more to do with the perpetual process of production. The process of analogue always had inbuilt poetics of delay. In an age fuelled by continuously progressive notions of immediacy, tactics of delay are increasingly more important. This can be witnessed by the process between the taking of the picture, the film processing and the viewing. This delay was temporal and spatial, creating a space for contemplation and reflection before the 'rewind' moment of viewing. Another key feature of the analogue was the role of the *haptic*.

Researchers in screen cultures soon began to realize that it was the haptic space of the cinema, or the domestic sphere, that transformed modes of engagement. This was evident in John Ellis's *Visible Fictions* (1987) in which he demonstrated how unproductive the emphasis on visual comparison between film and TV could be – such an exercise only served to reduce the cultures to binary oppositions whereby TV became about the glance and cinema about the gaze. This is what led new media theorist Chris Chesher (2004) to argue that mobile gaming cultures are about the 'sticky reflexivity' of the 'glaze' (gaze and glance conflated). Drawing on console games cultures, Chesher identifies three types of glaze spaces – the glazed over, sticky and identity-reflective. For Chesher, these three 'dimensions' of the glaze move beyond a visual economy, deploying the filters of the other senses such as aural and haptic. The glaze is more about the haptic than the visual. The haptic involves often dialectical tensions between mobility and immobility, delay and immediacy; such concepts that spill outside the frame.

Beyond the frame: emerging mobile media and the politics of the haptic

In order to engage with mobile media we need to think beyond the frame and contemplate the haptic procedural practices. In an epoch dominated by a 'mobility turn' (Urry 2000), the tactic of immobility and delay are increasingly evolving. For Bryan Turner (2007), global mobility (technological, cultural, and economic) is creating more enclaves and immobilities rather than flows. For Maria Bakardjieva (Bakardjieva 2003; Bakardjieva & Feenberg, 2004), we should not stop focusing upon 'mobile privatization' (Williams 1974) and instead consider the productive tactics of 'immobile socialization'. Bakardjieva's case is particularly prevalent in Korea – a country crowded with high broadband capabilities (OECD 2006) and 4 G (fourth generation) mobile media – whereby the continuing significance of the immobile and social *PC bang* (PC room) is the preferred space for most youth to engage with online and offline communities.

Through the lens of localized convergent mobile and immobile technologies we can gain insight into emerging forms of social capital, individualism and a sense of public discourse. In studies on the localization of the Internet, the role of the haptic is becoming of more prevalence as a key factor in how people negotiate online and offline co-presence. Where and how people access the Internet influences the relationship between mobility and mobilism; that is, the localized practice of being mobile and immobile that traverses online and offline spaces. The accessing of the Internet via the mobile phone creates a different sense of embodiment between online and offline co-presence than utilising the stationary and bigger PC. For Kenichi Fujimoto, mobilism is the 'broader cultural and social dimensions such as malleability, fluctuation and mobilization' (Fujimoto 2005, 80). Unlike mobilism, 'mobility has tended to refer to functional dimensions of portability and freedom from social and geographic constraint' (Fujimoto 2005, 80). In sum, mobilism is tied to socio-geographic factors, whereas mobility infers transcendence, particularly around geographic constraints. In the case of mobile communication, we are seeing new forms of mobilism and mobility.

In this space of mobilism and mobility, we could argue that new forms of mobility and immobility become apparent. These concurrent forces operate dialectically, in tandem with forces such as convergence and divergence (Jenkins 2006) across various social, cultural, industrial, and technological levels. If we stay fixated on the frame and visuality, such notions as mobility and immobility, delay and immediacy, convergence and divergence, public and private remain unproductive and simplistic binaries. However, in the phenomenological haptic space just outside the frame we can see a complex play around temporal and spatial currencies. In the case of mobile media practices from camera phone images to mobile gaming, visual binaries – and thus the fixture of the screen and frame – are perpetually displaced.

The inertia of mobile media: delay and immediacy

Mobile media requires us to reconsider the role of the visual – whether it is beyond a frame or a screen – in the light of haptic modes of mobility and immobility. These concepts are prevalent in the rise of customization in the form user created content (UCC) and emerging forms of social and creative labour. In my (aforementioned) ethnographic studies into camera phone practices in Seoul, Tokyo, Hong Kong and Melbourne from 2004-2007, one of the key features of co-presence around mobile media customization is the tension and oscillation between immediacy and delay.

Many respondents spoke of their pretence not to see the SMS or MMS so that they could savour and contemplate – partake in *the poetics of delay* – rather than impulsively respond to the relentless 'leash' (Qiu 2007) of immediate technologies. In the rise of mobile media one can note the initial move away from synchronous media such as voice calling towards asynchronous media such as SMS, MMS and camera phone practices. It is this asynchronous media that creates new forms of paradoxes that seem to be inherent to contemporary new media practices. The more innovative the media, the more it taxes, rather than saves, user's time. However, built into the increasing acceleration of immediacy politics is the tactics of resistance, the poetics of delay.

Mobile media is fecund with invisible nodes of delay that users attempt to deploy in order to resist the tyranny of increasing work/life demands. This is demonstrated by the fact that the applications that have been most popular within a diversity of cultures have, along with the variety of socio-cultural factors, been technologies of delay. As social and creative labour becomes all-pervasive and customization transforms into an involuntary act of individualism (Castells et al. 2007, 251), it is the built-in pauses that become increasingly important. This trend has been a key characteristic in my ethnographic research of mobile media personalization in the Asia-Pacific (Hjorth 2005; Hjorth 2009). For example, a female university student in Korea aged 22 noted how she had become the unofficial documenter of hers and her friend's events. The respondent detailed how she had to spend time photographing, deleting, editing, saving and sharing the images. The role of caretaker for the group's memories of their everyday activities was initially fun and rewarding, but after a while the respondent found the job exceptionally time consuming. In order to resign without scorn, the respondent pretended the camera on her phone ceased to work so the role of customisation could be shared with other members.

This tactic of deferring responsibility for customization is not uncommon in other case study locations. Rather, it is but one example of everyday practice of delay. For example, many respondents in my Melbourne case study (2004 – 2006) spoke of the pretence of 'immediately' responding to a message when, actually, they often contemplated their responses. Increasingly, as the mobile phone has grown into a multimedia device, so too has the amount of time needed to customize also risen. This can be conceptualized more broadly as emerging cartographies of personalization whereby the mapping of identity and socio-emotional economies moves and freezes across material and immaterial terrains. While the rise in multimedia device has been heralded in prosumer rhetoric as a democracy of multimedia and new media discourses, the darker, less productive side in which social and creative labour is exploited remains under-explored. This becomes particularly prevalent in case studies conducted in Seoul (2007) and Tokyo (2003) where media such as the Internet are intrinsically interwoven within the space of mobile media and Web 2.0 SNS such as mixi (in Japan) and Cyworld mini-hompy (in Korea); spaces in which the demand for high social and creative outputs was often relentless.

Undoubtedly, part of the explanation for the under-explored realms of mobile media is the fact that they are still discussed and engaged as an extension of the 20th century screen cultures. On one hand, mobile media, like all new media, are 'remediated', reconfiguring older media genres and modes of authorship. Practices, such as camera phone imagery clearly draw on the discourses of analogue photography (Gye 2005; Lee 2005; Hjorth 2007a). On the other hand, mobile media emerges with new paradigms of authorship and affect. Factors such as the 'portable, pedestrian and personal' (Ito et al. 2005) mean that mobile media creates a new intimate discourse with the body (Fortunati 2003).

Moreover, the multimodality entails the opening across various screens – what has been called cross-platform media. It is this cross-platform nature – which creates convergence and divergence (Jenkins 2006) across industrial, technological and cultural contexts – which is so particular to mobile media. With the new and yet remediated modes of engagement and context, emerging notions such as the 'producer' (Bruns 2007) prevail as testaments to both the joys and frustrations of the increasing conflations between work and life (Wajcman et al. 2009).

Returning to Koskinen's notion, the multimedia of mobile media is undoubtedly ordered by the logic of banality (Koskinen 2007, 48). The visuality of camera phone images is often low resolution 'snapshots' of the everyday, inflections of the users' subjectivity and social capital. Echoing Ito's and Okabe's emphasis on context rather than content, Koskinen's banality notion is significant in signposting the need of mobile media research to move beyond the focus on visuality in and between different frames, focussing instead upon the politics of what Chesher defines as 'glaze' cultures (Chesher 2004).

Reels of the banal: mobile media as new media

Discourses on the possibilities for experimentation have seen many artists and theorists orientating themselves around the role of mobile media as not just as a miniature and mobile version of the conventional gallery space. UK's The-phonebook Limited have explored the emergent genres of SMS, MMS and ring tones to highlight the conventions and codes (compression, immediacy, intimacy) of these remediated and vernacular-driven discourses. For example, SMS poems being poems restricted to the formats of SMS compression (i.e. 160 characters). In Proboscis' 'urban tapestries' project, a section of London is navigated and reorientated through mobile location devices, making one recognise that mobile media reinforces place rather than destroys it; highlighting the persistence of delay in the practice of immediate co-presence (Lane & Thelwall 2006; Fleuriot et al. 2004).

In Seoul, Interactive and Practice (INP) consisting of artists, engineers and media theorists headed by Taeyoon Choi, attempts to circumnavigate everyday practices with mobile media inventions (Hjorth 2007b). Initially re-enacting the success of the pervasive mobile game PacManhattan (Pac Man played out on the streets of Manhattan coordinated by geographic positioning systems and walkie talkies) in the streets of shopping district Myeong-dong, INP moved onto projects such as 'shoot me if you can' consisting of teams competing to camera phone without being 'shot'. Here the allegory of the photographic genre of snapshot (once used as a military term) is re-enacted by the function of the camera phone to shoot people and thereby eliminate them from the game. Having conducted residencies at the only Korean new media centre, Nabi, in 2005 and 2006, INP's autonomy from the centre (which is funded by the South Korean giant, SK Telecommunication) has resulted in the development of much more experimental projects such as DOTPLAY, a mobile hacking workshop. In many of INP projects, the significance of the haptic cannot be underestimated.

And yet, what has been significant about these various projects around mobile media – from location aware projects conducted by INP to mobile movie making – has been the re-occurrence of the reel/real, delay/immediacy paradoxes. This undoubtedly has to do with mobile media's ability to epitomise the paradox Michael Arnold calls 'Janus-faced' (2003) and Jack Qiu describes as 'wireless leash' (2007). The experience of the virtual is always at play in the offline space of the haptic; far from them becoming seamless, the politics of immediately is always the *poetics of delay*.

In June 2007, the Pompidou Museum (Paris) featured its annual Pocket Films festival (http://www.festivalpocketfilms.fr/). The basement of the Pompidou was awash with a sea of dangling mobile phones. Once viewers adapted to the 'newness' of the media and stopped looking at the mobile phones as commodities and objects of desire and began peering into them as portals for creative product, they began to engage. In this case, the engagement of mobile media users and viewers is similar whether partaking in 'new media' realms (as the context of the Pompidou would entail) or experiencing the everyday context of the 'normal' mobile media user. In both cases the engagement is not the gaze nor the glance, but it is rather akin to the aforementioned notion of the 'glaze' (Chesher 2004).

This formation of the glaze – a combination of aural and haptic into what I would call the 'hapral'– was apparent in the fact that spectators often stood with their ear towards the mobile phone, as if to listen to the pictures. The aural and haptic spectre of the domestic technology of the TV lingered. The movies that were most popular were not those that featured vivid visuals, but rather those that featured compelling aural narratives. Over-riding these factors was the significance of the holding of the device, with viewers often hugging or cradling the item. Viewers seemed to spend much time 'trying on' the device so that it became an intimate part of the viewer's body. While much work by social scientists has explored camera phone ethnographies in locations such as Tokyo (Ito & Okabe 2002; 2005) and Seoul (Lee 2005; Hjorth 2007a), one of the features that is becoming increasingly apparent is the rise of other senses such as aural and haptic in the contextualization and making 'reel' these images.

Indeed, one of the compelling factors to arise from mobile media, and this links back to its fusion with remediation and domestic genealogies, is the persistence of the ontology of the reel. Like the 20th century 'reel' – and its various modes of 'screen-ness' address – the mobile reel, and thus possible creative worlds and realities, is undoubtedly governed by the haptic (Richardson 2007). Thus, to analyse the multiple realities of mobile media we need to focus upon both the movement and stasis of the reel.

Haptic screens: glazing at banality

If, as art critic Robert Hughes (1991) said, the 20th century modernism was the 'shock of the new', then could mobile media not be defined, as indicative of the 21st century new media, as the 'banality of the new'? That is, as Terry Flew (2002) asks, what is so 'new' about new media? Certainly, Koskinen's prescient work in the field of mobile media as multimedia suggests so. However, it is important to realise that the politics of banality is one deeply entrenched in the practice of the everyday. As Meaghan Morris (1988) notes, the politics of what is conceived as banal partakes in power relations of normalization and naturalization that should not be overlooked. Indeed, many of the senses, such as smell, touch and sound –that are so pivotal to memories and subjectivity-have been rendered insignificant to the tyranny of visual culture dominating the 19th and especially 20th century media cultures. However, in the case of mobile media, with its history firmly entrenched in aural media such as telephone, radio and TV, the regime of the glaze could take hold in this century.

In Ingrid Richardson's compelling argument about mobile media she calls on the need to harness the importance of the haptic. Departing from what Lucas Intora and Fernando Ilharco (2004) characterize as the multiple 'screen-ness' inhabiting contemporary life, Richardson (2007, 210) argues, 'yet this "frontal" relationship which is typical of our engagement with most screens-where the mediums of cinema, television and computer can be said to discipline the body more or less into a face-to-face interaction-is thoroughly challenged by the mobile screen'. In conclusion, Richardson avows that mobile media disrupts 'any notion of a disembodied telepresence' deployed by much screen-based media; in turn, we can 'see emergent spatial ontologies of a kind never before experienced in such a collective and interactive fashion' (Richardson 2007, 214). While Richardson's argues for a future in mobile media, particularly in the case of location aware mobile gaming, where the virtual and the actual become seamless, I would argue that the future, like the past, is ordered by the persistence of the reel and delay. Two key features that will always be mediated by the glaze and its legacy in gaze and glance genealogies.

Whether it is a pervasive location aware game, or a mobile movie, the exciting contextual possibilities of mobile media are its related networked avenues and challenges to the notions of co-presence and intimacy. That is, the more we try to overcome difference and distance, the less we do so. This recites what aforementioned Arnold (2003) identified as the janus-faced nature of mobile media that operates to push and pull us, setting us free to roam and yet attach us to a perpetual leash. For anyone that has participated in a mobile pervasive game, they will quickly identify the lack of coherence-or janus-faced relationship-between online and offline co-presence. The more we try to partake in the politics of immediacy, the more we succumb to the poetics of delay. This paradox, which governs the practice and theory of contemporary location aware mobile media, is a phenomenon not to overcome (which is impossible anyway). Rather, it is in the gap between immediacy and delay that we can reflect upon, and indeed glaze, the practice of the game of what it means to be intimate and co-present today.

References

Arnold M. 'On the Phenomenology of Technology: The "Janus-Faces" of Mobile Phones' Information and Organization 13 (2003) pp. 231-256

Bakardjieva M. 'Virtual Togetherness: An Everyday-life Perspective' Media Culture Society 25 (2003) pp. 291-313

Bakardjieva M., Feenberg A. 'Virtual Community: No "Killer Implication"' New Media & Society 6 (2004) pp. 37-43

Bolter J., Grusin R. Remediation: Understanding New Media Cambridge, MA: The MIT Press (1999)

Bruns A. 'Produsage: Towards a Broader Framework for User-Led Content' URL: http://snurb.info/files/12132812018_towards_produser_0.pdf(2007)(accessed January 2009)

Castells M., Fernandez-Ardevol M., Linchuan Qui J., Araba S. Mobile Communication and Society: A Global Perspective Cambridge, MA: The MIT Press (2004)

Chesher C. 'Neither Gaze nor Glance, but Glaze: Relating to Console Game Screens' SCAN: Journal of Media Arts Culture 1: 1 URL: http://scan.net.au/journal/ (2004) (accessed January 2009)

Ellis J. Visible Fictions: Cinema, Television, Video London: Routledge and Kegan Paul (1987)

Fleuriot C., Wood L., Williams M., Jones O. 'Contextual Geographies and Children's Wireless Soundscapes' URL: http://www.ordnancesurvey.co.uk (2004) (accessed January 2009)

Flew T. New Media: An Introduction South Melbourne: Oxford University Press (2002)

Fortunati L. 'Real People, Artificial Bodies' eds. Fortunati L., Katz J. E., Riccini R. Mediating the Human Body: Technology, Communication and Fashion Mahwah, NJ: Lawrence Erlbaum (2003)

Fujimoto K. 'The Third-Stage Paradigm: Territory Machine from the Girls' Pager Revolution to Mobile Aesthetics' eds. M. Ito M., Okabe D., Matsuda M. Personal, Portable, Pedestrian: Mobile Phones in Japanese Life, Cambridge, MA: The MIT Press (2005)

Gye L. 'Picture This' Vital Signs Conference, September, ACMI, Melbourne (2005)

Hjorth L. 'Postal Presence: The Persistence of the Post Metaphor in Current SMS/MMS Practices' Fibreculture Journal 6 URL: http://journal.fibreculture.org (2005) (accessed January 2009)

Hjorth L. 'Snapshots of Almost Contact: Case Study on South Korea' Continuum 21: 2 (2007a) pp. 227-238

Hjorth L. 'Domesticating New Media: A Discussion on Locating Mobile Media' eds. Goggin G., Hjorth L. Mobile Media Sydney: University of Sydney (2007b)

Hjorth L. Mobile Media in Asia-Pacific: Gender and the Art of Being Mobile London: Routledge (2008)
Hughes R. The Shock of the New London: Thames and Hudson (1991)
Huhtamo E. 'From Kaleidoscomaniac to Cybernerd: Notes Toward an Archaeology of the Media' Leonardo 30 (1997) pp. 221-224
Intora L. D., Ilharco F. M. 'The Ontological Screening of Contemporary Life: A Phenomenological Analysis of Screens' European Journal of Information Systems 13 (2004) pp. 221-234
Ito M., Okabe D. 'Camera Phones Changing the Definition of Picture-Worthy' Japan Media Review URL: http://www.ojr.org/japan/wireless/1062208524.php (2003) (accessed January 2009)
Ito M., Okabe D. 'Intimate Visual Co-Presence' Paper presented at UbiComp 2005, 11-14 September, Tokyo, Japan URL: http://www.itofisher.com/mito (2005) (accessed January 2009)
Ito M., Okabe D., Matsuda M. eds. Personal, Portable, Pedestrian: Mobile Phones in Japanese Life Cambridge, MA: The MIT Press (2005)
Jenkins H. Convergence Culture: Where Old and New Media Collide: Where Old and New Media Collide New York: New York University Press (2006)
Kopoma T. The City in Your Pocket: Birth of the Mobile Information Society Helsinki: Gaudemus (2000)
Koskela H. (2004) 'Webcams, TV Shows and Mobile phones: Empowering Exhibitionism' Surveillance & Society 1 (2004) pp. 199-215
Koskinen I. 'Managing Banality in Mobile Multimedia' ed. Pertierra R. The Social Construction and Usage of Communication Technologies: European and Asian Experiences Singapore: Singapore University Press (2007)
Lane G., Thelwall S. 'Urban Tapestries: Public Authoring, Place and Mobility' URL: http://socialtapestries.net/outcomes/reports/UT_Report_2006.pdf (2006) (accessed January 2009)
Lee D. H. 'Women's Making of Camera Phone Culture' Fibreculture Journal 6 URL: http://journal.fibreculture.org (2005) (accessed January 2009)
Luke R. 'The Phoneur: Mobile Commerce and the Digital Pedagogies of the Wireless Web' ed. Pericles Trifonas P. Communities of Difference: Culture, Language, Technology New York: Palgrave MacMillan (2005)
Manovich L. 'The paradoxes of Digital Photography' ed. Wells L. The Photography Reader London: Routledge (2003)
Miller D. Material Culture and Mass Consumption London: Blackwell (1987)
Morris M. 'Banality in Cultural Studies' Discourse 10 (1988) pp. 3-29
Morse M. Virtualities: Television, Media Art, and Cyberculture. Bloomington: Indiana University Press (1998)

Organization for Economic Co-operation and Development OECD Broadband Statistics URL: http://www.oecd.org/sti/ict/broadband (2006) (accessed January 2009)

Qiu J. 'The Wireless Leash: Mobile Messaging Service as a Means of Control' International Journal of Communication 1 (2007) pp. 74-91

Richardson I. 'Pocket Technoscapes: The Bodily Incorporation of Mobile Media' Continuum: Journal of Media & Cultural Studies 21 (2007) pp. 205-216

Silverstone R., Hirsch E. eds. Consuming Technologies: Media and Information in Domestic Spaces London: Routledge (1992)

Taylor A., Harper R. 'Age-old Practices in the "New World": A Study of Gift-giving between Teenage Mobile Phone Users' Changing Our World, Changing Ourselves. The Proceedings of the SIGCHI Conference on Human Factors in Computing Systems, Minneapolis (2002)

Turner B. 'The Enclave Society: Towards a Sociology of immobility' European Journal of Social Theory 10 (2007) pp. 287-303

Urry J. Sociology beyond Societies: Mobilities for the Twenty-first Century London: Routledge (2000)

Wajcman J. 'Intimate Connections: The Impact of the Mobile Phone on Work Life Boundaries' eds. Goggin G., Hjorth L. Mobile Technologies London: Routledge (2008)

Williams R. Television: Technology and Cultural Form London: Collins (1974)

Authors

Sharon Baurley is a Reader at the Central Saint Martins College of Art & Design, University of the Arts London. Baurley's research is concerned with using design probes to gain an insight into the catalysts and drivers, and potential emergent consumer behaviour for a new genre of clothing where fashion converges with smart materials and digital technologies. With Philippa Brock, Erik Geelhoed and Andrew Moore he has co-authored a number of papers in the last few years. The most recent ones are: 'Communication-Wear: User Feedback as Part of a Co-Design Process' published in *Proceedings of the 2nd International Workshop on Haptic and Audio Interaction Design* (HAID 2007) (Springer 2007) and 'Communication-Wear' published in *Adjunct Proceedings of Ubicomp 2007 – Transitive materials: Towards an integrated approach to material technology, a workshop of the 9th International Conference on Ubiquitous Computing* (Springer 2007).

Marina Borovik graduated from the Moscow State Institute of International Relations (MGIMO-University), School of International Economic Relations. She holds a Ph.D. in economics and works as a Senior Researcher at the Institute of Scientific Information for Social Sciences (INION) of the Russian Academy of Sciences. Borovik's areas of research interest are: the influence of ICT on users' behaviour searching for economic information, improvement of social sciences retrieval, the creation of a thesaurus on economics, the formation of a problem-oriented database on economics and demography. With Liudmila Shemberko she was recently published 'Information Support of Demographic Researches: Electronic Resources and Services)' in Russian in *Proceedings of the All-Russia Conference: National Identity of Russia and Demographic Crisis* (Scientific Expert 2007) and 'Information Support of Economic Researches using Electronic Resources in the journal *Scientific and Technical Information Processing (NTI) (Vol. 1, 2009)*.

Philippa Brock is a Woven Textiles Specialist Subject Leader at the Central Saint Martins College of Art & Design, University of the Arts London, and also works as a textile designer, consultant and researcher. Brock's research interests include developing smart textile systems (circuits, switches and sensors), exploring in particular aesthetics, handle, drape and conductivity. Her selected publications include: 'Communication-Wear: User Feedback as Part of a Co-Design Process' published in *Proceedings of the 2nd International Workshop on Haptic and Au-*

dio Interaction Design (HAID 2007) (Springer 2007) and 'Communication-Wear' published in the *Adjunct Proceedings of Ubicomp 2007 – Transitive materials: Towards an integrated approach to material technology, a workshop of the 9th International Conference on Ubiquitous Computing* (Springer 2007) – both with Andrew Moore, Erik Geelhoed and Sharon Baurley.

María Beatriz Galán is a Professor of the Methodology of Industrial and Graphic Design at the Creation Centre of the University of Buenos Aires. She directs the programme of the Transference of Design at the University of Buenos Aires, and is a co-founder of Itaca Net (Latin-American Net of the Transference of Design and Innovation to emerging communities). She has given presentations conferences at universities in France, Brazil, Colombia, Finland and Ecuador on the topics of innovation, design for development and the social economy. Recently she published 'Transferencia de diseño a comunidades productivas emergentes [Design Transference to Emerging Productive Communities]', in *Diseño & territorio* (National University of Colombia 2007) and 'Diseño y complejidad [Design and Complexity]' in *Huellas Review* (Universidad de Cuyo 2008).

Sarah Gallez has a master's degree in Sociology and Communication Studies. She works as a researcher at the CITA (Cellule Interdisciplibaire de Technology Assessment), University of Namur (Belgium). Her field of research concerns cultural studies regarding the appropriation of information-communication technology by teens.

Erik Geelhoed is a Senior Researcher at Hewlett-Packard Laboratories, Bristol, UK. Geelhoed has a strong interest in applying sound psychological method and sound statistical technique, and has undertaken a diverse range of qualitative and quantitative studies including field trials, controlled laboratory experiments, large-scale surveys and in-depth interview studies in the areas of mobile appliances/mediated communication, multi-media and lifestyle research. His current work in this field is outlined in 'Probing Experiences: Logs, Traces, Self-report and a Sense of Wonder' published along with Sharon Baurley, Josephine Reid and Richard Hull in *Probing Experiences: From Academic Research to Commercial Propositions* (Springer 2007).

Kirsten Gram-Hanssen, Ph.D., is a Senior Researcher at the Danish Building Research Institute, Aalborg University. She works on qualitative and quantitative research in housing and consumption with a special focus on lifestyle and energy consumption, and the meaning and use of the home. Theoretically, her research builds on sociological consumer theory and recent practice theory. She has been involved in both international and national projects and has published in several international journals, including Energy Policy, Housing Studies, the Journal of Consumer Policy and Building Research and Information.

Larissa Hjorth is an artist and Senior Lecturer in the Games and Digital Art Programmes at the RMIT University, Melbourne, Australia. Since 2000, Hjorth has been researching and publishing on the gendered customising of mobile communication, gaming and virtual communities in the Asia–Pacific – these studies are outlined in her book, *Mobile Media in the Asia-Pacific* (Routledge 2009). Hjorth has published widely on the topic in national and international journals such as the Games and Culture journal, Convergence journal, Journal of Intercultural Studies, Continuum, ACCESS, Fibreculture and Southern Review and she recently co-edited two Routledge anthologies, *Games of Locality: Gaming Cultures in the Asia-Pacific* (with Dean Chan) and *Mobile technologies: From Telecommunication to Media* (with Gerard Goggin). In 2007, Hjorth co-convened the International *Mobile Media* conference with Gerard Goggin and the *Interactive Entertainment* (IE) conference with Esther Milne.

Jesper Ole Jensen, Ph.D., is a Senior Researcher at the Danish Building Research Institute, Aalborg University. He works within the field of urban sustainability, comprising issues such as lifestyle and consumption in households, sustainable buildings, infrastructure and building operation, and policies for urban sustainability. Theoretically, his research includes various social theories applied at the interaction between humans and the built environment. He has contributed to several international books and journals.

Carlos Andrés Maidana Legal is a founding member of GUIAS (*Grupo Universitario de Investigación para la Acción Social* – a Social Action Research university group) that works on topics related to city and society. He is a Professor and Investigator of the Urbanism Superior Institute at the University of Buenos Aires in the areas of local development, new technologies, technologies and the environment. He is the co-author of 'Design for Development: A Focus on Expansion' (University of Chile 2006).

Claire Lobet-Maris has a master's in Sociology and a Ph.D. in *Sciences du Travail* (Catholic University of Louvain). She is a Senior Professor at the Computer Science Faculty at University of Namur and the current Director of *Cellule Interdisciplinaire de Technology Assessment* (CITA) – focussing on scientific issues regarding interactions between ICTs and society. Her research career covers a large spectrum of topics which have in common the objective of providing the foundations for a democratic and sustainable information society: the democratic governance of IT projects, programmes and infrastructures, capabilities of end-users to impact on IT artefacts through their social practices and appropriation, trust and its necessary re-construction to interact in virtual spheres, actors and their self-determination capabilities confronted to new 'numeric cages' (profiling, body surveillance, facial recognition of emotion). Her recent publications include *Variation sur la Confiance* (together with Robin Lucas and Benjamin Six) (Peter Lang, forthcoming).

Andrew Moore is a freelance electronics engineer and designer working with both academic and commercial clients on projects which range from research and development to finished products. He worked for four years at Philips Research Laboratories on wearable technology and received a master of arts degree in Industrial Design Engineering from the Royal College of Art, London, UK. Moore is the author/co-author of several papers in journals and conference proceedings. The most recent are: 'Communication-Wear: User Feedback as Part of a Co-Design Process' published in *Proceedings of the 2nd International Workshop on Haptic and Audio Interaction Design* (HAID 2007) (Springer 2007) and 'Communication-Wear' published in the *Adjunct Proceedings of Ubicomp 2007 – Transitive materials: Towards an integrated approach to material technology, a workshop of the 9th International Conference on Ubiquitous Computing* (Springer 2007) – both with Philippa Brock, Erik Geelhoed and Sharon Baurley.

Anne-Claire Orban holds a master's in Communication Studies. She works as a Co-ordinator at the ACMJ (*Action Ciné Médias Jeunes*) in Brussels, Belgium. Her research interests span the area of the media's education for teens and, more specifically, education with blogging.

Jo Pierson is a Senior Researcher at SMIT (Studies on Media, Information and Telecommunication) – part of the IBBT (Interdisciplinary Institute for BroadBand Technology) – and holds a Ph.D. in social science (communication studies). As an Assistant Professor he lectures bachelor and master's courses on socio-economic issues of the information society and on qualitative research methods at the Vrije Universiteit Brussel in the Department of Communication Studies (Faculty of Arts and Philosophy). His core scientific expertise involves the field of innovation strategic research on the meaning and use of fixed and mobile media technologies at home, at work and in public settings. In this domain he is managing a range of national and international projects. His research focus is on involving users in the technological development process based on ethnographic study and the Living Lab approach.

Inge Røpke, Ph.D., is an Associate Professor at the Department of Management Engineering, Technical University of Denmark. Her research examines the history of ecological-economic thought and environmental implications of economic growth, international trade, technological change, and consumption. Her ongoing research projects investigate the environmental aspects of changes in everyday life, technology, and consumption. She has published her research in journals such as Ecological Economics and the Journal of Consumer Policy and co-edited *The Ecological Economics of Consumption* published by Edward Elgar in 2004.

Céline Scholler holds a master's in Law. She holds the position of a Research Fellow at the CRID (*Centre de Recherche Informatique et Droit*), University of Namur. Her field of research concerns regulation of the Internet and the legal framework that regulates the freedom of the press.

Pedro Senar is the Co-ordinator of the area of Technology of the Secretary of Investigation, and a Professor of Signature Industrial Design at the Architecture, Design and Urbanism School, University of Buenos Aires. At present, Senar is working on his Ph.D. thesis in the field of the social sciences. He has been the Director and Co-director of projects for strengthening handcraft productive sectors, funded by the Ministry of Social Development and Education, Science and Technology. In 2007 he published '*Diseño e innovación para el desarrollo del capital social* [Design and Innovation for the Development of Social Capital]' in the journal *Other Economy*.

Liudmila Shemberko graduated from the Lomonosov Moscow State University (MGU) Philological Department with a degree in Structural and Applied Linguistics. She is Head of the Information Retrieval Service at the Institute of Scientific Information for the Social Sciences (INION) of the Russian Academy of Sciences. Her professional interests cover the areas of social sciences databases retrieval, the implementation of linguistic tools in retrieval systems, the development of searching strategies to support communication between social science information users, and the creation of problem-oriented databases by downloading information from different information systems. Her recent publications include: 'Information Culture of Digital Information Users' (Case Study. Social and Humanitarian Sciences), a paper presented at the International Conference 'UNESCO between two phases of the World Summit on the Information Society' Saint Petersburg, May 2005, and an article in Russian (with V. Gloukhov) 'Main Stages of INION Information System Development' published in the journal *Liberia* (Vol. 3, 2007).

Maria Sourbati is a Lecturer in the Division of Media and Information Studies, School of CMIS, University of Brighton. After completing her Ph.D. on the co-evolution of media policies, technologies and markets, her research has integrated the study of communications policy and media use. Currently this research is developing along the following strands: media access as an analytical and regulatory concept; and the position of media users in public policy discourses on digital ICTs. Maria has appeared at conferences, been invited to make presentations, taken advisory roles and issued publications. Her publications encompass: 'On older people, internet access and electronic service delivery: A study of sheltered homes', in *The Social Dynamics of Information and Communication Technology* (Ashgate 2008).

Tim Van Lier is a Junior Researcher at SMIT (Studies on Media, Information and Telecommunication), which is part of the IBBT (Interdisciplinary Institute for BroadBand Technology). In 2006, he acquired a master's degree in Communication Studies from the Faculty of Arts and Philosophy at the Vrije Universiteit Brussel. His thesis concerning online communities and children, with Ketnet Kick as a case study, was very well received. He currently works on several IBBT projects such as ROMAS (on mobile media), VIN (on communities), Teleon (on games) and High Masquerade (on virtual experiences). His main interest lies in the convergence of these three topics.

Kerstin Wüstner, Ph.D., currently holds the position of a Senior Lecturer in Psychology at the Helmut-Schmidt-University Hamburg, Germany. She is interested in different aspects of science and society, such as the individual and social construction of risk, and employment studies. Her thematic publications are: 'Attitudes towards Preimplantation Genetic Diagnosis – A German and Japanese Comparison' (together with U. Heinze) published in *New Genetics and Society* (2007) and 'Technological development and society: The discourse about PGD in Germany' which appeared in *New Technologies in Global Societies: The Co-construction of Society and Technology in a Global World* (World Scientific 2006).

Participation in Broadband Society

Edited by Leopoldina Fortunati / Julian Gebhardt / Jane Vincent

This series publishes peer-reviewed monographs and edited volumes by internationally renowed scholars in the field of the 'social use of information and communication technologies (mass media included)', 'communication studies' and 'science and technology social studies'. It provides an editorial space specifically dedicated to the collection of work that integrates new research regarding theoretical discourse, methodologies and studies from multiple disciplines such as sociology, anthropology, psychology, geography, linguistics, information science, engeneering and more.

The editors particularly welcome texts elaborating new theories, original methodological approaches and challenges to existing knowledge. Proposals aimed at scholars, professionals and operators working in the diverse field of participation in broadband society are invited from all disciplines.

Vol. 1   Leopoldina Fortunati / Jane Vincent / Julian Gebhardt / Andraz Petrovčič / Olga Vershinskaya (eds.): Interacting with Broadband Society. 2010.

Vol. 2   Julian Gebhardt / Hajo Greif / Lilia Raycheva / Claire Lobet-Maris / Amparo Lasen (eds.): Experiencing Broadband Society. 2010.

www.peterlang.de

www.ingramcontent.com/pod-product-compliance
Ingram Content Group UK Ltd.
Pitfield, Milton Keynes, MK11 3LW, UK
UKHW021823140426
5217IPUK00004B/56